DATABASE MANAGEMENT
SYSTEM CONCEPTS

K.PREMA
A.GOWRI SHANKAR REDDY
K.REDDY PRADEEP

INDIA · SINGAPORE · MALAYSIA

Notion Press

Old No. 38, New No. 6
McNichols Road, Chetpet
Chennai - 600 031

First Published by Notion Press 2020
Copyright © K. Prema, A. Gowri Shankar Reddy,
K. Reddy Pradeep 2020
All Rights Reserved.

ISBN 978-1-64783-635-1

Dedication

To My Parents, Sister, Husband and Well-Wishers for their love and Support

— Mrs. K. Prema

To My Parents and Wife for their Love and Encouragement

— Mr. A. Gowri Shankar Reddy

To My Family and My Wife (G. Sreehitha Reddy) and especially to my daughter(K. Khasvi)

— Mr. K. Reddy Pradeep

Contents

Preface *9*

Acknowledgements *11*

1. Introduction **13**
  1.1   History of Database Systems 13
  1.2   Introduction to Database Management Systems
        (DBMS) 14
  1.3   DBMS vs. File System 15
  1.4   Database System Applications 16
  1.5   Purpose of Database Systems 18
  1.6   View of Data.. 19
  1.7   Data Models 22
  1.8   Database Languages: DDL, DML, DCL, TCL 24
  1.9   Database Architecture 30
  1.10 Database Users and Administrators 34

2. Introduction to Database Design **39**
  2.1   Introduction to Database Design 39
  2.2   ER Diagrams 40
  2.3   Additional Features of ER Model 53
  2.4   Conceptual Design with the ER Model 58
  2.5   conceptual Design for Large Enterprises 62

3. Relational Model **67**
  3.1   Introduction to the Relational Model 67
  3.2   Integrity Constraints.. 69
  3.3   Querying Relational Data 75
  3.4   Views... 77

4.   Relational Algebra and Calculus **85**
   4.1   Relational Algebra... 85
   4.2   Joins 93
   4.3   Division Operator (÷) 100
   4.4   Relational Calculus 102
   4.5   Tuple Relational Calculus (TRC)........................... 102
   4.6   Domain Relational Calculus (DRC) 103
   4.7   Expressive Power of Algebra and Calculus.............. 104
   4.8   Form of Basic SQL Query 104
   4.9   Basic Structure of SQL 106
   4.10 Nested Queries 108
   4.11 Set – Comparison Operators................................... 111
   4.12 Order By Clause 123
   4.13 Group By Clause 125
   4.14 SQL Having Clause... 126
   4.15 Aggregate Operators 127
   4.16 SQL Joins.. 133
   4.17 Triggers... 141

5.   Introduction to Schema Refinement **145**
   5.1   Problems Caused By Redundancy........................... 145
   5.2   Decompositions – Problem Related to
         Decomposition 146
   5.3   Functional Dependencies.. 150
   5.4   Normalization... 153
   5.5   Fourth Normal Form (4NF) 160
   5.6   Fifth Normal Form (5NF) 162

6.   Transactions Management **165**
   6.1   Transaction 165
   6.2   Implementation of Atomicity.................................. 168
   6.3   Implementation of Consistency 169
   6.4   Implemention of Isolation 170
   6.5   Implemention of Durability..................................... 171
   6.6   Transaction States 171

6.7   Schedule 173
6.8   Serializability 176
6.9   Concurrent Execution................................. 185
6.10 Recoverability 186

7. **Concurrency Control** **191**
7.1   Concurrency Control................................. 191
7.2   Lock Based Protocol 196
7.3   Timestamp Ordering Protocol 204
7.4   Validation Based Protocol 205
7.5   Multiple Granularity................................. 208
7.6   Deadlock 211
7.7   Multiversion Concurrency Control
      Techniques (MVCC) 217

8. **Query Processing and Optimization** **221**
8.1   Query Processing...................................... 221
8.2   Query Algorithms 224
8.3   Query Optimization 228
8.4   Basic Algorithms for Executing Query Operations.....243
8.5   Introduction to Database Tuning.................. 251
8.6   Physical Database Design Decisions.............. 255
8.7   An Overview of Database Tuning in
      Relational Systems 260

9. **Recovery System** **271**
9.1   Objectives.. 271
9.2   What is Recovery?..................................... 272
9.3   Failure Classification 275
9.4   Storage Structure...................................... 276
9.5   Log Based Recovery 278
9.6   Categorization of Recovery Algorithms 281
9.7   Recovery Techniques Based on Deferred Update ... 290
9.8   Recovery Techniques Based on
      Immediate Update 297

9.9   Shadow Paging 300
9.10   Database Backup and Recovery from
       Catastrophic Failures 302

10.   **Overview of Storage and Indexing**. **305**
      10.1   Data on External Storage 305
      10.2   Secondary Storage Devices.................................... 306
      10.3   Operations on Files... 314
      10.4   File Organization 319
      10.5   Indexing 326
      10.6   Tree Based Indexing.. 332
      10.7   Hashing.. 343
      10.8   Extendible Hashing 347
      10.9   Linear Hashing.. 359

11.   **Distributed Database** **371**
      11.1   Introduction 371
      11.2   Distributed Database Management System........... 371
      11.3   Advantages of Distributed Databases 373
      11.4   Adversities of Distributed Databases 374
      11.5   Types of Distributed Databases............................ 374
      11.6   Distributed Dbms Architectures 376
      11.7   Multi – Dbms Architectures 378
      11.8   Design Alternatives.. 380
      11.9   Data Replication.. 381
      11.10 Fragmentation 383
      11.11 Distribution Transparency.................................... 385

Preface

The goal of this book is to provide a complete knowledge on DBMS which is said to be a heart of Computer science department for both Under Graduate & Post Graduates. DBMS stands for **D**atabase **M**anagement **S**ystem. We can break it like this DBMS = Database + Management System. Database is a collection of data and Management System is a set of programs to store and retrieve those data. Based on this we can **define DBMS** like this: DBMS is a collection of inter-related data and set of programs to store & access those data in an easy and effective manner. The traditional mechanism for storing computer data was data files. Data files have been immensely popular since the 1960s. The earlier commercially successful programming languages such as COBOL had extensive features related to file processing.

In fact, even today, many major computer applications run on file-based computer systems. Database management has evolved from a specialized computer application to a central component of a modern computing environment, and, as a result, knowledge about database systems has become an essential part of an education in computer science. In this text, we present the fundamental concepts of database management. These concepts include aspects of database design, database languages, and database-system implementation, an overview on Structured query Language(SQL) and distributed databases along with corresponding examples and keen diagrams which represent the complete concept.

The text is organized into the following set of 11 chapters

1.   Introduction
2.   Introduction to Database Design
3.   Relational Model
4.   Relational Algebra & Calculus
5.   Introduction to Schema Refinement
6.   Transaction Management
7.   Concurrency Control
8.   Query Processing and Optimization
9.   Recovery System
10. Overview of storage and Indexing
11. Introduction to Distributed Databases

Acknowledgements

We would like to thank who have provided invaluable feedback on the textbook. The result, we hope, is greater clarity for readers. We would also like to acknowledge the contributions, influence, and support of the following people. We have included organization affiliation if we could figure it out.

Dr. A. V. Sriharsha	Professor, Sree Vidyanikethan Engineering college, Tirupati, India
Dr. M. Sunil Kumar	Professor, HOD(CSE), SreeVidyanikethan Engineering college, Tirupati, India
Dr. L. Venkateswara Reddy	Professor, Sree Vidyanikethan Engineering college, Tirupati, India
Dr. N. M. Saravana Kumar	Professor and HOD, Vivekanandha Engineering College For (Women), Nammakal, India
Dr. Pavan Kumar Pagadala	Assistant Professor, SVEC, Tirupati, India
Dr. N. Sudhakara Reddy	Principal, SVPCET, Puttur, India
Dr. A. Rama Mohan Reddy	Professor, S. V University, Tirupati, India
Dr. D. Vivekananda Reddy	Assistant professor, S. V University, Tirupati, India
Dr. B. Ramasubba Reddy	Vice Principal, SVEC, Tirupati, India
Mr. Suresh Avula	Design Engineer, Adtran, Huntsville.

Our gratitude towards the following dearest persons.

| Mr. K. Yogindra Reddy & Mrs. K. Sujatha |
| Ms. K. Pavani |
| Mr. A. Rajasekhar Reddy & Mrs. A. Vani |
| Mr. Y. Jayachandra Reddy & Mrs. Y. Bharathi |
| Mr. G. Rama Murthy Reddy & Mrs. N. Bhoodevi |
| Mr. K. Kodanda Ram & Mrs. K. Uma Maheswari |
| Mr. G. Srikar Senior Android Engineer, Finbox, Banglore, India. |
| Mr. K. Reddy Sandeep Application Support Engineer, Clover Infotech, Banglore, India. |

Finally, our special thanks to our well wishers for their encouragement.

1.1 HISTORY OF DATABASE SYSTEMS

Database management systems (DBMSs) have played an outsized role in the history of software development and in the creation and growth of the software products industry. Recognizing the major role played by these products, the Annals is publishing two special issues on the subject. These two issues will be the fourth and fifth sponsored by the Software Industry Special Interest Group of the Computer History Museum (formerly the Software History Center). This issue (the first) is focused on the products, companies, and people who designed, programmed, and sold mainframe DBMS software products beginning in the 1960s and 1970s. The second issue will be devoted to the relational DBMS products, which were developed during the 1970s and came to prominence (and some say dominance) during the 1980s and 1990s.

What was so important about these DBMS products? Why did they have such a major impact on the growth of the software products industry and, more importantly, on the way that almost all major commercial applications were built from the 1970s on? It is a complex story, part of which is told in this issue. Thomas Haigh begins this issue by describing the world prior to DBMSs and some of the early DBMS products. Tim Bergin and Thomas Haigh then examine the database management products that dominated the IBM environment and other major computer platforms in the 1970s and 1980s.

This issue tells the rest of the story through a series of pioneer recollections, principally from people who founded the major DBMS companies or were heavily involved in the growth and development of these products and companies. These eight recollections cover the principal DBMS software products for IBM mainframe computers.[1] IBM itself was a significant player in this marketplace with its IMS product, but all the other products were produced and marketed by independent software companies. Many historians and industry analysts believe that these products and these companies formed the foundation on which the mainframe software products industry was built.

Here, are the important landmarks from the history:

- ✧ 1960 – Charles Bachman designed first DBMS system
- ✧ 1970 – Codd introduced IBM'S Information Management System (IMS)
- ✧ 1976 – Peter Chen coined and defined the Entity-relationship model also know as the ER model
- ✧ 1980 – Relational Model becomes a widely accepted database component
- ✧ 1985 – Object-oriented DBMS develops.
- ✧ 1990s – Incorporation of object-orientation in relational DBMS.
- ✧ 1991 – Microsoft ships MS access, a personal DBMS and that displaces all other personal DBMS products.
- ✧ 1995: – First Internet database applications
- ✧ 1997: – XML applied to database processing. Many vendors begin to integrate XML into DBMS products.

1.2   INTRODUCTION TO DATABASE MANAGEMENT SYSTEMS (DBMS)

Firstly let us know what is database and then about DBMS

DATABASE: A database is a collection of related data which represents some aspect of the real world. A database system is designed to be built and populated with data for a certain task.

DBMS: Database Management System (also known as DBMS) is a software for storing and retrieving users' data by considering appropriate security measures. It allows users to create their own databases as per their requirement.

Characteristics of Database Management System

- ⋏   Provides security and removes redundancy
- ⋏   Self-describing nature of a database system
- ⋏   Insulation between programs and data abstraction
- ⋏   Support of multiple views of the data
- ⋏   Sharing of data and multiuser transaction processing
- ⋏   DBMS allows entities and relations among them to form tables.
- ⋏   It follows the ACID concept (Atomicity, Consistency, Isolation, and Durability).
- ⋏   DBMS supports multi-user environment that allows users to access and manipulate data in parallel.

1.3   DBMS VS. FILE SYSTEM

DBMS	File System
Multi-user access	It does not support multi-user access
Design to fulfill the need for small and large businesses	It is only limited to smaller DBMS system.
Remove redundancy and Integrity	Redundancy and Integrity issues
Expensive. But in the long term Total Cost of Ownership is cheap	It's cheaper
Easy to implement complicated transactions	No support for complicated transactions

1.4   DATABASE SYSTEM APPLICATIONS

1. Railway Reservation System

Database is required to keep record of ticket booking, train's departure and arrival status. Also if trains get late then people get to know it through database update.

2. Library Management System

There are thousands of books in the library so it is very difficult to keep record of all the books in a copy or register. So DBMS used to maintain all the information relate to book issue dates, name of the book, author and availability of the book.

3. Banking

We make thousands of transactions through banks daily and we can do this without going to the bank. So how banking has become so easy that by sitting at home we can send or get money through banks. That is all possible just because of DBMS that manages all the bank transactions.

4. Universities and colleges

Examinations are done online today and universities and colleges maintain all these records through DBMS. Student's registrations details, results, courses and grades all the information are stored in database.

5. Credit Card Transactions

For purchase of credit cards and all the other transactions are made possible only by DBMS. A credit card holder knows the importance of their information that all are secured through DBMS.

6. Social Media Sites

We all are on social media websites to share our views and connect with our friends. Daily millions of users signed up for these social media accounts like facebook, twitter, pinterest and Google plus. But how all the information of users are stored and how we become able to connect to other people, yes this all because DBMS.

7. Telecommunications

Any telecommunication company cannot even think about their business without DBMS. DBMS is must for these companies to store the call details and monthly post paid bills.

8. Finance

Those days have gone far when information related to money was stored in registers and files. Today the time has totally changed because there are lots f thing to do with finance like storing sales, holding information and finance statement management etc.

9. Military

Military keeps records of millions of soldiers and it has millions of files that should be keep secured and safe. As DBMS provides a big security assurance to the military information so it is widely used in militaries. One can easily search for all the information about anyone within seconds with the help of DBMS.

10. Online Shopping

Online shopping has become a big trend of these days. No one wants to go to shops and waste his time. Everyone wants to shop from home. So all these products are added and sold only with the help of DBMS. Purchase information, invoice bills and payment, all of these are done with the help of DBMS.

11. Human Resource Management

Big firms have many workers working under them. Human resource management department keeps records of each employee's salary, tax and work through DBMS.

12. Manufacturing

Manufacturing companies make products and sales them on the daily basis. To keep records of all the details about the products like quantity, bills, purchase, supply chain management, DBMS is used.

13. Airline Reservation system

Same as railway reservation system, airline also needs DBMS to keep records of flights arrival, departure and delay status. So in short, one can say the DBMS is used everywhere around us and we cannot rely without DBMS.

So these were the **Application and Uses of Database Management System (DBMS)**. If you liked them then please share them with your friends

1.5   PURPOSE OF DATABASE SYSTEMS

Advantages of DBMS

ᴧ   DBMS offers a variety of techniques to store & retrieve data
ᴧ   DBMS serves as an efficient handler to balance the needs of multiple applications using the same data
ᴧ   Uniform administration procedures for data

▲ Application programmers never exposed to details of data representation and storage.

▲ A DBMS uses various powerful functions to store and retrieve data efficiently.

▲ Offers Data Integrity and Security

▲ The DBMS implies integrity constraints to get a high level of protection against prohibited access to data.

▲ A DBMS schedules concurrent access to the data in such a manner that only one user can access the same data at a time

▲ Reduced Application Development Time

Disadvantage of DBMS

DBMS may offer plenty of advantages but, it has certain flaws-

✧ Cost of Hardware and Software of a DBMS is quite high which increases the budget of your organization.

✧ Most database management systems are often complex systems, so the training for users to use the DBMS is required.

✧ In some organizations, all data is integrated into a single database which can be damaged because of electric failure or database is corrupted on the storage media

✧ Use of the same program at a time by many users sometimes lead to the loss of some data.

✧ DBMS can't perform sophisticated calculations.

1.6   VIEW OF DATA

Abstraction is one of the main features of database systems. Hiding irrelevant details from user and providing abstract view of data to users, helps in easy and efficient **user-database** interaction. In the previous tutorial, we discussed the **three levels of DBMS architecture,** The top level of that architecture is "view level".

The view level provides the **"view of data"** to the users and hides the irrelevant details such as data relationship, database schema, **constraints**, security etc from the user.

To fully understand the view of data, you must have a basic knowledge of data abstraction and instance & schema. Refer these two tutorials to learn them in detail.

1. Data abstraction
2. Instance and schema

1. Data abstraction

Database systems are made-up of complex data structures. To ease the user interaction with database, the developers hide internal irrelevant details from users. This process of hiding irrelevant details from user is called data abstraction.

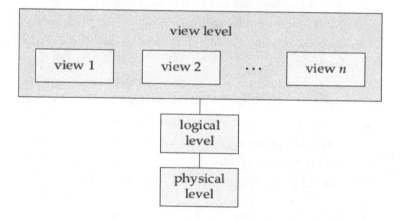

Fig.1.1: Three levels of data abstraction

Physical level

The lowest level of abstraction describes how the data are actually stored. The physical level describes complex low-level data structures in detail.

Logical level

The next-higher level of abstraction describes what data are stored in the database, and what relationships exist among those data. The logical level thus describes the entire database in terms of a small number of relatively simple structures. Although implementation of the simple structures at the logical level may involve complex physical-level structures, the user of the logical level does not need to be aware of this complexity.

This is referred to as physical data independence. Database administrators, who must decide what information to keep in the database, use the logical level of abstraction.

View level

The highest level of abstraction describes only part of the entire database. Even though the logical level uses simpler structures, complexity remains because of the variety of information stored in a large database. Many users of the database system do not need all this information; instead, they need to access only a part of the database. The view level of abstraction exists to simplify their interaction with the system. The system may provide many views for the same database.

Figure 1.1 shows the relationship among the three levels of abstraction. An analogy to the concept of data types in programming languages may clarify the distinction among levels of abstraction. Many high-level programming

2. Instances and Schemas

Databases change over time as information is inserted and deleted. The collection of information stored in the database at a particular moment is called an instanc of the database. The overall design of the database is called the database schema. Schemas are changed in frequently, if at all The concept of database schemas and instances can be understood by analogy to a program written in a programming language.

A database schema corresponds to the variable declarations (along with associated type definitions) in a program. Each variable has a particular value at a given instant. The values of the variables in a program at a point in time correspond to an instance of a database schema. Database systems have several schemas, partitioned according to the levels of abstraction.

The physical schema describes the database design at the physical level, while the logical schema describes the database design at the logical level. A database may also have several schemas at the view level, sometimes called subschemas, that describe different views of the database. Of these, the logical schema is by far the most important, in terms of its effect on application programs, since programmers construct applications by using the logical schema.

The physical schema is hidden beneath the logical schema, and can usually be changed easily without affecting application programs. Application programs are said to exhibit physical data independence if they do not depend on the physical schema, and thus need not be rewritten if the physical schema changes.

1.7 DATA MODELS

Underlying the structure of a database is the data model: a collection of conceptual tools for describing data, data relationships, data semantics, and consistency constraints. A data model provides a way to describe the design of a database at the physical, logical, and view levels. There are a number of different data models that we shall cover in the text. The data models can be classified into four different categories:

Relational Model

The relational model uses a collection of tables to represent both data and the relationships among those data. Each table has multiple columns, and each column has a unique name. Tables are also know as relations.

The relational model is an example of a record-based model. Record-based models are so named because the database is structured in fixed-format records of several types. Each table contains records of a particular type. Each record type defines a fixed number of fields, or attributes.

The columns of the table correspond to the attributes of the record type. The relational data model is the most widely used data model, and a vast majority of current database systems are based on the relational model.

Entity-Relationship Model

The entity-relationship (E-R) data model uses a collection of basic objects, called entities, and relationships among these objects. An entity is a "thing" or "object" in the real world that is distinguishable from other objects. The entity-relationship model is widely used in database design.

Object-Based Data Model

Object-oriented programming (especially in Java, C++, or C#) has become the dominant software-development methodology. This led to the development of an object-oriented data model that can be seen as extending the E-R model with notions of encapsulation, methods (functions), and object identity. The object-relational data model combines features of the object-oriented data model and relational data model.

Semistructured Data Model

The semistructured data model permits the specification of data where individual data items of the same type may have different sets of attributes. This is in contrast to the data models mentioned earlier, where every data item of a particular type must have the same set of attributes. The Extensible Markup Language (XML) is widely used to represent semistructured data.

Historically, the network data model and the hierarchical data model preceded the relational data model. These models were tied closely to the underlying implementation, and complicated the task of modeling data. As a result they are used little now, except in old database code that is still in service in some places.

1.8 DATABASE LANGUAGES: DDL, DML, DCL, TCL

Database languages are used to read, update and store data in a database. There are several such languages that can be used for this purpose; one of them is SQL (Structured Query Language)

Types of DBMS languages

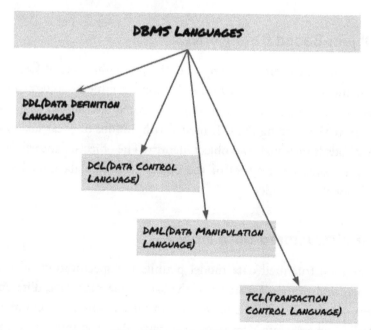

Fig.1.2: Database Languages

Data Definition Language (DDL)

DDL is used for specifying the database schema. It is used for creating tables, schema, indexes, constraints etc. in database. Lets see the operations that we can perform on database using DDL:

Create

Data Definition Language provides reserved keyword **create** to create tables, views, database etc.

Syntax

Create table <Table name>

(

Column1 name data-type <constraint>,

Column2 name data-type <constraint>,

Column3 name data-type <constraint>

);

Note: – Constraint is optional

Example

CREATE TABLE EMPLOYEE(Name VARCHAR2(20), Email VARCHAR2(100), DOB DATE);

Drop

It is used to delete both the structure and record stored in the table.

Syntax

DROP TABLE;

Example

DROP TABLE EMPLOYEE;

Alter

It is used to alter the structure of the database. This change could be either to modify the characteristics of an existing attribute or probably to add a new attribute.

Syntax

To add a new column in the table

   1. ALTER TABLE table_name ADD column_name COLUMN-definition;

To modify existing column in the table:

   1. ALTER TABLE MODIFY(COLUMN DEFINITION....);

Example

1. ALTER TABLE STU_DETAILS ADD(ADDRESS VARCHAR2(20));
2. ALTER TABLE STU_DETAILS MODIFY (NAME VARCHAR2(20));

Truncate

It is used to delete all the rows from the table and free the space containing the table.

Syntax

TRUNCATE TABLE table_name;

Example

TRUNCATE TABLE EMPLOYEE;

Data Manipulation Language (DML)

DML commands are used to modify the database. It is responsible for all form of changes in the database. The command of DML is not auto-committed that means it can't permanently save all the changes in the database. They can be rollback.

Here are some commands that come under DML:

Select

This is the same as the projection operation of relational algebra. It is used to select the attribute based on the condition described by WHERE clause.

Syntax

SELECT expressions   FROM TABLES   WHERE conditions;

Example

SELECT emp_name   FROM employee   WHERE age > 20;

Insert

The INSERT statement is a SQL query. It is used to insert data into the row of a table.

Syntax

INSERT INTO TABLE_NAME (col1, col2, col3,... col N) VALUES (value1, value2, value3,... valueN);

Or

INSERT INTO TABLE_NAME VALUES (value1, value2, value3,... valueN);

Example

INSERT INTO BOOKS (Author, Subject) VALUES ("Sonoo", "DBMS");

Update

This command is used to update or modify the value of a column in the table.

Syntax

UPDATE table_name SET [column_name1= value1,... column_nameN = valueN] [WHERE   CONDITION]

Example

UPDATE students SET User_Name = 'Sonoo' WHERE Student_Id = ‹3›

Delete

It is used to remove one or more row from a table.

Syntax

DELETE FROM table_name [WHERE condition];

Example

DELETE FROM BOOKS WHERE Author= "Sonoo";

Data Control Language (DCL)

DCL commands are used to grant and take back authority from any database user.

Grant

It is used to give user access privileges to a database.

Example

GRANT SELECT, UPDATE ON MY_TABLE TO SOME_USER, ANOTHER_USER;

Revoke

It is used to take back permissions from the user.

Example

REVOKE SELECT, UPDATE ON MY_TABLE FROM USER1, USER2;

Transaction Control Language (TCL)

TCL commands can only use with DML commands like INSERT, DELETE and UPDATE only. These operations are automatically committed in the database that's why they cannot be used while creating tables or dropping them.

Commit

Commit command is used to save all the transactions to the database.

Syntax

COMMIT;

Example

DELETE FROM CUSTOMERS WHERE AGE = 25;
COMMIT;

Rollback

Rollback command is used to undo transactions that have not already been saved to the database.

Syntax

ROLLBACK;

Example

DELETE FROM CUSTOMERS WHERE AGE = 25;
ROLLBACK;

Savepoint

It is used to roll the transaction back to a certain point without rolling back the entire transaction.

Syntax

SAVEPOINT SAVEPOINT_NAME;

1.9 DATABASE ARCHITECTURE

The DBMS design depends upon its architecture. The basic client/ server architecture is used to deal with a large number of PCs, web servers, database servers and other components that are connected with networks. The client/server architecture consists of many PCs and a workstation which are connected via the network. DBMS architecture depends upon how users are connected to the database to get their request done.

Types of DBMS Architecture

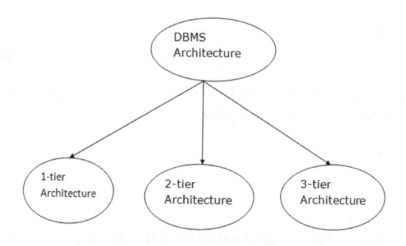

Fig.1.3: Types of Database Architecture

Database architecture can be seen as a single tier or multi-tier. But logically, database architecture is of two types like: **2-tier architecture** and **3-tier architecture.**

1-Tier Architecture

In this architecture, the database is directly available to the user. It means the user can directly sit on the DBMS and uses it. Any changes done here will directly be done on the database itself. It doesn't provide a handy tool for end users. The 1-Tier architecture is used for development of the local application, where programmers can directly communicate with the database for the quick response. The simplest of Database Architecture are **1 tier** where the Client, Server, and Database all reside on the same machine. Anytime you install a DB in your system and access it to practise SQL queries it is 1 tier architecture. But such architecture is rarely used in production.

For example, lets say you want to fetch the records of employee from the database and the database is available on your computer system, so the request to fetch employee details will be done by your computer and the records will be fetched from the database by your computer as well. This type of system is generally referred as local database system.

2-Tier Architecture

The 2-Tier architecture is same as basic client-server. In the two-tier architecture, applications on the client end can directly communicate with the database at the server side. In two-tier architecture, the Database system is present at the server machine and the DBMS application is present at the client machine, these two machines are connected with each other through a reliable network as shown in the below fig1.4.

For this interaction, API's like: ODBC, JDBC are used. The user interfaces and application programs are run on the client-side. The server side is responsible to provide the functionalities like: query processing and transaction management. To communicate with the DBMS, client-side application establishes a connection with the server side.

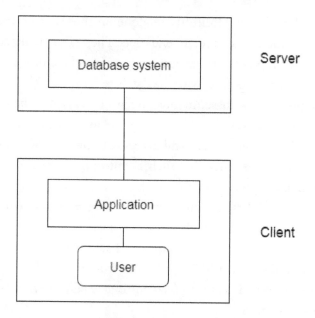

Fig.1.4: 2-tier Architecture

3-Tier Architecture

The 3-Tier architecture contains another layer between the client and server. In this architecture, client can't directly communicate with the server. The application on the client-end interacts with an application server which further communicates with the database system. End user has no idea about the existence of the database beyond the application server. The database also has no idea about any other user beyond the application. The 3-Tier architecture is used in case of large web application.

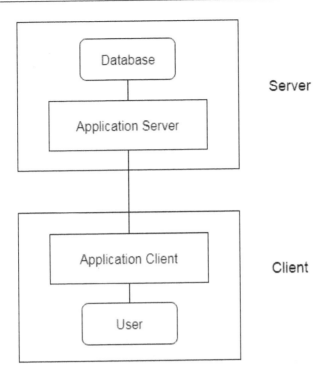

Fig.1.5: 3-TIER ARCHITECTURE

Three tier architecture is the most popular DBMS architecture. The Goal of Three-Teir Architecture is

✧ To separate the user applications and physical database
✧ Proposed to support DBMS characteristics
✧ Program-data independence
✧ Support of multiple views of the data

Overview Of Database Architecture

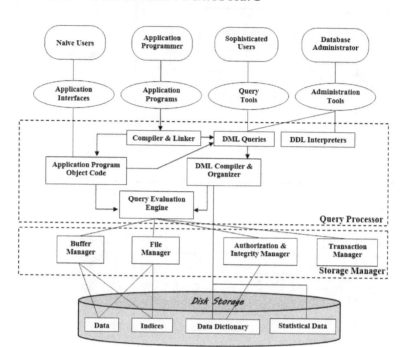

Fig. 1.6: Overall System Structure Of The Database Management System

1.10 DATABASE USERS AND ADMINISTRATORS

Database users are the one who really use and take the benefits of database. There will be different types of users depending on their need and way of accessing the database.

Naïve Users

Naive users are unsophisticated users who interact with the system by invoking one of the application programs that have been written previously. For example, a bank teller who needs to transfer $50 from account A to account B invokes a program called transfer. This program asks the teller for the amount of money to be transferred, the account from which the money is to be transferred, and the account to which the money is to be transferred.

Application Programmers

They are the developers who interact with the database by means of DML queries. These DML queries are written in the application programs like C, C++, JAVA, Pascal etc. These queries are converted into object code to communicate with the database. For example, writing a C program to generate the report of employees who are working in particular department will involve a query to fetch the data from database. It will include a embedded SQL query in the C Program.

Sophisticated Users

They are database developers, who write SQL queries to select/insert/delete/update data. They do not use any application or programs to request the database. They directly interact with the database by means of query language like SQL. These users will be scientists, engineers, analysts who thoroughly study SQL and DBMS to apply the concepts in their requirement. In short, we can say this category includes designers and developers of DBMS and SQL.

Database Administrator

The life cycle of database starts from designing, implementing to administration of it. A database for any kind of requirement needs to be designed perfectly so that it should work without any issues. Once all the design is complete, it needs to be installed. Once this step is complete, users start using the database. The database grows as the data grows in the database. When the database becomes huge, its performance comes down. Also accessing the data from the database becomes challenge. There will be unused memory in database, making the memory inevitably huge. These administration and maintenance of database is taken care by database Administrator – DBA. The database administrator has a good understanding of the enterprise's information resources and needs. Database administrator's duties include:

Schema Definition

The DBA creates the original database schema by executing a set of data definition statements in the DDL.
Storage structure and access-method definition

Schema and Physical-Organization Modification

The DBA carries out changes to the schema and physical organization to reflect the changing needs of the organization, or to alter the physical organization to improveperformance.

Granting of Authorization for Data Access

By granting different types of authorization, the database administrator can regulate which parts of the database various users can access. The authorization information is kept in a special system structure that the database system consults whenever someone attempts to access the data in the system.

Routine Maintenance

Examples of the database administrator's routine maintenance activities are:

   ✧ Periodically backing up the database, either onto tapes or onto remote servers, to prevent loss of data in case of disasters such as flooding.

- ✦ Ensuring that enough free disk space is available for normal operations, and upgrading disk space as required.
- ✦ Monitoring jobs running on the database and ensuring that performance is not degraded by very expensive tasks submitted by some users.

Other components of DBMS apart from database users and administrators are discussed below

Query Processor

The query processor will accept query from user and solves it by accessing the database.

Parts of Query Processor

➤ DDL interpreter

This will interprets DDL statements and fetch the definitions in the data dictionary.

➤ DML compiler

a. This will translates DML statements in a query language into low level instructions that the query evaluation engine understands.

b. A query can usually be translated into any of a number of alternative evaluation plans for same query result DML compiler will select best plan for query optimization.

➤ Query evaluation engine

This engine will execute low-level instructions generated by the DML compiler on DBMS.

Storage Manager/Storage Management

➤ A storage manager is a program module which acts like interface between the data stored in a database and the application programs and queries submittted to the system.

▲   Thus, the storage manager is responsible for storing, retrieving and updating data in the database.

▲   The storage manager components include:

✧   **Authorization and integrity manager:** Checks for integrity constraints and authority of users to access data.

✧   **Transaction manager:** Ensures that the database remains in a consistent state although there are system failures.

✧   **File manager:** Manages the allocation of space on disk storage and the data structures used to represent information stored on disk.

✧   **Buffer manager:** It is responsible for retrieving data from disk storage into main memory. It enables the database to handle data sizes that are much larger than the size of main memory.

+   **Data structures implemented by storage manager.**

+   **Data files:** Stored in the database itself.

+   **Data dictionary:** Stores metadata about the structure of the database.

+   **Indices:** Provide fast access to data items.

Chapter 2

Introduction to Database Design

2.1 INTRODUCTION TO DATABASE DESIGN

The database design process can be divided into six steps. The ER model is most relevant to the first three steps.

1. Requirement Analysis

The very first step in designing a database application is to understand what data is to be stored in the database, what application must be built in top of it, and whatoperations are most frequent and subject to performancerequirements. In other words, we must find out what the userswant from the database.

2. Conceptual Database Design

The information gathered in the requirements analysisstep is used to develop a high-level description of the datato be stored in the database, along with the constraints known to hold over this data. The ER model is one of several high-level or semantic, data models used in database design.

3. Logical Database Design

We must choose a database to convert the conceptual database design into a database schema in the data model of the chosen DBMS. Normally we will consider the Relational DBMS and therefore, the task in the logical design step is to

Convert an ER schema into a relational database schema.

Beyond ER Design

4. Schema Refinement

This step is to analyze the collection of relations in our relational database schema to identify potential problems, and refine it.

5. Physical Database Design

This step may simply involve building indexes on some table and clustering some tables or it may involve substantial redesign of parts of database schema obtained from the earlier steps.

6. Application and security Design

Any software project that involves a DBMS must consider aspects of the application that go beyond the database itself. We must describe the role of each entity (users, user group, departments) in every process that is reflected in some application task, as part of a complete workflow for the task.

2.2   ER DIAGRAMS

ER model stands for an Entity-Relationship model. It is a high-level data model. This model is used to define the data elements and relationship for a specified system. It develops a conceptual design for the database. It also develops a very simple and easy to design view of data. In ER modeling, the database structure is portrayed as a diagram called an entity-relationship diagram. A diagram representing entities and relationships among them is known as entity relationship diagram. The major elements used in an ER diagram are entities, attributes, identifiers and relationships that express a reality for which the database is designed.

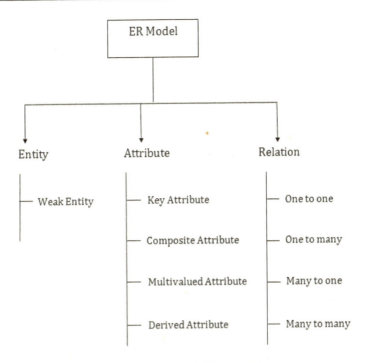

Fig.2.1: Components Of Er Diagram

Entity

An entity may be any object, class, person or place. In the ER diagram, an entity can be represented as rectangles. Consider an organization as an example – manager, product, employee, department etc. can be taken as an entity.

Weak Entity

An entity that depends on another entity called a weak entity. The weak entity doesn't contain any key attribute of its own. The weak entity is represented by a double rectangle.

Attribute: An oval shape is used to represent the attributes. these are the propertities of an entity Name of the attribute is written inside the oval shape and is connected to its entity by a line.

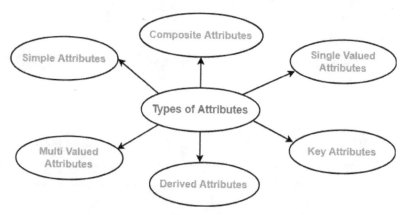

Fig.2.2: TYPES OF ATTRIBUTE

Composite Attribute

An attribute **composed of many other attribute** is called as composite attribute. For example, Address attribute of student Entity type consists of Street, City, State, and Country. In ER diagram, composite attribute is represented by an oval comprising of ovals.

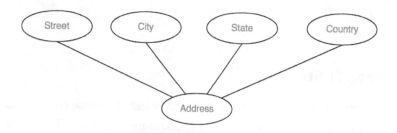

Multivalued Attribute

An attribute consisting **more than one value** for a given entity. For example, Phone_No (can be more than one for a given student). In ER diagram, multivalued attribute is represented by double oval.

Derived Attribute

An attribute which can be **derived from other attributes** of the entity type is known as derived attribute. e.g.; Age (can be derived from DOB). In ER diagram, derived attribute is represented by dashed oval. The complete entity type **Student** with its attributes can be represented as:

Key Attribute

The attribute which **uniquely identifies each entity** in the entity set is called key attribute. For example, Roll_No will be unique for each student. In ER diagram, key attribute is represented by an oval with underlying lines.

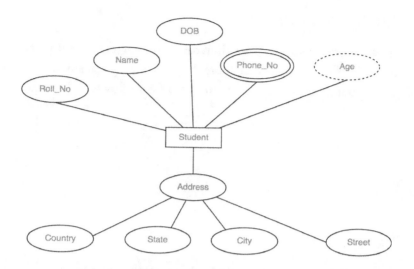

Fig. 2.3 Er Diagram Comprising Of All Attributes

Types of Keys

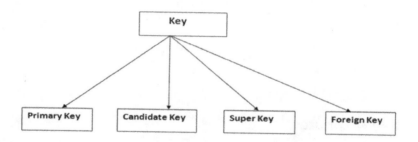

1. Primary key

It is the first key which is used to identify one and only one instance of an entity uniquely. An entity can contain multiple keys as we saw in PERSON table. The key which is most suitable from those lists become a primary key. In the EMPLOYEE table, ID can be primary key since it is unique for each employee. In the EMPLOYEE table, we can even select License_Number and Passport_Number as primary key since they are also unique. For each entity, selection of the primary key is based on requirement and developers.

Notes

⋏ The value of primary key can never be NULL.

⋏ The value of primary key must always be unique.

⋏ The values of primary key can never be changed i.e. no updation is possible.

⋏ The value of primary key must be assigned when inserting a record.

⋏ A relation is allowed to have only one primary key.

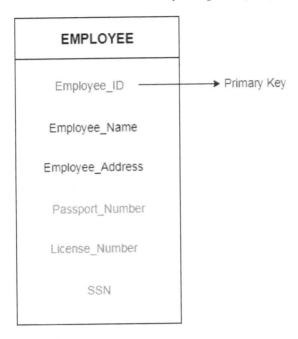

2. Candidate key

A candidate key is an attribute or set of an attribute which can uniquely identify a tuple. The remaining attributes except for primary key are considered as a candidate key. The candidate keys are as strong as the primary key.

For example: In the EMPLOYEE table, id is best suited for the primary key. Rest of the attributes like SSN, Passport_Number, and License_Number, etc. are considered as a candidatekey.

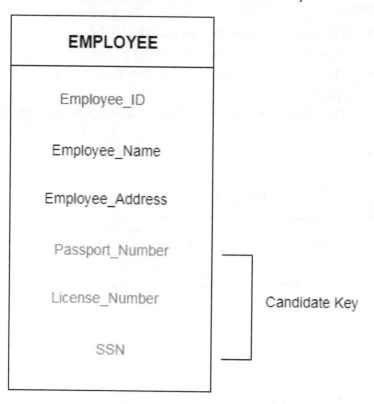

3. Super Key

Super key is a set of an attribute which can uniquely identify a tuple. Super key is a superset of a candidate key.

For example: In the above EMPLOYEE table, for(EMPLOEE_ ID, EMPLOYEE_NAME) the name of two employees can be the same, but their EMPLYEE_ID can't be the same. Hence, this combination can also be a key.

The super key would be EMPLOYEE-ID, (EMPLOYEE_ID, EMPLOYEE-NAME), etc.

4. Foreign key

Foreign keys are the column of the table which is used to point to the primary key of another table. In a company, every employee works in a specific department, and employee and department are two different entities. So we can't store the information of the department in the employee table. That's why we link these two tables through the primary key of one table. We add the primary key of the DEPARTMENT table, Department_Id as a new attribute in the EMPLOYEE table. Now in the EMPLOYEE table, Department_Id is the foreign key, and both the tables are related.

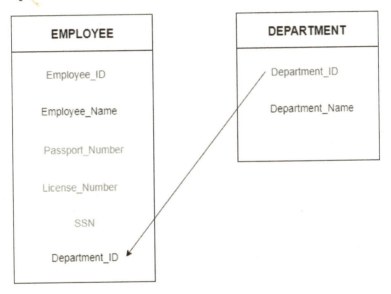

Difference Between Primary key & Foreign key

Primary Key	Foreign Key
Helps you to uniquely identify a record in the table.	It is a field in the table that is the primary key of another table.
Primary Key never accept null values.	A foreign key may accept multiple null values.

Contd...

Primary Key	Foreign Key
Primary key is a clustered index and data in the DBMS table are physically organized in the sequence of the clustered index.	A foreign key cannot automatically create an index, clustered or non-clustered. However, you can manually create an index on the foreign key.
You can have the single Primary key in a table.	You can have multiple foreign keys in a table.

Relationship Type and Relationship Set

A relationship type represents the **association between entity types**. For example, 'Enrolled in' is a relationship type that exists between entity type Student and Course. In ER diagram, relationship type is represented by a diamond and connecting the entities with lines.

A set of relationships of same type is known as relationship set. The following relationship set depicts S1 is enrolled in C2, S2 is enrolled in C1 and S3 is enrolled in C3.

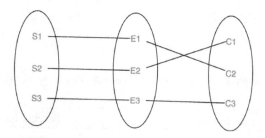

Degree of a Relationship Set

The number of different entity sets **participating in a relationship set** is called as degree of a relationship set.

Unary Relationship

When there is **only ONE entity set participating in a relation**, the relationship is called as unary relationship. For example, one person is married to only one person.

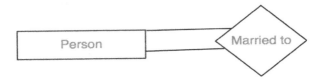

Binary Relationship

When there are **TWO entities set participating in a relation**, the relationship is called as binary relationship. For example, Student is enrolled in Course.

Ternary Relationship

Ternary relationship set is a relationship set where three entity sets participate in a relationship set.

Example

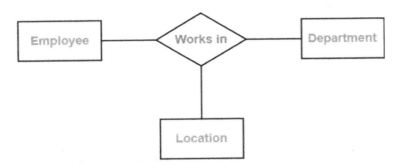

Ternary Relationship Set

N-ary Relationship

N-ary relationship set is a relationship set where 'n' entity sets participate in a relationship set.

A relationship is used to describe the relation between entities. Diamond or rhombus is used to represent the relationship.

Types of relationship are as follows:

a. One-to-One Relationship

When only one instance of an entity is associated with the relationship, then it is known as one to one relationship.

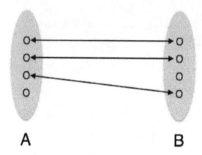

For example, A female can marry to one male, and a male can marry to one female.

b. One-to-Many Relationship

When only one instance of the entity on the left, and more than one instance of an entity on the right associates with the relationship then this is known as a one-to-many relationship.

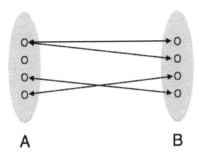

For example, Scientist can invent many inventions, but the invention is done by the only specific scientist.

c. Many-to-one relationship

When more than one instance of the entity on the left, and only one instance of an entity on the right associates with the relationship then it is known as a many-to-one relationship.

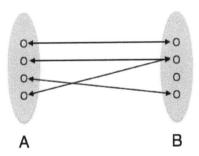

For example, Student enrolls for only one course, but a course can have many students.

d. Many-to-Many Relationship

When more than one instance of the entity on the left, and more than one instance of an entity on the right associates with the relationship then it is known as a many-to-many relationship.

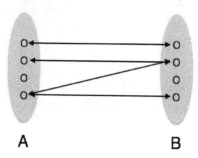

For example, Employee can assign by many projects and project can have many employees.

Notations of ER Diagram

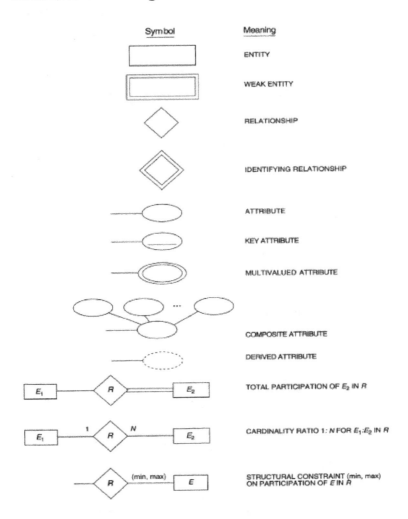

Symbol	Meaning
	ENTITY
	WEAK ENTITY
	RELATIONSHIP
	IDENTIFYING RELATIONSHIP
	ATTRIBUTE
	KEY ATTRIBUTE
	MULTIVALUED ATTRIBUTE
	COMPOSITE ATTRIBUTE
	DERIVED ATTRIBUTE
	TOTAL PARTICIPATION OF E_2 IN R
	CARDINALITY RATIO 1: N FOR E_1:E_2 IN R
	STRUCTURAL CONSTRAINT (min, max) ON PARTICIPATION OF E IN R

2.3   ADDITIONAL FEATURES OF ER MODEL

Participation Constraint

Participation Constraint is applied on the entity participating in the relationship set.

1. **Total Participation** – Each entity in the entity set **must participate** in the relationship. If each student must enroll in a course, the participation of student will be total. Total participation is shown by double line in ER diagram.
2. **Partial Participation** – The entity in the entity set **may or may NOT participate** in the relationship. If some courses are not enrolled by any of the student, the participation of course will be partial.

The diagram depicts the 'Enrolled in' relationship set with Student Entity set having total participation and Course Entity set having partial participation.

Using set, it can be represented as,

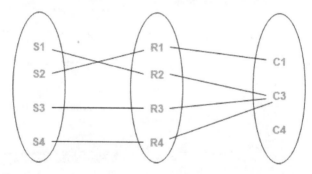

Every student in Student Entity set is participating in relationship but there exists a course C4 which is not taking part in the relationship.

Weak Entity Type and Identifying Relationship

As discussed before, an entity type has a key attribute which uniquely identifies each entity in the entity set. But there exists **some entity type for which key attribute can't be defined.** These are called Weak Entity type. For example, A company may store the information of dependants (Parents, Children, Spouse) of an Employee. But the dependents don't have existence without the employee. So Dependent will be weak entity type and Employee will be Identifying Entity type for Dependant. A weak entity type is represented by a double rectangle. The participation of weak entity type is always total. The relationship between weak entity type and its identifying strong entity type is called identifying relationship and it is represented by double diamond.

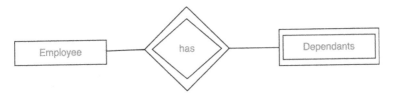

Class Hierarchies

Generalization, Specialization and Aggregation in ER model are used for data abstraction in which abstraction mechanism is used to hide details of a set of objects.

Generalization

Generalization is the process of extracting common properties from a set of entities and create a generalized entity from it. It is a bottom-up approach in which two or more entities can be generalized to a higher level entity if they have some attributes in common. For Example, STUDENT and FACULTY can be generalized to a higher level entity called PERSON as shown in below Figure. In this case, common attributes like P_NAME, P_ADD become part of higher entity (PERSON) and specialized attributes like S_FEE become part of specialized entity (STUDENT).

Example

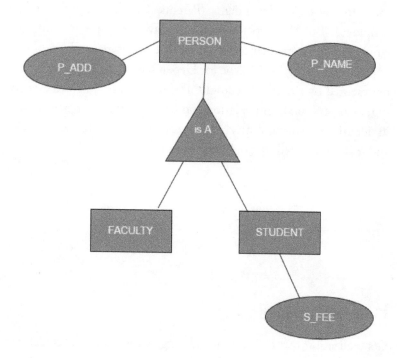

Specialization

In specialization, an entity is divided into sub-entities based on their characteristics. It is a top-down approach where higher level entity is specialized into two or more lower level entities. For Example, EMPLOYEE entity in an Employee management system can be specialized into DEVELOPER, TESTER etc. as shown in below figure. In this case, common attributes like E_NAME, E_SAL etc. become part of higher entity (EMPLOYEE) and specialized attributes like TES_TYPE become part of specialized entity (TESTER).

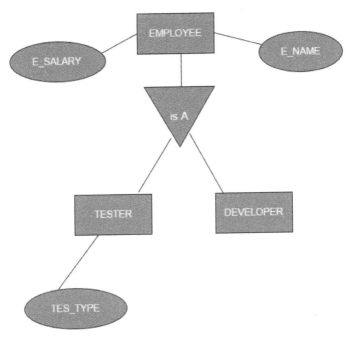

Specialization

Aggregation

An ER diagram is not capable of representing relationship between an entity and a relationship which may be required in some scenarios. In those cases, a relationship with its corresponding entities is aggregated into a higher level entity. For Example, Employee working for a project may require some machinery. So, REQUIRE relationship is needed between relationship WORKS_ FOR and entity MACHINERY. Using aggregation, WORKS_ FOR relationship with its entities EMPLOYEE and PROJECT is aggregated into single entity and relationship REQUIRE is created between aggregated entity and MACHINERY.

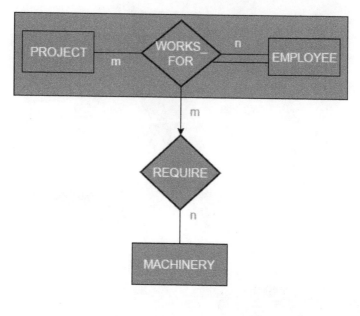

Aggregation

2.4 CONCEPTUAL DESIGN WITH THE ER MODEL

It is most important to recognize that there is more than one way to model a given situation. Our next goal is to start to compare the pros and cons of common choices.

➤ **Should a concept be modeled as an entity or an attribute?**

- ✧ Consider the scenario, if we want to add address information to the Employees entity set? We might choose to add a single attribute address to the entity set. Alternatively, we could introduce a new entity set, Addresses and then a relationship associating employees with addresses. What are the pros and cons?

- ✧ Adding a new entity set is more complex model. It should only be done when there is need for the complexity. For example, if some employees have multiple address to be associated, then the more complex model is needed. Also, representing addresses as a separate entity would allow a further breakdown, for example by zip code or city.

✧ What if we wanted to modify the Works_In relationship to have both a start and end date, rather than just a start date. We could add one new attribute for the end date; alternatively, we could create a new entity set Duration which represents intervals, and then the Works_In relationship can be made ternary (associating an employee, a department and an interval). What are the pros and cons?

If the duration is described through descriptive attributes, only a single such duration can be modeled. That is, we could not express an employment history involving someone who left the department yet later returned.

⋏ Should a concept be modeled as an entity or a relationship?

✧ Consider a situation in which a manager controls several departments. Let's presume that a company budgets a certain amount (budget) for each department. Yet it also wants managers to have access to some discretionary budget (dbudget). There are two corporate models. A discretionary budget may be created for each individual department; alternatively, there may be a discretionary budget for each manager, to be used as she desires.

✧ Which scenario is represented by the following ER diagram? If you want the alternate interpretation, how would you adjust the model?

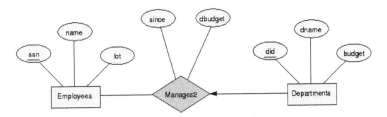

Should We Use Binary or Ternary Relationships?

▲   Consider the following ER diagram, representing insurance policies owned by employees at a company. Each employee can own several polices, each policy can be owned by several employees, and each dependent can be covered by several polices.

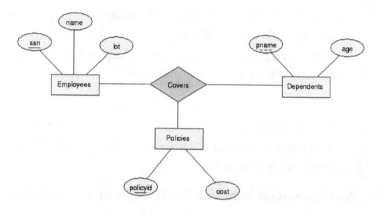

What if we wish to model the following additional requirements:

- ✧ A policy cannot be owned jointly by two or more employees.
- ✧ Every policy must be owned by some employee.
- ✧ Dependents is a weak entity set, and each dependent entity is uniquely identified by taking pname in conjunction with the policyid of a policy entity (which, intuitively, covers the given dependent).
- ✧ The best way to model this is to switch away from the ternary relationship set, and instead use two distinct binary relationship sets.

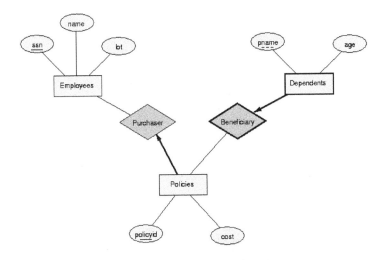

⋏   Should We Use Aggregation?

Consider again the following ER diagram

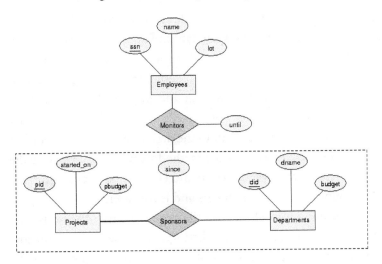

If we did not need the until or since attributes. In tihs case, we could model the identical setting using the following ternary relationship:

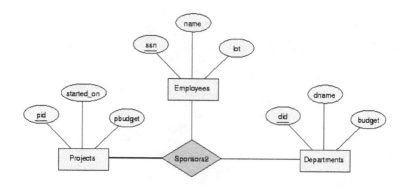

2.5   CONCEPTUAL DESIGN FOR LARGE ENTERPRISES

The process of conceptual design consists of more than just describing small fragments of the application in terms of ER diagrams. For a large enterprise, the design may require the efforts of more than one designer and span data and application code used by a number of user groups. Using a high-level, semantic data model, such as ER diagrams, for conceptual design in such an environment offers theadditional advantage that the high-level design can be diagrammatically representedand easily understood by the many people who must provide input to the design process. An important aspect of the design process is the methodology used to structure the development of the overall design and ensure that the design takes into account all user requirements and is consistent.

The usual approach is that the requirements of various user groups are considered, any conflicting requirements are somehow resolved, and a single set of global requirements is generated at the end of the. requirements analysis phase. Generating a single set of global requirements is a difficult task, but it allows the conceptual design phase to proceed with the development of a logical schema that spans all the data and applications throughout the enterprise.

An alternative approach is to develop separate conceptual schema for different user groups and then integrate these conceptual schemas. To integrate multiple conceptual schemas, we must establish correspondences between entities, relationships, and attributes, and we must resolve numerous kinds of conflicts (e.g., naming conflicts, domain mismatches, differences in measurement units). This task is difficult in its own right. In some situations, schema integration cannot be avoided; for example, when one organization merges with another, existing databases may have to be integrated. Schema integration is also increasing in importance as users demand access to heterogeneous data sources, often maintained by different organizations.

ER Diagramfor Company Database

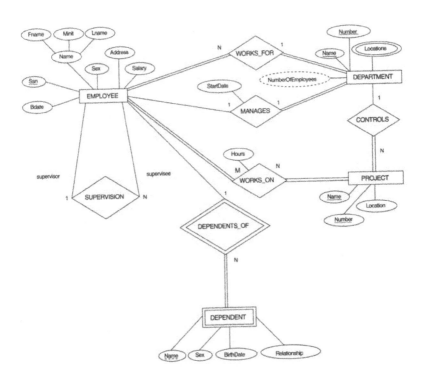

ER Diagram for University Database

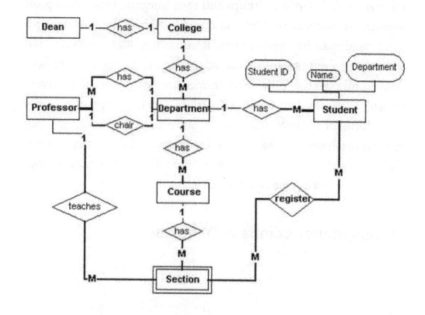

ER Diagram for Bank Database Management System

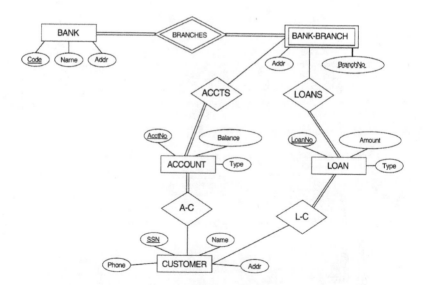

ER Diagram for Online Library Management System

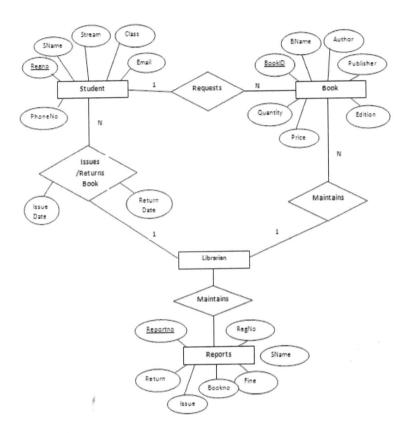

Chapter 3

Relational Model

3.1 INTRODUCTION TO THE RELATIONAL MODEL

➤ A relational database consists of a collection of tables, each of which is assigned a unique name.

➤ A row in table represents a relationship among a set of values.

➤ Table is a collection of rows or relationships which is similar to a mathematical relation i.e. a set of tuples.

Relational Model Concepts

1. **Attribute:** Each column in a Table. Attributes are the properties which define a relation. e.g., Student_Rollno, NAME, etc.

2. **Tables** – In the Relational model the, relations are saved in the table format. It is stored along with its entities. A table has two properties rows and columns. Rows represent records and columns represent attributes.

3. **Tuple** – It is nothing but a single row of a table, which contains a single record.

4. **Relation Schema:** A relation schema represents the name of the relation with its attributes.

5. **Degree:** The total number of attributes which in the relation is called the degree of the relation.

6. **Cardinality:** Total number of rows present in the Table.

7. **Column:** The column represents the set of values for a specific attribute.

8. **Relation instance** – Relation instance is a finite set of tuples in the RDBMS system. Relation instances never have duplicate tuples.
9. **Relation key** – Every row has one, two or multiple attributes, which is called relation key.
10. **Attribute domain** – Every attribute has some pre-defined value and scope which is known as attribute domain

Best Practices for Creating a Relational Model

⊿ Data need to be represented as a collection of relations
⊿ Each relation should be depicted clearly in the table
⊿ Rows should contain data about instances of an entity
⊿ Columns must contain data about attributes of the entity
⊿ Cells of the table should hold a single value
⊿ Each column should be given a unique name
⊿ No two rows can be identical
⊿ The values of an attribute should be from the same domain

Advantages of Using Relational Model

⊿ **Simplicity**: A relational data model is simpler than the hierarchical and network model.
⊿ **Structural Independence**: The relational database is only concerned with data and not with a structure. This can improve the performance of the model.
⊿ **Easy to use**: The relational model is easy as tables consisting of rows and columns is quite natural and simple to understand
⊿ **Query capability**: It makes possible for a high-level query language like SQL to avoid complex database navigation.
⊿ **Data independence**: The structure of a database can be changed without having to change any application.
⊿ **Scalable**: Regarding a number of records, or rows, and the number of fields, a database should be enlarged to enhance its usability.

Disadvntages of Using Relational Model

⋏ Few relational databases have limits on field lengths which can't be exceeded.

⋏ Relational databases can sometimes become complex as the amount of data grows, and the relations between pieces of data become more complicated.

⋏ Complex relational database systems may lead to isolated databases where the information cannot be shared from one system to another.

3.2 INTEGRITY CONSTRAINTS

Integrity constraints are a set of rules. It is used to maintain the quality of information. Integrity constraints ensure that the data insertion, updating, and other processes have to be performed in such a way that data integrity is not affected. Thus, integrity constraint is used to guard against accidental damage to the database. There are many types of integrity constraints. Constraints on the Relational database management system is mostly divided into

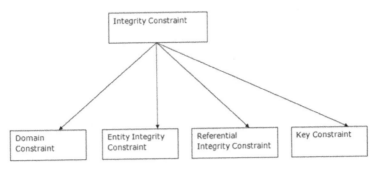

Domain Constraints

Domain constraints can be violated if an attribute value is not appearing in the corresponding domain or it is not of the appropriate data type. Domain constraints specify that within each tuple, and the value of each attribute must be unique. This is specified as data types which include standard datatypes integers, real numbers, characters, Booleans, variable length strings, etc. The value of the attribute must be available in the corresponding domain.

Example

Create DOMAIN CustomerName CHECK (value not NULL)

The example shown demonstrates creating a domain constraint such that CustomerName is not NULL

Entity integrity constraints

The entity integrity constraint states that primary key value can't be null. This is because the primary key value is used to identify individual rows in relation and if the primary key has a null value, then we can't identify those rows. A table can contain a null value other than the primary key field.

Example

EMPLOYEE

EMP_ID	EMP_NAME	SALARY
123	Jack	30000
142	Harry	60000
164	John	20000
	Jackson	27000

Not allowed as primary key can't contain a NULL value

Referential Integrity Constraints

A referential integrity constraint is specified between two tables. In the Referential integrity constraints, if a foreign key in Table 1 refers to the Primary Key of Table 2, then every value of the Foreign Key in Table 1 must be null or be available in Table 2.

Example

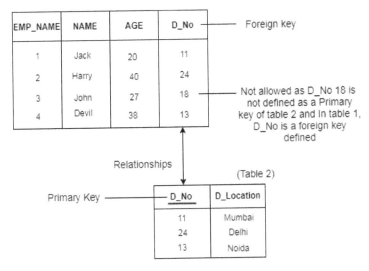

Key constraints

An attribute that can uniquely identify a tuple in a relation is called the key of the table. The value of the attribute for different tuples in the relation has to be unique.

Example

In the given table, CustomerID is a key attribute of Customer Table. It is most likely to have a single key for one customer, CustomerID =1 is only for the CustomerName =" Google".

CustomerID	CustomerName	Status
1	Google	Active
2	Amazon	Active
3	Apple	Inactive

Constraints are the rules that we can apply on the type of data in a table. That is, we can specify the limit on the type of data that can be stored in a particular column in a table using constraints.

The available constraints in SQL are:

- ✧ **NOT NULL**: This constraint tells that we cannot store a null value in a column. That is, if a column is specified as NOT NULL then we will not be able to store null in this particular column any more.
- ✧ **UNIQUE**: This constraint when specified with a column, tells that all the values in the column must be unique. That is, the values in any row of a column must not be repeated.
- ✧ **PRIMARY KEY**: A primary key is a field which can uniquely identify each row in a table. And this constraint is used to specify a field in a table as primary key.
- ✧ **FOREIGN KEY**: A Foreign key is a field which can uniquely identify each row in a another table. And this constraint is used to specify a field as Foreign key.
- ✧ **CHECK**: This constraint helps to validate the values of a column to meet a particular condition. That is, it helps to ensure that the value stored in a column meets a specific condition.
- ✧ **DEFAULT**: This constraint specifies a default value for the column when no value is specified by the user.

How to specify constraints?

We can specify constraints at the time of creating the table using CREATE TABLE statement. We can also specify the constraints after creating a table using ALTER TABLE statement.

Syntax

Below is the syntax to create constraints using CREATE TABLE statement at the time of creating the table.

CREATE TABLE sample_table
(
column1 data_type(size) constraint_name,

column2 data_type(size) constraint_name,

column3 data_type(size) constraint_name,

....

);

sample_table: Name of the table to be created.

data_type: Type of data that can be stored in the field.

constraint_name: Name of the constraint. for example – NOT NULL, UNIQUE, PRIMARY KEY etc.

Let us see each of the constraint in detail.

NOT NULL Constraint

If we specify a field in a table to be NOT NULL. Then the field will never accept null value. That is, you will be not allowed to insert a new row in the table without specifying any value to this field.

For example, the below query creates a table Student with the fields ID and NAME as NOT NULL. That is, we are bound to specify values for these two fields every time we wish to insert a new row.

CREATE TABLE Student(ID int(6) NOT NULL, NAME varchar(10) NOT NULL, ADDRESS varchar(20));

UNIQUE Constraint

This constraint helps to uniquely identify each row in the table. i.e. for a particular column, all the rows should have unique values. We can have more than one UNIQUE columns in a table.

For example, the below query creates a tale Student where the field ID is specified as UNIQUE. i.e, no two students can have the same ID.

CREATE TABLE Student (ID int(6) NOT NULL UNIQUE, NAME varchar(10), ADDRESS varchar(20));

PRIMARY KEY Constraint

Primary Key is a field which uniquely identifies each row in the table. If a field in a table as primary key, then the field will not be able to contain NULL values as well as all the rows should have unique values for this field. So, in other words we can say that this is combination of NOT NULL and UNIQUE constraints.

A table can have only one field as primary key. Below query will create a table named Student and specifies the field ID as primary key.

CREATE TABLE Student(ID int(6) NOT NULL UNIQUE, NAME varchar(10), ADDRESS varchar(20), PRIMARY KEY(ID));

FOREIGN KEY Constraint

Foreign Key is a field in a table which uniquely identifies each row of a another table. That is, this field points to primary key of another table. This usually creates a kind of link between the tables. Consider the two tables as shown below

Orders

O_ID	ORDER_NO	C_ID
1	2253	3
2	3325	3
3	4521	2
4	8532	1

Customers

C_ID	NAME	ADDRESS
1	RAMESH	DELHI
2	SURESH	NOIDA
3	DHARMESH	GURGAON

As we can see clearly that the field C_ID in Orders table is the primary key in Customers table, i.e. it uniquely identifies each row in the Customers table. Therefore, it is a Foreign Key in Orders table.

Syntax

CREATE TABLE Orders(O_ID int NOT NULL, ORDER_NO int NOT NULL, C_ID int, PRIMARY KEY (O_ID), FOREIGN KEY (C_ID) REFERENCES Customers(C_ID));

CHECK Constraint

Using the CHECK constraint we can specify a condition for a field, which should be satisfied at the time of entering values for this field.

For example, the below query creates a table Student and specifies the condition for the field AGE as (AGE >= 18). That is, the user will not be allowed to enter any record in the table with AGE < 18.

CREATE TABLE Student(ID int(6) NOT NULL, NAME varchar(10) NOT NULL, AGE int NOT NULL CHECK (AGE >= 18));

DEFAULT Constraint

This constraint is used to provide a default value for the fields. That is, if at the time of entering new records in the table if the user does not specify any value for these fields then the default value will be assigned to them.

For example, the below query will create a table named Student and specify the default value for the field AGE as 18.

CREATE TABLE Student(ID int(6) NOT NULL, NAME varchar(10) NOT NULL, AGE int DEFAULT 18);

3.3 QUERYING RELATIONAL DATA

The SQL **SELECT** statement is used to fetch the data from a database table which returns this data in the form of a result table. These result tables are called result-sets.

Syntax

The basic syntax of the SELECT statement is as follows –

SELECT column1, column2, columnN FROM table_name;

Here, column1, column2... are the fields of a table whose values you want to fetch. If you want to fetch all the fields available in the field, then you can use the following syntax.

SELECT * FROM table_name;

Example

Consider the CUSTOMERS table having the following records –

ID	NAME	AGE	ADDRESS	SALARY
1	Ramesh	32	Ahmedabad	2000.00
2	Khilan	25	Delhi	1500.00
3	kaushik	23	Kota	2000.00
4	Chaitali	25	Mumbai	6500.00
5	Hardik	27	Bhopal	8500.00
6	Komal	22	MP	4500.00
7	Muffy	24	Indore	10000.00

The following code is an example, which would fetch the ID, Name and Salary fields of the customers available in CUSTOMERS table.

SQL> SELECT ID, NAME, SALARY FROM CUSTOMERS;

This would produce the following result –

ID	NAME	SALARY
1	Ramesh	2000.00
2	Khilan	1500.00
3	kaushik	2000.00
4	Chaitali	6500.00
5	Hardik	8500.00

| 6 | Komal | 4500.00 |
| 7 | Muffy | 10000.00 |

If you want to fetch all the fields of the CUSTOMERS table, then you should use the following query.

SQL> SELECT * FROM CUSTOMERS;

This would produce the result as shown below.

ID	NAME	AGE	ADDRESS	SALARY
1	Ramesh	32	Ahmedabad	2000.00
2	Khilan	25	Delhi	1500.00
3	kaushik	23	Kota	2000.00
4	Chaitali	25	Mumbai	6500.00
5	Hardik	27	Bhopal	8500.00
6	Komal	22	MP	4500.00
7	Muffy	24	Indore	10000.00

3.4   VIEWS

Views in SQL are kind of virtual tables. A view also has rows and columns as they are in a real table in the database. We can create a view by selecting fields from one or more tables present in the database. A View can either have all the rows of a table or specific rows based on certain condition. In this we will learn about creating, deleting and updating Views.

Sample Tables

StudentDetails

S_ID	NAME	ADDRESS
1	Harsh	Kolkata
2	Ashish	Durgapur
3	Pratik	Delhi
4	Dhanraj	Bihar
5	Ram	Rajasthan

Student Marks

ID	NAME	MARKS	AGE
1	Harsh	90	19
2	Suresh	50	20
3	Pratik	80	19
4	Dhanraj	95	21
5	Ram	85	18

Creating Views

We can create View using **CREATE VIEW** statement. A View can be created from a single table or multiple tables.

Syntax

CREATE VIEW view_name AS SELECT column1, column2.....
FROM table_nameWHERE condition;

view_name: Name for the View

table_name: Name of the table

condition: Condition to select rows

Examples:

⋏   **Creating View from a single table:**
  ❖ In this example we will create a View named DetailsView from the table StudentDetails.

Query

CREATE VIEW DetailsView AS SELECT NAME, ADDRESS FROM StudentDetails WHERE S_ID < 5;

To see the data in the View, we can query the view in the same manner as we query a table.

SELECT * FROM DetailsView;

Output

NAME	ADDRESS
Harsh	Kolkata
Ashish	Durgapur
Pratik	Delhi
Dhanraj	Bihar

⋏ In this example, we will create a view named StudentNames from the table StudentDetails.

Query

CREATE VIEW StudentNames AS SELECT S_ID, NAME FROM StudentDetails ORDER BY NAME;

If we now query the view as,

SELECT * FROM StudentNames;

Output

S_ID	NAMES
2	Ashish
4	Dhanraj
1	Harsh
3	Pratik
5	Ram

⋏ **Creating View from multiple tables**

❖ In this example we will create a View named MarksView from two tables StudentDetails and StudentMarks. To create a View from multiple tables we can simply include multiple tables in the SELECT statement.

Query

CREATE VIEW MarksView AS SELECT StudentDetails. NAME, StudentDetails. ADDRESS, StudentMarks. MARKS FROM StudentDetails, StudentMarks WHERE StudentDetails. NAME = StudentMarks. NAME;

To display data of View MarksView:

SELECT * FROM MarksView;

Output

NAME	ADDRESS	MARKS
Harsh	Kolkata	90
Pratik	Delhi	80
Dhanraj	Bihar	95
Ram	Rajasthan	85

Deleting Views

We have learned about creating a View, but what if a created View is not needed any more? Obviously we will want to delete it. SQL allows us to delete an existing View. We can delete or drop a View using the DROP statement.

Syntax

DROP VIEW view_name;
view_name: Name of the View which we want to delete.
For example, if we want to delete the View **MarksView**, we can do this as:
DROP VIEW MarksView;

Updating Views

There are certain conditions needed to be satisfied to update a view. If any one of these conditions is **not** met, then we will not be allowed to update the view.

1. The SELECT statement which is used to create the view should not include GROUP BY clause or ORDER BY clause.
2. The SELECT statement should not have the DISTINCT keyword.
3. The View should have all NOT NULL values.
4. The view should not be created using nested queries or complex queries.
5. The view should be created from a single table. If the view is created using multiple tables then we will not be allowed to update the view.

➤ We can use the **CREATE OR REPLACE VIEW** statement to add or remove fields from a view.

Syntax

CREATE OR REPLACE VIEW view_name AS SELECT column1, coulmn2,... FROM table_name WHERE condition;

For example, if we want to update the view **MarksView** and add the field AGE to this View from **StudentMarks** Table, we can do this as:

CREATE OR REPLACE VIEW MarksView AS SELECT StudentDetails. NAME, StudentDetails. ADDRESS, StudentMarks. MARKS, StudentMarks. AGE FROM StudentDetails, StudentMarks WHERE StudentDetails. NAME = StudentMarks. NAME;

If we fetch all the data from MarksView now as:

SELECT * FROM MarksView;

Output

NAME	ADDRESS	MARKS	AGE
Harsh	Kolkata	90	19
Pratik	Delhi	80	19
Dhanraj	Bihar	95	21
Ram	Rajasthan	85	18

⅄   **Inserting a row in a view**

We can insert a row in a View in a same way as we do in a table. We can use the INSERT INTO statement of SQL to insert a row in a View.

Syntax

INSERT   view_name(column1,   column2,   column3,..) VALUES(value1, value2, value3..); view_name: Name of the View

Example:

In the below example we will insert a new row in the View DetailsView which we have created above in the example of "creating views from a single table".

INSERT   INTO   DetailsView(NAME,   ADDRESS) VALUES("Suresh", "Gurgaon");

If we fetch all the data from DetailsView now as,

SELECT * FROM DetailsView;

Output

NAME	ADDRESS
Harsh	Kolkata
Ashish	Durgapur
Pratik	Delhi
Dhanraj	Bihar
Suresh	Gurgaon

↗ Deleting a row from a View:

Deleting rows from a view is also as simple as deleting rows from a table. We can use the DELETE statement of SQL to delete rows from a view. Also deleting a row from a view first delete the row from the actual table and the change is then reflected in the view.

Syntax

DELETE FROM view_name WHERE condition;

view_name: Name of view from where we want to delete rows

condition: Condition to select rows

Example

In this example we will delete the last row from the view DetailsView which we just added in the above example of inserting rows.

DELETE FROM DetailsView WHERE NAME= "Suresh";

If we fetch all the data from DetailsView now as,

SELECT * FROM DetailsView;

Output

NAME	ADDRESS
Harsh	Kolkata
Ashish	Durgapur
Pratik	Delhi
Dhanraj	Bihar

With Check Option

The WITH CHECK OPTION clause in SQL is a very useful clause for views. It is applicable to a updatable view. If the view is not updatable, then there is no meaning of including this clause in the CREATE VIEW statement.

- ❖ The WITH CHECK OPTION clause is used to prevent the insertion of rows in the view where the condition in the WHERE clause in CREATE VIEW statement is not satisfied.
- ❖ If we have used the WITH CHECK OPTION clause in the CREATE VIEW statement, and if the UPDATE or INSERT clause does not satisfy the conditions then they will return an error.

Example

In the below example we are creating a View SampleView from StudentDetails Table with WITH CHECK OPTION clause.

CREATE VIEW SampleView AS SELECT S_ID, NAME FROM StudentDetails WHERE NAME IS NOT NULLWITH CHECK OPTION;

In this View if we now try to insert a new row with null value in the NAME column then it will give an error because the view is created with the condition for NAME column as NOT NULL. For example, though the View is updatable but then also the below query for this View is not valid:

INSERT INTO SampleView(S_ID) VALUES(6);

NOTE: The default value of NAME column is null.

Chapter 4

Relational Algebra and Calculus

4.1 RELATIONAL ALGEBRA

Relational algebra is a procedural query language. It gives a step by step process to obtain the result of the query. It uses operators to perform queries. In relational algebra, input is a relation(table from which data has to be accessed) and output is also a relation(a temporary table holding the data asked for by the user).

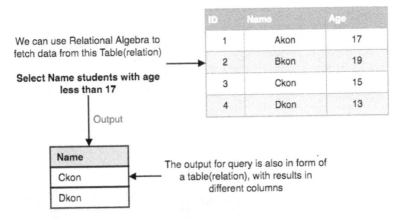

We can use Relational Algebra to fetch data from this Table(relation)

Select Name students with age less than 17

Output

ID	Name	Age
1	Akon	17
2	Bkon	19
3	Ckon	15
4	Dkon	13

Name
Ckon
Dkon

The output for query is also in form of a table(relation), with results in different columns

Relational Algebra works on the whole table at once, so we do not have to use loops etc to iterate over all the rows(tuples) of data one by one. All we have to do is specify the table name from which we need the data, and in a single line of command, relational algebra will traverse the entire given table to fetch data for you.

The primary operations that we can perform using relational algebra are:

1. Select
2. Project
3. Union
4. Intersection
5. Set Difference
6. Cartesian product
7. Rename

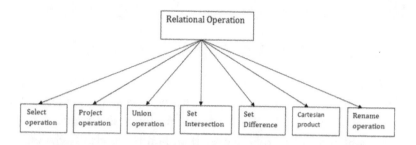

Table 1: STUDENT_SPORT

ROLL_NO	SPORTS
1	Badminton
2	Cricket
2	Badminton
4	Badminton

Table 2: EMPLOYEE

EMP_NO	NAME	ADDRESS	PHONE	AGE
1	RAM	DELHI	9455123451	18
5	NARESH	HISAR	9782918192	22
6	SWETA	RANCHI	9852617621	21
4	SURESH	DELHI	9156768971	18

Table 3: STUDENT

ROLL_NO	NAME	ADDRESS	PHONE	AGE
1	RAM	DELHI	9455123451	18
2	RAMESH	GURGAON	9652431543	18
3	SUJIT	ROHTAK	9156253131	20
4	SURESH	DELHI	9156768971	18

1. Selection Operator (σ)

The SELECT operation is used for selecting a subset of the tuples according to a given selection condition. Sigma(σ) Symbol denotes it. It is used as an expression to choose tuples which meet the selection condition. Select operation selects tuples that satisfy a given predicate. We will use STUDENT_SPORTS, EMPLOYEE and STUDENT relations as given in Table 1, Table 2 and Table 3 respectively to understand the various operators.

Selection operator is used to select tuples from a relation based on some condition.

Syntax

σ $_{(Cond)}$ **(Relation Name)**

Extract students whose age is greater than 18 from STUDENT relation given in Table 1

σ $_{(AGE>18)}$ **(STUDENT)**

Result

ROLL_NO	NAME	ADDRESS	PHONE	AGE
3	SUJIT	ROHTAK	9156253131	20

2. Projection Operator (π)

Projection operator is used to project particular columns from a relation.

Syntax

$\Pi_{(Column\ 1,\ Column\ 2.... Column\ n)}$ **(Relation Name)**

Extract ROLL_NO and NAME from STUDENT relation given in Table 3

$\Pi_{(ROLL\_NO,\ NAME)}$**(STUDENT)**

Result

ROLL_NO	NAME
1	RAM
2	RAMESH
3	SUJIT
4	SURESH

Note: If resultant relation after projection has duplicate rows, it will be removed. For Example: $\Pi_{(ADDRESS)}$(STUDENT) will remove one duplicate row with value DELHI and return three rows.

3. Union (∪)

Union on two relations R1 and R2 can only be computed if R1 and R2 are **union compatible** (These two relation should have same number of attributes and corresponding attributes in two relations have same domain). Union operator when applied on two relations R1 and R2 will give a relation with tuples which are either in R1 or in R2. The tuples which are in both R1 and R2 will appear only once in result relation.

Syntax

Relation1 U Relation2

Find person who are either student or employee, we can use Union operator like:

STUDENT U EMPLOYEE

Result:

ROLL_NO	NAME	ADDRESS	PHONE	AGE
1	RAM	DELHI	9455123451	18
2	RAMESH	GURGAON	9652431543	18
3	SUJIT	ROHTAK	9156253131	20
4	SURESH	DELHI	9156768971	18
5	NARESH	HISAR	9782918192	22
6	SWETA	RANCHI	9852617621	21

4. Intersection ($\cap$)

Intersection on two relations R1 and R2 can only be computed if R1 and R2 are union compatible (These two relation should have same number of attributes and corresponding attributes in two relations have same domain). Intersection operator when applied on two relations as R1$\cap$R2 will give a relation with tuples which are in R1 as well as R2.

Syntax

Relation1 $\cap$ Relation2

Example: Find a person who is student as well as employee –
STUDENT $\cap$ EMPLOYEE

In terms of basic operators (union and set difference):

STUDENT $\cap$ EMPLOYEE = STUDENT + EMPLOYEE – (STUDENT U EMPLOYEE)

Result

ROLL_NO	NAME	ADDRESS	PHONE	AGE
1	RAM	DELHI	9455123451	18
4	SURESH	DELHI	9156768971	18

5. Set Difference (-)

Minus on two relations R1 and R2 can only be computed if R1 and R2 are **union compatible**. Minus operator when applied on two relations as R1-R2 will give a relation with tuples which are in R1 but not in R2.

Syntax

Relation1 – Relation2

Find person who are student but not employee, we can use minus operator like:

STUDENT – EMPLOYEE

Result

ROLL_NO	NAME	ADDRESS	PHONE	AGE
2	RAMESH	GURGAON	9652431543	18
3	SUJIT	ROHTAK	9156253131	20

6. Cartesian Product (X)

Cross product is used to join two relations. For every row of Relation1, each row of Relation2 is concatenated. If Relation1 has m tuples and and Relation2 has n tuples, cross product of Relation1 and Relation2 will have m X n tuples. Syntax:

Relation1 X Relation2

To apply Cross Product on STUDENT relation given in Table 1 and STUDENT_SPORTS relation given in Table 2,

STUDENT X STUDENT_SPORTS

Result

ROLL_NO	NAME	ADDRESS	PHONE	AGE	ROLL_NO	SPORTS
1	RAM	DELHI	9455123451	18	1	Badminton
1	RAM	DELHI	9455123451	18	2	Cricket
1	RAM	DELHI	9455123451	18	2	Badminton
1	RAM	DELHI	9455123451	18	4	Badminton
2	RAMESH	GURGAON	9652431543	18	1	Badminton
2	RAMESH	GURGAON	9652431543	18	2	Cricket
2	RAMESH	GURGAON	9652431543	18	2	Badminton
2	RAMESH	GURGAON	9652431543	18	4	Badminton
3	SUJIT	ROHTAK	9156253131	20	1	Badminton
3	SUJIT	ROHTAK	9156253131	20	2	Cricket
3	SUJIT	ROHTAK	9156253131	20	2	Badminton
3	SUJIT	ROHTAK	9156253131	20	4	Badminton
4	SURESH	DELHI	9156768971	18	1	Badminton
4	SURESH	DELHI	9156768971	18	2	Badminton
4	SURESH	DELHI	9156768971	18	2	Cricket
4	SURESH	DELHI	9156768971	18	4	Badminton

7. Rename(ρ)

Rename operator is used to give another name to a relation.

Syntax

ρ(Relation2, Relation1)

To rename STUDENT relation to STUDENT1, we can use rename operator like:

ρ(STUDENT1, STUDENT)

If you want to create a relation STUDENT_NAMES with ROLL_NO and NAME from STUDENT, it can be done using rename operator as:

ρ(STUDENT_NAMES, $\Pi_{(ROLL\_NO,\ NAME)}$(STUDENT))

4.2   JOINS

Join is used to fetch data from two or more tables, which is joined to appear as single set of data. It is used for combining column from two or more tables by using values common to both tables. Join operation is essentially a cartesian product followed by a selection criterion.

Join operation denoted by ⋈.

JOIN operation also allows joining variously related tuples from different relations.

Types of JOIN

Various forms of join operation are:

Inner Joins

⋏ Theta join
⋏ EQUI join
⋏ Natural join

Outer Join

⋏ Left Outer Join
⋏ Right Outer Join
⋏ Full Outer Join

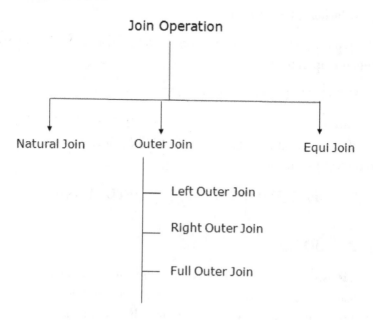

4.2.1 Inner Join

In an inner join, only those tuples that satisfy the matching criteria are included, while the rest are excluded. Let's study various types of Inner Joins:

1. Theta Join

The general case of JOIN operation is called a Theta join. It is denoted by symbol θ

Example

$A \bowtie_{\theta} B$

Theta join can use any conditions in the selection criteria.

For example

$A \bowtie_{\text{A. column 2} > \text{B. column 2}} (B)$

A ⋈ A. column 2 > B. column 2 (B)	
column 1	column 2
1	2

2. Equi Join

It is also known as an inner join. It is the most common join. It is based on matched data as per the equality condition. The equi join uses the comparison operator(=).

Example
Customer Relation

CLASS_ID	NAME
1	John
2	Harry
3	Jackson

Product

PRODUCT_ID	CITY
1	Delhi
2	Mumbai
3	Noida

Input
1. Customer ⋈ Product

Output

CLASS_ID	NAME	PRODUCT_ID	CITY
1	John	1	Delhi
2	Harry	2	Mumbai
3	Harry	3	Noida

3. Natural Join

A natural join is the set of tuples of all combinations in R and S that are equal on their common attribute names. It is denoted by ⋈.

Example: Let's use the above EMPLOYEE table and SALARY table:

Input

1. ΠEMP_NAME, SALARY (EMPLOYEE ⋈ SALARY)

Output

EMP_NAME	SALARY
Stephan	50000
Jack	30000
Harry	25000

4.2.2 Outer Join

In an outer join, along with tuples that satisfy the matching criteria, we also include some or all tuples that do not match the criteria.

Example
Employee

EMP_NAME	STREET	CITY
Ram	Civil line	Mumbai
Shyam	Park street	Kolkata
Ravi	M. G. Street	Delhi
Hari	Nehru nagar	Hyderabad

Fact_workers

EMP_NAME	BRANCH	SALARY
Ram	Infosys	10000
Shyam	Wipro	20000
Kuber	HCL	30000
Hari	TCS	50000

1. Left Outer Join (⋈)

In the left outer join, operation allows keeping all tuple in the left relation. However, if there is no matching tuple is found in right relation, then the attributes of right relation in the join result are filled with null values. Left outer join contains the set of tuples of all combinations in R and S that are equal on their common attribute names. In the left outer join, tuples in R have no matching tuples in S. It is denoted by ⋈.

All rows from Left Table.

Example: Using the above EMPLOYEE table and FACT_WORKERS table

Input
EMPLOYEE ⋈ FACT_WORKERS

Output

EMP_NAME	STREET	CITY	BRANCH	SALARY
Ram	Civil line	Mumbai	Infosys	10000
Shyam	Park street	Kolkata	Wipro	20000
Hari	Nehru street	Hyderabad	TCS	50000
Ravi	M. G. Street	Delhi	NULL	NULL

2. Right Outer Join(⋈)

In the right outer join, operation allows keeping all tuple in the right relation. However, if there is no matching tuple is found in the left relation, then the attributes of the left relation in the join result are filled with null values. Right outer join contains the set of tuples of all combinations in R and S that are equal on their common attribute names. In right outer join, tuples in S have no matching tuples in R. It is denoted by ⋈.

All rows from Right Table.

Example: Using the above EMPLOYEE table and FACT_WORKERS Relation

Input

EMPLOYEE ⋈ FACT_WORKERS

Output

EMP_NAME	BRANCH	SALARY	STREET	CITY
Ram	Infosys	10000	Civil line	Mumbai
Shyam	Wipro	20000	Park street	Kolkata

EMP_NAME	BRANCH	SALARY	STREET	CITY
Hari	TCS	50000	Nehru street	Hyderabad
Kuber	HCL	30000	NULL	NULL

3. Full Outer Join(⋈)

In a full outer join, all tuples from both relations are included in the result, irrespective of the matching condition. Full outer join is like a left or right join except that it contains all rows from both tables. In full outer join, tuples in R that have no matching tuples in S. and tuples in S that have no matching tuples in R in their common attribute name. It is denoted by ⋈.

Example: Using the above EMPLOYEE table and FACT_ WORKERS table

Input

EMPLOYEE ⋈ FACT_WORKERS

Output

EMP_NAME	STREET	CITY	BRANCH	SALARY
Ram	Civil line	Mumbai	Infosys	10000
Shyam	Park street	Kolkata	Wipro	20000
Hari	Nehru street	Hyderabad	TCS	50000
Ravi	M. G. Street	Delhi	NULL	NULL
Kuber	NULL	NULL	HCL	30000

Summary

OPERATION	PURPOSE
Select(σ)	The SELECT operation is used for selecting a subset of the tuples according to a given selection condition
Projection(π)	The projection eliminates all attributes of the input relation but those mentioned in the projection list.

Contd...

OPERATION	PURPOSE
Union Operation(∪)	UNION is symbolized by symbol. It includes all tuples that are in tables A or in B.
Set Difference(-)	– Symbol denotes it. The result of A – B, is a relation which includes all tuples that are in A but not in B.
Intersection(∩)	Intersection defines a relation consisting of a set of all tuple that are in both A and B.
Cartesian Product(X)	Cartesian operation is helpful to merge columns from two relations.
Inner Join	Inner join, includes only those tuples that satisfy the matching criteria.
Theta Join(θ)	The general case of JOIN operation is called a Theta join. It is denoted by symbol θ.
EQUI Join	When a theta join uses only equivalence condition, it becomes a equi join.
Natural Join(⋈)	Natural join can only be performed if there is a common attribute (column) between the relations.
Outer Join	In an outer join, along with tuples that satisfy the matching criteria.
Left Outer Join(⟖)	In the left outer join, operation allows keeping all tuple in the left relation.
Right Outer join(⟗)	In the right outer join, operation allows keeping all tuple in the right relation.
Full Outer Join(⟗)	In a full outer join, all tuples from both relations are included in the result irrespective of the matching condition.

4.3   DIVISION OPERATOR (÷)

Division operator A÷B can be applied if and only if:

- ✧ Attributes of B is proper subset of Attributes of A.
- ✧ The relation returned by division operator will have attributes = (All attributes of A – All Attributes of B)

✦ The relation returned by division operator will return those tuples from relation A which are associated to every B's tuple.

Table 2: ALL_SPORTS

SPORTS
Badminton
Cricket

Table 3: EMPLOYEE

EMP_NO	NAME	ADDRESS	PHONE	AGE
1	RAM	DELHI	9455123451	18
5	NARESH	HISAR	9782918192	22
6	SWETA	RANCHI	9852617621	21
4	SURESH	DELHI	9156768971	18

Consider the relation STUDENT_SPORTS and ALL_SPORTS given in Table 2 and Table 3 above.

To apply division operator as

STUDENT_SPORTS÷ ALL_SPORTS

➤ The operation is valid as attributes in ALL_SPORTS is a proper subset of attributes in STUDENT_SPORTS.

➤ The attributes in resulting relation will have attributes {ROLL_NO, SPORTS}-{SPORTS}=ROLL_NO

➤ The tuples in resulting relation will have those ROLL_NO which are associated with all B's tuple {Badminton, Cricket}. ROLL_NO 1 and 4 are associated to Badminton only. ROLL_NO 2 is associated to all tuples of B. So the resulting relation will be:

ROLL_NO
2

4.4 RELATIONAL CALCULUS

In non-procedural query language and has no description about how the query will work or the data will b fetched. It only focusses on what to do, and not on how to do it.

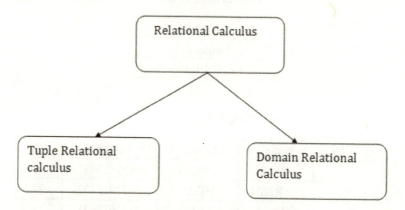

Relational Calculus exists in two forms:

1. Tuple Relational Calculus (TRC)
2. Domain Relational Calculus (DRC)

4.5 TUPLE RELATIONAL CALCULUS (TRC)

In tuple relational calculus, we work on filtering tuples based on the given condition. The tuple relational calculus is specified to select the tuples in a relation. In TRC, filtering variable uses the tuples of a relation. The result of the relation can have one or more tuples.

Syntax: {T | Condition}

In this form of relational calculus, we define a tuple variable, specify the table(relation) name in which the tuple is to be searched for, along with a condition. We can also specify column name using a. dot operator, with the tuple variable to only get a certain attribute(column) in result. A lot of informtion, right! Give it some time to sink in.

A tuple variable is nothing but a name, can be anything, generally we use a single alphabet for this, so let's say T is a tuple variable. To specify the name of the relation(table) in which we want to look for data, we do the following:

Relation(T), where T is our tuple variable.

For example if our table is **Student**, we would put it as Student(T)

Then comes the condition part, to specify a condition applicable for a particular attribute(column), we can use the. dot variable with the tuple variable to specify it, like in table **Student**, if we want to get data for students with age greater than 17, then, we can write it as, T. age > 17, where T is our tuple variable. Putting it all together, if we want to use Tuple Relational Calculus to fetch names of students, from table **Student**, with age greater than **17**, then, for T being our tuple variable, T. name | Student(T) AND T. age > 17

4.6   DOMAIN RELATIONAL CALCULUS (DRC)

In domain relational calculus, filtering is done based on the domain of the attributes and not based on the tuple values. The second form of relation is known as Domain relational calculus. In domain relational calculus, filtering variable uses the domain of attributes. Domain relational calculus uses the same operators as tuple calculus. It uses logical connectives ∧ (and), ∨ (or) and ¬ (not). It uses Existential (∃) and Universal Quantifiers (∀) to bind the variable.

Syntax: {c1, c2, c3,..., cn | F(c1, c2, c3,..., cn)}

where, c1, c2... etc represents domain of attributes(columns) and F defines the formula including the condition for fetching the data.

For Example,

{< name, age > | ∈ Student ∧ age > 17}

Again, the above query will return the names and ages of the students in the table **Student** who are older than 17.

4.7   EXPRESSIVE POWER OF ALGEBRA AND CALCULUS

We presented two formal query languages for the relational model. Are they equivalent in power? Can every query that can be expressed in relational algebra also be expressed in relational calculus? The answer is yes, it can.

Regarding expressiveness, we can show that every query that can be expressed using a safe relational calculus query can also be expressed as a relational algebra query. The expressive power of relational algebra is often used as a metric of how powerful a relational database query language is. If a query language can express all the queries that we can express in relational algebra, it is said to be relationally complete. A practical query language is expected to be relationally complete; in addition, commercial query languages typically support features that allow us to express some queries that cannot be expressed in relational algebra.

4.8   FORM OF BASIC SQL QUERY

Introduction

Structured Query Language (SQL) is the most widely used commercial relational database language. It was originally developed at IBM in the SEQUEL XRM and System-R projects (1974-1977). Almost immediately, other vendors introduced DBMS products based on SQL, and it is now a de facto standard. SQL continues to evolve in response to changing needs in the database area.

Overview

The SQL language has several aspects to it.

The Data Manipulation Language (DML): This subset of SQL allows users to pose queries and to insert, delete, and modify rows. Queries are the main focus of this chapter. We covered DML commands to insert, delete, and modify rows

The Data Definition Language (DDL): This subset of SQL supports the creation, deletion, and modification of definitions for tables and views. Integrity constraints can be defined on tables, either when the table is created or later. Although the standard does not discuss indexes, commercial implementations also provide commands for creating and deleting indexes.

Triggers and Advanced Integrity Constraints: The new SQL: 1999 standard includes support for triggers, which are actions executed by the DBMS whenever changes to the database meet conditions specified in the trigger.

Embedded and Dynamic SQL: Embedded SQL features allow SQL code to be called from a host language such as C or COBOL. Dynamic SQL features allow a query to be constructed (and executed) at run-time.

Client-Server Execution and Remote Database Access: These commands control how a client application program can connect to an SQL database server, or access data from a database over a network.

Transaction Management: Various commands allow a user to explicitly control aspects of how a transaction is to be executed.

Security: SQL provides mechanisms to control users' access to data objects such as tables and views.

Advanced features: The SQL: 1999 standard includes object-oriented features, recursive queries, decision support queries, and also addresses emerging areas such as data mining, spatial data, and text and XML data management

4.9   BASIC STRUCTURE OF SQL

The basic structure of an SQL consists of three clauses: **select, from** and **where.**

- ✧ **select:** it corresponds to the projection operation of relational algebra. Used to list the attributes desired in the result.
- ✧ **from:** corresponds to the Cartesian product operation of relational algebra. Used to list the relations to be scanned in the evaluation of the expression
- ✧ **where:** corresponds to the selection predicate of the relational algebra. It consists of a predicate involving attributes of the relations that appear in the **from** clause.
- ✧ A typical SQL query has the form:

    select $A_1, A_2, ..., A_n$
    from $r_1, r_2, ..., r_m$
    where P

- ✧ A_i represents an attribute
- ✧ r_j represents a relation
- ✧ P is a predicate
- ✧ It is equivalent to following relational algebra expression:

[**Note:** The words marked in dark in this text work as keywords in SQL language. For example "select", "from" and "where" in the above paragraph are shown in bold font to indicate that they are keywords]

Select Clause

Let us see some simple queries and use of **select** clause to express them in SQL.

Find the names of all branches in the Loan relation
select branch-name **from** Loan

✧ By default the **select** clause includes duplicate values. If we want to force the elimination of duplicates the **distinct** keyword is used as follows:

select distinct branch-name **from** Loan

✧ The **all** key word can be used to specify explicitly that duplicates are not removed. Even if we not use **all** it means the same so we don't require **all** to use in **select** clause.

select all branch-name **from** Loan

✧ The asterisk "*" can be used to denote "all attributes". The following SQL statement will select and all the attributes of Loan.

SELECT * FROM LOAN;

✧ The arithmetic expressions involving operators, +, −, *, and / are also allowed in **select** clause. The following statement will return the amount multiplied by 100 for the rows in Loan table.

SELECT BRANCH-NAME, LOAN-NUMBER, AMOUNT * 100 **FROM** LOAN;

Where Clause

⋏ Find all loan numbers for loans made at "Sadar" branch with loan amounts greater than Rs 1200

SELECT LOAN-NUMBER **FROM** LOAN **WHERE** BRANCH-NAME= "SADAR" **AND** AMOUNT > 1200;

⋏ **where** clause uses uses logival connectives **and**, **or**, and **not**

Operands of the logical connectives can be expressions involving the comparison operators <, <=, >, >=, =, and < >.

➤   **between** can be used to simplify the comparisons

> **SELECT** LOAN-NUMBER **FROM** LOAN **WHERE** AMOUNT BETWEEN 90000 AND 100000;

From Clause

➤   The **from** clause by itself defines a Cartesian product of the relations in the clause.

➤   When an attribute is present in more than one relation they can be referred as relation-name. attribute-name to avoid the ambiguity.

➤   For all customers who have loan from the bank, find their names and loan numbers

SELECT DISTINCT CUSTOMER-NAME, BORROWER. LOAN-NUMBER **FROM** BORROWER, LOAN **WHERE** BORROWER. LOAN-NUMBER = LOAN. LOAN-NUMBER

4.10 NESTED QUERIES

One of the most powerful features of SQL is nested queries. A nested query is a query that has another query embedded within it; the embedded query is called a subquery. The embedded query can of course be a nested query itself; thus queries that have very deeply nested structures are possible. When writing a query, we sometimes need to express a condition that refers to a table that must itself be computed. The query used to compute this subsidiary table is a subquery and appears as part of the main query. A subquery typically appears within the WHERE clause of a query. Subqueries can sometimes appear in the FROM clause or the HAVING clause.

In nested queries, a query is written inside a query. The result of inner query is used in execution of outer query. We will use **STUDENT, COURSE, STUDENT_COURSE tables for understanding nested queries.**

Student

S_ID	S_NAME	S_ADDRESS	S_PHONE	S_AGE
S1	RAM	DELHI	9455123451	18
S2	RAMESH	GURGAON	9652431543	18
S3	SUJIT	ROHTAK	9156253131	20
S4	SURESH	DELHI	9156768971	18

Course

C_ID	C_NAME
C1	DSA
C2	Programming
C3	DBMS

Student_course

S_ID	C_ID
S1	C1
S1	C3
S2	C1
S3	C2
S4	C2
S4	C3

There are mainly two types of nested queries:

Independent Nested Queries
In independent nested queries, query execution starts from innermost query to outermost queries. The execution of inner query is independent of outer query, but the result of inner query is used

in execution of outer query. Various operators like IN, NOT IN, ANY, ALL etc are used in writing independent nested queries.

IN: If we want to find out **S_ID** who are enrolled in **C_NAME** 'DSA' or 'DBMS', we can write it with the help of independent nested query and IN operator. From **COURSE** table, we can find out **C_ID** for **C_NAME** 'DSA' or DBMS' and we can use these **C_ID**s for finding **S_ID**s from **STUDENT_COURSE** TABLE.

STEP 1: Finding **C_ID** for **C_NAME** = 'DSA' or 'DBMS'

> SELECT **C_ID** FROM **COURSE** WHERE **C_NAME** = 'DSA' OR **C_NAME** = 'DBMS'

STEP 2: USING **C_ID** OF STEP 1 FOR FINDING **S_ID**

> SELECT **S_ID** FROM **STUDENT_COURSE** WHERE **C_ID** IN
>
> (SELECT **C_ID** FROM **COURSE** WHERE **C_NAME** = 'DSA' OR **C_NAME**= 'DBMS');

The inner query will return a set with members C1 and C3 and outer query will return those **S_ID**s for which **C_ID** is equal to any member of set (C1 and C3 in this case). So, it will return S1, S2 and S4.

Note: If we want to find out names of **STUDENT**s who have either enrolled in 'DSA' or 'DBMS', it CAN BE DONE AS:

> SELECT **S_NAME** FROM **STUDENT** WHERE **S_ID** IN
>
> (SELECT **S_ID** FROM **STUDENT_COURSE** WHERE **C_ID** IN
>
> (SELECT **C_ID** FROM **COURSE** WHERE **C_NAME**= 'DSA' OR **C_NAME**= 'DBMS'));

NOT IN: If we want to find out **S_ID**s of **STUDENT**s who have neither enrolled in 'DSA' nor in 'DBMS', it can be done as:

SELECT **S_ID** FROM **STUDENT** WHERE **S_ID** NOT IN

(SELECT **S_ID** FROM **STUDENT_COURSE** WHERE **C_ID** IN

(SELECT **C_ID** FROM **COURSE** WHERE **C_NAME**= 'DSA' OR **C_NAME**= 'DBMS'));

The innermost query will return a set with members C1 and C3. Second inner query will return those **S_ID**s for which **C_ID** is equal to any member of set (C1 and C3 in this case) which are S1, S2 and S4. The outermost query will return those **S_ID**s where **S_ID** is not a member of set (S1, S2 and S4). So it will return S3.

CO-RELATED NESTED QUERIES

In co-related nested queries, the output of inner query depends on the row which is being currently executed in outer query. e.g.; If we want to find out **S_NAME** of **STUDENT**s who are enrolled in **C_ID** 'C1', it can be done with the help of co-related nested query as:

SELECT S_NAME FROM **STUDENT** S WHERE EXISTS

(SELECT * FROM **STUDENT_COURSE** SC WHERE S.**S_ID**=SC.**S_ID** AND SC.**C_ID**= 'C1');

For each row of **STUDENT** S, it will find the rows from **STUDENT_COURSE** where S. **S_ID** = SC. **S_ID** and SC. **C_ID**= 'C1'. If for a **S_ID** from **STUDENT** S, atleast a row exists in **STUDENT_COURSE** SC with **C_ID**= 'C1', then inner query will return true and corresponding **S_ID** will be returned as output.

4.11 SET – COMPARISON OPERATORS

SQL supports few Set operations which can be performed on the table data. These are used to get meaningful results from data stored in the table, under different special conditions.

There are 4 different types of SET operations, they are discussed below:

1. UNION
2. UNION ALL
3. INTERSECT
4. MINUS

1. UNION Operation

UNION is used to combine the results of two or more SELECT statements. However it will eliminate duplicate rows from its resultset. In case of union, number of columns and datatype must be same in both the tables, on which UNION operation is being applied.

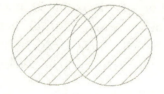

Example of UNION

The First table,

ID	Name
1	abhi
2	adam

The Second table,

ID	Name
2	Adam
3	Chester

Union SQL query will be,

SELECT * FROM First UNION SELECT * FROM Second;

The resultset table will look like,

ID	NAME
1	abhi
2	adam
3	Chester

2. UNION All

This operation is similar to Union. But it also shows the duplicate rows.

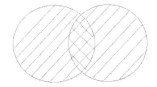

Example of Union All

The First table,

ID	NAME
1	abhi
2	adam

The Second table,

ID	NAME
2	Adam
3	Chester

Union All sql query will be like,

SELECT * FROM First UNION ALL SELECT * FROM Second;

The resultset table will look like,

ID	NAME
1	Abhi
2	Adam
2	Adam
3	Chester

3. Intersect

Intersect operation is used to combine two SELECT statements, but it only retuns the records which are common from both SELECT statements. In case of Intersect the number of columns and datatype must be same.

NOTE: MySQL does not support INTERSECT operator.

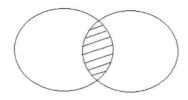

Example of Intersect

The First table,

ID	NAME
1	Abhi
2	Adam

The Second table,

ID	NAME
2	Adam
3	Chester

Intersect query will be,

SELECT * FROM First INTERSECT SELECT * FROM Second;

The resultset table will look like

ID	NAME
2	Adam

4. MINUS

The Minus operation combines results of two SELECT statements and return only those in the final result, which belongs to the first set of the result.

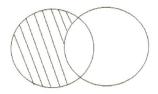

Example of Minus

The First table,

ID	NAME
1	Abhi
2	Adam

The Second table,

ID	NAME
2	Adam
3	Chester

Minus sql query will be,

SELECT * FROM First MINUS SELECT * FROM Second;

The resultset table will look like,

ID	NAME
1	Abhi

There are three Logical Operators namely, AND, OR, and NOT. These operators compare two conditions at a time to determine whether a row can be selected for the output. When retrieving data using a SELECT statement, you can use logical operators in the WHERE clause, which allows you to combine more than one condition.

Logical Operators	Description
OR	For the row to be selected at least one of the conditions must be true.
AND	For a row to be selected all the specified conditions must be true.
NOT	For a row to be selected the specified condition must be false.

"OR" Logical Operator

If you want to select rows that satisfy at least one of the given conditions, you can use the logical operator, OR. **For example:** if you want to find the names of students who are studying either Maths or Science, the query would be like,

SELECT first_name, last_name, subject FROM student_details WHERE subject = 'Maths' OR subject = 'Science'

The output would be something like,

first_name	last_name	subject
Anajali	Bhagwat	Maths
Shekar	Gowda	Maths
Rahul	Sharma	Science
Stephen	Fleming	Science

The following table describes how logical "OR" operator selects a row.

Column1 Satisfied?	Column2 Satisfied?	Row Selected
YES	YES	YES
YES	NO	YES
NO	YES	YES
NO	NO	NO

"AND" Logical Operator

If you want to select rows that must satisfy all the given conditions, you can use the logical operator, AND. **For Example:** To find the names of the students between the age 10 to 15 years, the query would be like:

SELECT FIRST_NAME, LAST_NAME, AGE FROM STUDENT_DETAILS WHERE AGE >= 10 AND AGE <= 15;

The output would be something like,

first_name	last_name	age
Rahul	Sharma	10
Anajali	Bhagwat	12
Shekar	Gowda	15

The following table describes how logical "AND" operator selects a row.

Column1 Satisfied?	Column2 Satisfied?	Row Selected
YES	YES	YES
YES	NO	NO
NO	YES	NO
NO	NO	NO

"NOT" Logical Operator

If you want to find rows that do not satisfy a condition, you can use the logical operator, NOT. NOT results in the reverse of a condition. That is, if a condition is satisfied, then the row is not returned.

For example: If you want to find out the names of the students who do not play football, the query would be like:

SELECT first_name, last_name, games FROM student_details WHERE NOT games = ‹Football›

The output would be something like,

first_name	last_name	Games
Rahul	Sharma	Cricket
Stephen	Fleming	Cricket
Shekar	Gowda	Badminton
Priya	Chandra	Chess

The following table describes how logical "NOT" operator selects a row.

Column1 Satisfied?	NOT Column1 Satisfied?	Row Selected
YES	NO	NO
NO	YES	YES

Nested Logical Operators

You can use multiple logical operators in an SQL statement. When you combine the logical operators in a SELECT statement, the order in which the statement is processed is

1. NOT
2. AND
3. OR

For example

If you want to select the names of the students who age is between 10 and 15 years, or those who do not play football, the SELECT statement would be

SELECT first_name, last_name, age, gamesFROM student_details WHERE age >= 10 AND age <= 15 OR NOT games = 'Football'

The output would be something like,

first_name	last_name	Age	games
Rahul	Sharma	10	Cricket
Priya	Chandra	15	Chess

In this case, the filter works as follows:

Condition1: All the students you do not play football are selected.

Condition2: All the students whose are aged between 10 and 15 are selected.

Condition 3: Finally the result is, the rows which satisfy atleast one of the above conditions is returned.

NOTE: The order in which you phrase the condition is important, if the order changes you are likely to get a different result.

There are other comparison keywords available in sql which are used to enhance the search capabilities of a sql query. They are "IN", "BETWEEN... AND", "IS NULL", "LIKE".

Comparision Operators	Description
LIKE	column value is similar to specified character(s).
IN	column value is equal to any one of a specified set of values.
BETWEEN... AND	column value is between two values, including the end values specified in the range.
IS NULL	column value does not exist.

SQL LIKE Operator

The LIKE operator is used to list all rows in a table whose column values match a specified pattern. It is useful when you want to search rows to match a specific pattern, or when you do not know the entire value. For this purpose we use a wildcard character '%'.

For example: To select all the students whose name begins with ‹S›

SELECT first_name, last_name FROM student_details WHERE first_name LIKE ‹S%›;

The output would be similar to:

first_name	last_name
Stephen	Fleming
Shekar	Gowda

The above select statement searches for all the rows where the first letter of the column first_name is 'S' and rest of the letters in the name can be any character.

There is another wildcard character you can use with LIKE operator. It is the underscore character, '_'. In a search string, the underscore signifies a single character.

For example: to display all the names with ‹a› second character,

SELECT first_name, last_name FROM student_details WHERE first_name LIKE '_a%';

The output would be similar to:

first_name	last_name
Rahul	Sharma

NOTE: Each underscore act as a placeholder for only one character. So you can use more than one underscore. Eg: ' __i%' - this has two underscores towards the left, 'S__j%' – this has two underscores between character 'S' and 'i'.

SQL BETWEEN... AND Operator

The operator BETWEEN and AND, are used to compare data for a range of values.

For Example: to find the names of the students between age 10 to 15 years, the query would be like,

SELECT first_name, last_name, age FROM student_details WHERE age BETWEEN 10 AND 15;

The output would be similar to:

first_name	last_name	age
Rahul	Sharma	10
Anajali	Bhagwat	12
Shekar	Gowda	15

SQL IN Operator

The IN operator is used when you want to compare a column with more than one value. It is similar to an OR condition. **For example:** If you want to find the names of students who are studying either Maths or Science, the query would be like,

SELECT first_name, last_name, subjectFROM student_details WHERE subject IN (‹Maths›, ‹Science›);

The output would be similar to:

first_name	last_name	subject
Anajali	Bhagwat	Maths
Shekar	Gowda	Maths
Rahul	Sharma	Science
Stephen	Fleming	Science

You can include more subjects in the list like ('maths', 'science', 'history')

NOTE: The data used to compare is case sensitive.

SQL Is NULL Operator

A column value is NULL if it does not exist. The IS NULL operator is used to display all the rows for columns that do not have a value. **For Example:** If you want to find the names of students who do not participate in any games, the query would be as given below

SELECT first_name, last_nameFROM student_details WHERE games IS NULL;

There would be no output as we have every student participate in a game in the table student_details, else the names of the students who do not participate in any games would be displayed.

SQL NOT IN

The NOT IN operator is used when you want to retrieve a column that has no entries in the table or referencing table.

This is important for keywords when we want to find records to management questions such as:

✧ Which customer has not done any transaction with us?
✧ Which product is not selling in the past few days?

For Example: If you want to find the names of customers who have not done any transactions

A customer table will be containing records of all the customers and the transaction table keeps the records of any transaction between the store and the customer.

Customers SQL table contains the following:

Cust_id	first_name	last_name
01	Jhon	Cramer
02	Mathew	George
03	Phillip	McCain
04	Andrew	Thomas

Transaction table contains:

Transaction_ID	Cust_id	Product_ID	Amount	subject
01	01	02	10	5.99
02	03	01	12	6.59
03	01	05	09	8.99
04	01	04	18	6.59
05	03	02	15	5.99

The NOT IN query would be like

Select first_name, last_name, cust_id from customer where cust_id NOT IN (Select cust_id from transactions)

The output will be:

first_name	last_name	Cust_id
Mathew	George	02
Andrew	Thomas	04

Thus: These are the 2 names of customers who have not done any transactions

4.12   ORDER BY CLAUSE

The ORDER BY clause is used in a SELECT statement to sort results either in ascending or descending order. Oracle sorts query results in ascending order by default.

Syntax for using SQL ORDER BY clause to sort data is:

SELECT column-list FROM table_name [WHERE condition] [ORDER BY column1 [, column2,.. columnN] [DESC]];

database table "employee";

id	name	dept	age	salary	location
100	Ramesh	Electrical	24	25000	Bangalore
101	Hrithik	Electronics	28	35000	Bangalore
102	Harsha	Aeronautics	28	35000	Mysore
103	Soumya	Electronics	22	20000	Bangalore
104	Priya	InfoTech	25	30000	Mangalore

For Example: If you want to sort the employee table by salary of the employee, the sql query would be.

SELECT name, salary FROM employee ORDER BY salary;

The output would be like,

Name	Salary
Soumya	20000
Ramesh	25000
Priya	30000
Hrithik	35000
Harsha	35000

The query first sorts the result according to name and then displays it. You can also use more than one column in the ORDER BY clause. If you want to sort the employee table by the name and salary, the query would be like,

SELECT name, salary FROM employee ORDER BY name, salary;

The output would be like:

Name	Salary
Soumya	20000
Ramesh	25000
Priya	30000
Harsha	35000
Hrithik	35000

NOTE: The columns specified in ORDER BY clause should be one of the columns selected in the SELECT column list.

You can represent the columns in the ORDER BY clause by specifying the position of a column in the SELECT list, instead of writing the column name. The above query can also be written as given below,

SELECT name, salary FROM employee ORDER BY 1, 2;

By default, the ORDER BY Clause sorts data in ascending order. If you want to sort the data in descending order, you must explicitly specify it as shown below.

SELECT name, salary FROM employee ORDER BY name, salary DESC;

The above query sorts only the column 'salary' in descending order and the column 'name' by ascending order. If you want to select both name and salary in descending order, the query would be as given below.

SELECT name, salary FROM employee ORDER BY name DESC, salary DESC;

How to use expressions in the ORDER BY Clause?

Expressions in the ORDER BY clause of a SELECT statement.

For example: If you want to display employee name, current salary, and a 20% increase in the salary for only those employees for whom the percentage increase in salary is greater than 30000 and in descending order of the increased price, the SELECT statement can be written as shown below

SELECT name, salary, salary*1.2 AS new_salary FROM employee WHERE salary*1.2 > 30000 ORDER BY new_salary DESC;

The output for the above query is as follows.

Name	Salary	new_salary
Hrithik	35000	37000
Harsha	35000	37000
Priya	30000	36000

NOTE: Aliases defined in the SELECT Statement can be used in ORDER BY Clause.

4.13 GROUP BY CLAUSE

The SQL GROUP BY Clause is used along with the group functions to retrieve data grouped according to one or more columns.

For Example: If you want to know the total amount of salary spent on each department, the query would be:

SELECT dept, SUM (salary) FROM employee GROUP BY dept;

The output would be like:

dept	salary
Electrical	25000
Electronics	55000
Aeronautics	35000
InfoTech	30000

NOTE: The group by clause should contain all the columns in the select list expect those used along with the group functions.

SELECT location, dept, SUM (salary) FROM employee GROUP BY location, dept;

The output would be like:

location	dept	salary
Bangalore	Electrical	25000
Bangalore	Electronics	55000
Mysore	Aeronautics	35000
Mangalore	InfoTech	30000

4.14   SQL HAVING CLAUSE

Having clause is used to filter data based on the group functions. This is similar to WHERE condition but is used with group functions. Group functions cannot be used in WHERE Clause but can be used in HAVING clause.

SQL HAVING Clause Example

If you want to select the department that has total salary paid for its employees more than 25000, the sql query would be like;

SELECT dept, SUM (salary) FROM employee GROUP BY dept HAVING SUM (salary) > 25000;

The output would be like:

Dept	Salary
Electronics	55000
Aeronautics	35000
InfoTech	30000

When WHERE, GROUP BY and HAVING clauses are used together in a SELECT statement, the WHERE clause is processed first, then the rows that are returned after the WHERE clause is executed are grouped based on the GROUP BY clause. Finally, any conditions on the group functions in the HAVING clause are applied to the grouped rows before the final output is displayed.

4.15 AGGREGATE OPERATORS

SQL aggregation function is used to perform the calculations on multiple rows of a single column of a table. It returns a single value. It is also used to summarize the data. ggregate Functions are all about

* ✧ Performing calculations on multiple rows
* ✧ Of a single column of a table
* ✧ And returning a single value.

Why use aggregate functions

From a business perspective, different organization levels have different information requirements. Top levels managers are usually interested in knowing whole figures and not necessary the individual details.

>Aggregate functions allow us to easily produce summarized data from our database.

For instance, from our myflix database, management may require following reports

- ✧ Least rented movies.
- ✧ Most rented movies.
- ✧ Average number that each movie is rented out in a month.

We easily produce above reports using aggregate functions.

Types of SQL Aggregation Function

The ISO standard defines five (5) aggregate functions namely;

1. COUNT ()
2. SUM ()
3. AVG ()
4. MIN ()
5. MAX ()

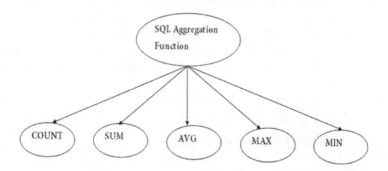

1. COUNT ()

COUNT function is used to Count the number of rows in a database table. It can work on both numeric and non-numeric data types. COUNT function uses the COUNT(*) that returns the count of all the rows in a specified table. COUNT(*) considers duplicate and Null.

Syntax

COUNT(*)   or   COUNT([ALL|DISTINCT] expression)

Sample table

PRODUCT_MAST

PRODUCT	COMPANY	QTY	RATE	COST
Item1	Com1	2	10	20
Item2	Com2	3	25	75
Item3	Com1	2	30	60
Item4	Com3	5	10	50
Item5	Com2	2	20	40
Item6	Cpm1	3	25	75
Item7	Com1	5	30	150
Item8	Com1	3	10	30
Item9	Com2	2	25	50
Item10	Com3	4	30	120

Example: COUNT()

SELECT COUNT(*) FROM PRODUCT_MAST;

Output

10

Example: COUNT with WHERE

SELECT COUNT(*) FROM PRODUCT_MAST WHERE RATE>=20;

Output

7

Example: COUNT() with DISTINCT

SELECT   COUNT(DISTINCT   COMPANY)   FROM
PRODUCT_MAST;

Output

3

Example: COUNT() with GROUP BY

SELECT COMPANY, COUNT(*) FROM PRODUCT_MAST
GROUP BY COMPANY;

Output

Com1 5

Com2 3

Com3 2

Example: COUNT() with HAVING

SELECT COMPANY, COUNT(*) FROM PRODUCT_MAST
GROUP BY COMPANY HAVING COUNT(*)>2;

Output

Com1 5

Com2 3

2. SUM ()

Sum function is used to calculate the sum of all selected columns. It works on numeric fields only. **SUM** function returns the sum of all the values in the specified column. SUM works on numeric fields only. Null values are excluded from the result returned.

Syntax

SUM()   or   SUM([ALL|DISTINCT] expression)

Example: SUM()

SELECT SUM(COST) FROM PRODUCT_MAST;

Output

670

Example: SUM() with WHERE

SELECT SUM(COST) FROM PRODUCT_MAST WHERE QTY>3;

Output

320

Example: SUM() with GROUP BY

SELECT SUM(COST) FROM PRODUCT_MAST WHERE QTY>3 GROUP BY COMPANY;

Output

Com1 150

Com2 170

Example: SUM() with HAVING

SELECT COMPANY, SUM(COST) FROM PRODUCT_MAST GROUP BY COMPANY HAVING SUM(COST)>=170;

Output

Com1 335

Com3 170

3. AVG ()
The AVG function is used to calculate the average value of the numeric type. AVG function returns the average of all non-Null values.

Syntax

AVG()   or   AVG([ALL|DISTINCT] expression)

Example

SELECT AVG(COST) FROM PRODUCT_MAST;

Output:

67.00

4. MAX ()

MAX function is used to find the maximum value of a certain column. This function determines the largest value of all selected values of a column.

Syntax

MAX ()   or   MAX([ALL|DISTINCT] expression)

Example

SELECT MAX(RATE) FROM PRODUCT_MAST;

Output

30

5. MIN ()

MIN function is used to find the minimum value of a certain column. This function determines the smallest value of all selected values of a column.

Syntax

MIN()   or   MIN([ALL|DISTINCT] expression)

Example

SELECT MIN(RATE) FROM PRODUCT_MAST;

Output

10

4.16 SQL JOINS

SQL Join is used to fetch data from two or more tables, which is joined to appear as single set of data. It is used for combining column from two or more tables by using values common to both tables. JOIN Keyword is used in SQL queries for joining two or more tables. Minimum required condition for joining table, is **(n-1)** where **n**, is number of tables. A table can also join to itself, which is known as, **Self Join.**

Types of JOIN

Following are the types of JOIN that we can use in SQL:

- ✧ Inner
- ✧ Outer
- ✧ Left
- ✧ Right

Cross JOIN or Cartesian Product

This type of JOIN returns the cartesian product of rows from the tables in Join. It will return a table which consists of records which combines each row from the first table with each row of the second table.

Cross JOIN Syntax is,

SELECT column-name-list FROM table-name1 CROSS JOIN table-name2;

Example of Cross JOIN

Following is the **class** table, and

ID	NAME
1	abhi
2	adam
4	alex

the **class_info** table,

ID	Address
1	DELHI
2	MUMBAI
3	CHENNAI

Cross JOIN query will be,

SELECT * FROM class CROSS JOIN class_info;

The resultset table will look like,

ID	NAME	ID	Address
1	Abhi	1	DELHI
2	adam	1	DELHI
4	alex	1	DELHI
1	abhi	2	MUMBAI
2	adam	2	MUMBAI
4	alex	2	MUMBAI
1	abhi	3	CHENNAI
2	adam	3	CHENNAI
4	alex	3	CHENNAI

As you can see, this join returns the cross product of all the records present in both the tables.

INNER Join or EQUI Join

This is a simple JOIN in which the result is based on matched data as per the equality condition specified in the SQL query.

Inner Join Syntax is,

SELECT column-name-list FROM table-name1 INNER JOIN table-name2 WHERE table-name1. column-name = table-name2. column-name;

Example of INNER JOIN

Consider a **class** table,

ID	NAME
1	abhi
2	adam
3	alex
4	anu

and the **class_info** table,

ID	Address
1	DELHI
2	MUMBAI
3	CHENNAI

Inner JOIN query will be,

SELECT * from class INNER JOIN class_info where class.id = class_info.id;

The resultset table will look like,

ID	NAME	ID	Address
1	abhi	1	DELHI
2	adam	2	MUMBAI
3	alex	3	CHENNAI

Natural JOIN

Natural Join is a type of Inner join which is based on column having same name and same datatype present in both the tables to be joined.

The syntax for Natural Join is,

SELECT * FROM table-name1 NATURAL JOIN table-name2;

Example of Natural JOIN

Here is the **class** table,

ID	NAME
1	abhi
2	adam
3	alex
4	anu

and the **class_info** table,

ID	Address
1	DELHI
2	MUMBAI
3	CHENNAI

Natural join query will be,
SELECT * from class NATURAL JOIN class_info;
The resultset table will look like,

ID	NAME	Address
1	Abhi	DELHI
2	Adam	MUMBAI
3	Alex	CHENNAI

In the above example, both the tables being joined have **ID** column(same name and same datatype), hence the records for which value of **ID** matches in both the tables will be the result of Natural Join of these two tables.

Outer Join

Outer Join is based on both matched and unmatched data. Outer Joins subdivide further into,

1. Left Outer Join
2. Right Outer Join
3. Full Outer Join

LEFT Outer Join

The left outer join returns a resultset table with the **matched data** from the two tables and then the remaining rows of the **left** table and null from the **right** table›s columns.

Syntax for Left Outer Join is,

SELECT column-name-list FROM table-name1 LEFT OUTER JOIN table-name2 ON table-name1. column-name = table-name2.column-name;

To specify a condition, we use the ON keyword with Outer Join.

Left outer Join Syntax for **Oracle** is,

SELECT column-name-list FROM table-name1, table-name2 on table-name1.column-name = table-name2.column-name(+);

Example of Left Outer Join

Here is the **class** table,

ID	NAME
1	abhi
2	adam
3	alex
4	anu
5	ashish

and the **class_info** table,

ID	Address
1	DELHI
2	MUMBAI
3	CHENNAI
7	NOIDA
8	PANIPAT

Left Outer Join query will be,

SELECT * FROM class LEFT OUTER JOIN class_info ON (class.id = class_info.id);

The resultset table will look like,

ID	NAME	ID	Address
1	abhi	1	DELHI
2	adam	2	MUMBAI
3	alex	3	CHENNAI
4	anu	null	null
5	ashish	null	null

RIGHT Outer Join

The right outer join returns a resultset table with the **matched data** from the two tables being joined, then the remaining rows of the **right** table and null for the remaining **left** table›s columns.

Syntax for Right Outer Join is,

SELECT column-name-list FROM table-name1 RIGHT OUTER JOIN table-name2 ON table-name1.column-name = table-name2.column-name;

Right outer Join Syntax for **Oracle** is,

SELECT column-name-list FROM table-name1, table-name2 ON table-name1.column-name(+) = table-name2.column-name;

Example of Right Outer Join

Once again the **class** table,

ID	NAME
1	abhi
2	adam
3	alex

ID	NAME
4	anu
5	Ashish

and the **class_info** table,

ID	Address
1	DELHI
2	MUMBAI
3	CHENNAI
7	NOIDA
8	PANIPAT

Right Outer Join query will be,

SELECT * FROM class RIGHT OUTER JOIN class_info ON (class.id = class_info.id);

The resultant table will look like,

ID	NAME	ID	Address
1	abhi	1	DELHI
2	adam	2	MUMBAI
3	alex	3	CHENNAI
null	null	7	NOIDA
null	null	8	PANIPAT

Full Outer Join

The full outer join returns a resultset table with the **matched data** of two table then remaining rows of both **left** table and then the **right** table.

Syntax of Full Outer Join is,

SELECT column-name-list FROM table-name1 FULL OUTER JOIN table-name2 ON table-name1.column-name = table-name2.column-name;

Example of Full outer join is,

The **class** table,

ID	NAME
1	Abhi
2	Adam
3	Alex
4	anu
5	ashish

and the **class_info** table,

ID	Address
1	DELHI
2	MUMBAI
3	CHENNAI
7	NOIDA
8	PANIPAT

Full Outer Join query will be like,

SELECT * FROM class FULL OUTER JOIN class_info ON (class.id = class_info.id);

The resultset table will look like,

ID	NAME	ID	Address
1	Abhi	1	DELHI
2	Adam	2	MUMBAI
3	Alex	3	CHENNAI
4	Anu	null	Null
5	Ashish	null	Null
null	Null	7	NOIDA
null	Null	8	PANIPAT

4.17 TRIGGERS

A trigger is a procedure that is automatically invoked by the DBMS in response to specified changes to the database, and is typically specified by the DBA. A database that has a set of associated triggers is called an active database. A trigger description contains three parts:

- ✧ **Event:** A change to the database that activates the trigger.
- ✧ **Condition:** A query or test that is run when the trigger is activated.
- ✧ **Action:** A procedure that is executed when the trigger is activated and its condition is true.

A trigger can be thought of as a 'daemon' that monitors a databa. se, and is executed when the database is modified in a way that matches the event specification. An insert, delete, or update statement could activate a trigger, regardless of which user or application invoked the activating statement; users may not even be aware that a trigger wa.'3 executed as a side effect of their program. A condition in a trigger can be a true/false statement (e.g., all employee salaries are less than $100, 000) or a query. A query is interpreted as true if the answer set is nonempty and false if the query ha.') no answers. If the condition partevaluates to true, the action a., sociated with the trigger is executed.

A trigger action can examine the answers to th(- query in the condition part of the trigger, refer to old and new values of tuples modified by the statement activating the trigger, execute Hew queries, and make changes to the database. In fact, an action can even execute a series of data-definition commands (e.g., create new tables, change authorizations) and transaction-oriented commands(e.g., commit) or call host-language procedures.

An important issue is when the action part of a trigger executes in relation tothe statement that activated the trigger. For example, a statement that inserts records into the Students table may activate a trigger that is used to maintain statistics on how many studen-s younger than 18 are inserted at a time by a typical insert statement. Depending on exactly what the trigger does, we may want its action to execute before changes are made to the Students table or afterwards: A trigger that initializes a variable used to count the nurnber of qualifying insertions should be executed before, and a trigger that executes onceper qualifying inserted record and increments the variable should be executedafter each record is inserted (because we may want to examine the values in the new record to determine the action).

Syntax

create trigger [trigger_name] [before | after] {insert | update | delete} on [table_name] [for each row] [trigger_body]

Explanation of Syntax

1. create trigger [trigger_name]: Creates or replaces an existing trigger with the trigger_name.
2. [before | after]: This specifies when the trigger will be executed.
3. {insert | update | delete}: This specifies the DML operation.
4. on [table_name]: This specifies the name of the table associated with the trigger.
5. [for each row]: This specifies a row-level trigger, i.e., the trigger will be executed for each row being affected.
6. [trigger_body]: This provides the operation to be performed as trigger is fired

Types of Triggers

Triggers are classified into

1. Row level triggers
2. Statement level triggers
3. After triggers
4. Before triggers

⋏ Row level trigger:

Row level trigger is executed when each row of the table is inserted/ updated/ deleted. If it is a row level trigger, then we have to explicitly specify while creating the trigger, as we did in the above example. Also, we have to specify the WHEN (condition) in the trigger.

⋏ Statement level trigger

This trigger will be executed only once for DML statement. This DML statement may insert / delete/ update one row or multiple rows or whole table. Irrespective of number of rows, this trigger will be fired for the statement. If we have not specified the type of trigger while creating, by default it would be a statement level trigger.

⋏ After triggers:

✧ **AFTER INSERT**

+ Activated after data is inserted into the table.

✧ **AFTER UPDATE:**

+ Activated after data in the table is modified.

✧ **AFTER DELETE:**

+ Activated after data is deleted/removed from the table.

⋏ Before triggers

✧ **BEFORE INSERT**

+ activated before data is inserted into the table.

✧ **BEFORE UPDATE**

+ activated before data in the table is modified.

✧ **BEFORE DELETE**

+ activated before data is deleted/removed from the table.

Chapter 5

Introduction to Schema Refinement

5.1 PROBLEMS CAUSED BY REDUNDANCY

Redundancy means having multiple copies of same data in the database. This problem arises when a database is not normalized. Suppose a table of student details attributes are: student Id, student name, college name, college rank, course opted.

Student_ID	Name	Contact	College	Course	Rank
100	Himanshu	7300934851	GEU	Btech	1
101	Ankit	7900734858	GEU	Btech	1
102	Aysuh	7300936759	GEU	Btech	1
103	Ravi	7300901556	GEU	Btech	1

As it can be observed that values of attribute college name, college rank, course is being repeated which can lead to problems. Problems caused due to redundancy are: Insertion anomaly, Deletion anomaly, and Updation anomaly.

Insertion Anomaly

If a student detail has to be inserted whose course is not being decided yet then insertion will not be possible till the time course is decided for student.

Student_ID	Name	Contact	College	Course	Rank
100	Himanshu	7300934851	GEU		1

This problem happens when the insertion of a data record is not possible without adding some additional unrelated data to the record.

Deletion Anomaly

If the details of students in this table is deleted then the details of college will also get deleted which should not occur by common sense. This anomaly happens when deletion of a data record results in losing some unrelated information that was stored as part of the record that was deleted from a table.

Updation Anomaly

Suppose if the rank of the college changes then changes will have to be all over the database which will be time-consuming and computationally costly.

Student _ID	Name	Contact	College	Course	Rank
100	Himanshu	7300934851	GEU	Btech	1
101	Ankit	7900734858	GEU	Btech	1
102	Aysuh	7300936759	GEU	Btech	1
103	Ravi	7300901556	GEU	Btech	1

All places should be updated

If updation do not occur at all places then database will be in inconsistent state.

5.2 DECOMPOSITIONS – PROBLEM RELATED TO DECOMPOSITION

A **decomposition of relation schema R** consists of replacing the relation schema by two or more relation schemas that each contain a subset of the attributes of R and together include all attributes in R.

Ex: We can decompose Hourly_Emps into two relations:

Hourly_Emps2(ssn, name, lot, rating, hours_worked)

Wages(rating, hourly_wages)

Problems Related to Decomposition

Two important questions must be asked during decomposition process:

1. Do we need to decompose a relation?
2. What problems does a given decomposition cause?

To answer a first question, several normal forms have been proposed for relations. If a relation schema is in one of these normal forms, we know that certain kinds of problems cannot arise.

With respect second question, two properties of decomposition are to be considered:

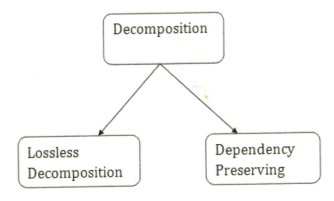

Lossless Decomposition

If the information is not lost from the relation that is decomposed, then the decomposition will be lossless. The lossless decomposition guarantees that the join of relations will result in the same relation as it was decomposed. The relation is said to be lossless decomposition if natural joins of all the decomposition give the original relation.

- ✧ Let R be a relation schema and let F be a set of FDs over R. A decomposition of R into two schemas with attribute sets X and Y is said to be a **lossless-join decomposition with respect to F** if, for every instance r of R that satisfies the dependencies in F, $\Pi_x(r) \bowtie \Pi_y(r) = r$. In other words, we can recover the original relation from the decomposed relations.

- ✧ From the definition it is easy to see that r is always a subset of natural join of decomposed relations. If we take projections of a relation and recombine them using natural join, we typically obtain some tuples that were not in the original relation.

Example

➤ By replacing the instance r shown in figure with the instances $\Pi_{SP}(r)$ and $\Pi_{PD}(r)$, we lose some information.

S	P	D
s1	p1	d1
s2	p2	d2
s3	p1	d3

S	P
s1	p1
s2	p2
s3	p1

P	D
p1	d1
p2	d2
p1	d3

Instance r $\Pi_{SP}(r)$ $\Pi_{PD}(r)$

$\Pi_{SP}(r) \bowtie \Pi_{PD}(r)$

S	P	D
s1	p1	d1
s2	p2	d2
s3	p1	d3
s1	p1	d3
s3	p1	d1

Fig.5.1: Instances illustrating Lossy Decompositions

Theorem: Let R be a relation and F be a set of FDs that hold over R. The decomposition of R into relations with attribute sets R1 and R2 is lossless if and only if F⁺ contains either the FD R1 ∩ R2 → R1 (or R1−R2) or the FD R1 ∩ R2 → R2 (or R2−R1).

Consider the Hourly_Emps relation. It has attributes SNLRWH, and the FD R→W causes a violation of 3NF. We dealt this violation by decomposing the relation into SNLRH and RW. Since R is common to both decomposed relations and R→W holds, this decomposition is lossless-join.

Dependency-Preserving Decomposition

Consider the Contracts relation with attributes CSJDPQV. The given FDs are C→CSJDPQV, JP→C, and SD→P. Because SD is not a key, the dependency SD→P causes a violation of BCNF.

We can decompose Contracts into relations with schemas CSJDQV and SDP to address this violation. The decomposition is lossless-join. But, there is one problem. If we want to enforce an integrity constraint JP→C, it requires an expensive join of the two relations. We say that this decomposition is not dependency-preserving.

Let R be a relation schema that is decomposed into two schemas with attributes sets X and Y, and let F be a set of FDs over R. The **projection of F on X** is the set of FDs in the closure F⁺ that involve only attributes in X. We denote the projection of F on attributes X as F_X. Note that a dependency U→V in F⁺ is in F_X only if all the attributes in U and V are in X.

The decomposition of relation schema R with FDs F into schemas with attribute sets X and Y is **dependency-preserving** if $(F_X \cup F_Y)^+ = F^+$.

Example

Consider the relation R with attributes ABC is decomposed into relations with attributes AB and BC. The set of FDs over R includes A→B, B→C, and C→A.

The closure of F contains all dependencies in F plus A→C, B→A, and C→B. Consequently F_{AB} contains

A→B and B→A, and F_{BC} contains B→C and C→B. Therefore, $F_{AB} \cup F_{BC}$ contains A→B, B→C, B→A

and C→B. The closure of F_{AB} and F_{BC} now includes C→A (which follows from C→B and B→A). Thus the decomposition preserves the dependency C→A.

5.3   FUNCTIONAL DEPENDENCIES

The functional dependency is a relationship that exists between two attributes. It typically exists between the primary key and non-key attribute within a table.

X   →   Y

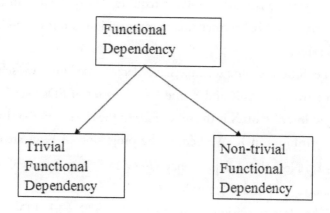

Trivial Functional Dependencies

A functional dependency $X \rightarrow Y$ is said to be trivial if and only if $Y \rightarrow X$.

- ❖ Thus, if RHS of a functional dependency is a subset of LHS, then it is called as a trivial functional dependency.

Examples

The examples of trivial functional dependencies are-

- ❖ $AB \rightarrow A$
- ❖ $AB \rightarrow B$
- ❖ $AB \rightarrow AB$

Non-Trivial Functional Dependencies

A functional dependency $X \rightarrow Y$ is said to be non-trivial if and only if $Y \rightarrow X$.

- ❖ Thus, if there exists at least one attribute in the RHS of a functional dependency that is not a part of LHS, then it is called as a non-trivial functional dependency.

Examples

The examples of non-trivial functional dependencies are-

- ❖ $AB \rightarrow BC$
- ❖ $AB \rightarrow CD$

Inference Rules

1. Reflexivity

If B is a subset of A, then $A \rightarrow B$ always holds.

2. Transitivity

If A → B and B → C, then A → C always holds.

3. Augmentation

If X → Y, then XZ → YZ for any Z

4. Union

If X → Y and X → Z, then X → YZ.

5. Decomposition

If X → YZ, then X → Y and X → Z.

Example

1. Consider a relation schema ABC with FDs
A→B and B→C

From transitivity, we get A → C.

From augmentation, we get AC→BC, AB→AC, AB→CB.

2. Contracts (contractid, supplierid, projectid, deptid, partid, qty, value) We denote the schema for Contracts as CSJDPQV.

The following are the given FDs

    i.   **C → CSJDPQV.**

    ii. **JP → C.**

    iii. **SD → P.**

Several additional FDs hold in the closure of the set of given FDs:

From JP→C and C→CSJDPQV, and transitivity, we infer JP→CSJDPQV.

From SD→P and augmentation, we infer SDJ→ JP.

From SDJ→JP, JP→CSJDPQV, and transitivity, we infer SDJ→CSJDPQV.

5.4 NORMALIZATION

▲ **Normalization** is a process of organizing the data in database to avoid data redundancy, insertion anomaly, update anomaly & deletion anomaly Normalization divides the larger table into the smaller table and links them using relationship. The normal form is used to reduce redundancy from the database table.

▲ Some of the undesirable properties that a bad database design may have

   ✦ Repetition of information
   ✦ Inability to represent certain information
   ✦ Incapability to maintain integrity of data

▲ The normal forms of relational database theory provide criteria for determining a table's degree of vulnerability to logical inconsistencies and anomalies.

▲ The higher the normal form applicable to a table, the less vulnerable it is to inconsistencies and anomalies.

▲ Each table has a "highest normal form" (HNF): by definition, a table always meets the requirements of its HNF and of all normal forms lower than its HNF; also by definition, a table fails to meet the requirements of any normal form higher than its HNF.

▲   Generally known hierarchy of normal forms is as follows First Normal Form(1NF), Second Normal Form(2NF), Third Normal Form(3NF), Fourth Normal Form(4NF), Fifth Normal Form(5NF).

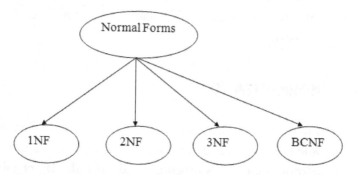

Normalization rule are divided into following normal form.

1. First Normal Form
2. Second Normal Form
3. Third Normal Form
4. BCNF

5.4.1 First Normal Form (1Nf)

As per First Normal Form, no two Rows of data must contain repeating group of information i.e eachset of column must have a unique value, such that multiple columns cannot be used to fetch thesame row., if a table is in 1NF if and only if it is "isomorphic to some relation", which means, specifically, that it satisfies the following five conditions:

1. There's no top-to-bottom ordering to the rows.
2. There's no left-to-right ordering to the columns.
3. There are no duplicate rows.
4. Every row-and-column intersection contains exactly one value from the applicable domain (and nothing else).

5. All columns are regular [i.e. rows have no hidden components such as row IDs, object IDs, or hidden timestamps].

Each table should be organized into rows, and each row should have a primary key thatdistinguishes it as unique. The Primary key is usually a single column, but sometimes more than one column can be combinedto create a single primary key. For example consider a table which is not in First normal form

Student Table:

Student	Age	Subject
Adam	15	Biology, Maths
Alex	14	Maths
Stuart	17	Maths

In First Normal Form, any row must not have a column in which more than one value is saved, likeseparated with commas. Rather than that, we must separate such data into multiple rows.

Student Table following 1NF will be

Student	Age	Subject
Adam	15	Biology
Adam	15	Maths
Alex	14	Maths
Stuart	17	Maths

Using the First Normal Form, data redundancy increases, as there will be many columns with same data in multiple rows but each row as a whole will be unique.

5.4.2 SECOND NORMAL FORM (2NF)

As per the Second Normal Form there must not be any partial dependency of any column on primary key. It means that for a table that has concatenated primary key, each column in the table that is not part of the primary key must depend upon the entire concatenated key for its existence. If any column depends only on one part of the concatenated key, then the table fails **Second normal form**. A 1NF table is in 2NF if and only if, given any candidate key **K** and any attribute **A** that is not a constituent of a candidate key, **A** depends upon the whole of **K** rather than just a part of it

- ❖ A 1NF table is in 2NF if and only if all its non-prime attributes are functionally dependent on the whole of every candidate key. (A non-prime attribute is one that does not belong to any candidate key.

- ❖ Note that when a 1NF table has no composite candidate keys (candidate keys consisting of more than one attribute), the table is automatically in 2NF.

In example of First Normal Form there are two rows for Adam, to include multiple subjects that he has opted for. While this is searchable, and follows First normal form, it is an inefficient use of space. Also in the above Table in First Normal Form, while the candidate key is {**Student, Subject**}, **Age** of Student only depends on Student column, which is incorrect as per Second Normal Form. To achieve second normal form, it would be helpful to split out the subjects into an independent table, and match them up using the student names as foreign keys.

New Student Table following 2NF will be

Student	Age
Adam	15
Alex	14
Stuart	17

In Student Table the candidate key will be **Student** column, because all other column i.e **Age** is dependent on it.

New Subject Table introduced for 2NF will be

Student	Subject
Adam	Biology
Adam	Maths
Alex	Maths
Stuart	Maths

In Subject Table the candidate key will be {Student, Subject} column. Now, both the above tables qualifies for Second Normal Form and will never suffer from Update Anomalies. Although there are a few complex cases in which table in Second Normal Form suffers Update Anomalies, and to handle those scenarios Third Normal Form is there.

5.4.3 HIRD NORMAL FORM (3NF)

A relation is said to be in 3NF, if it is already in 2NF and there exists no **transitive dependency** in that relation. Speaking inversely, if a table contains transitive dependency, then it is not in 3NF, and the table must be split to bring it into 3NF.

What is a transitive dependency? Within a relation if we see

$A \rightarrow B$ [B depends on A]

And

$B \rightarrow C$ [C depends on B]

Then we may derive

$A \rightarrow C$ [C depends on A]

Such derived dependencies hold well in most of the situations. For example if we have

Roll $\rightarrow$ Marks

And

Marks → Grade

Then we may safely derive

Roll → Grade.

This third dependency was not originally specified but we have derived it.

The derived dependency is called a transitive dependency when such dependency becomes

improbable.

For example we have been given

Roll → City

And

City→ STDCode

If we try to derive Roll → STDCode it becomes a transitive dependency, because obviously the STDCode of a city cannot depend on the roll number issued by a school or college. In such a case the relation should be broken into two, each containing one of these two dependencies:

Roll → City

And

City →STD code

5.4.4 Boyce-Code Normal Form (BCNF)

A relationship is said to be in BCNF if it is already in 3NF and the left hand side of every dependency is a candidate key. A relation which is in 3NF is almost always in BCNF. These could be same situation when a 3NF relation may not be in BCNF the following conditions are found true.

1. The candidate keys are composite.
2. There are more than one candidate keys in the relation.
3. There are some common attributes in the relation.

Professor Code	Department	Head of Dept.	Percent Time
P1	Physics	Ghosh	50
P1	Mathematics	Krishnan	50
P2	Chemistry	Rao	25
P2	Physics	Ghosh	75
P3	Mathematics	Krishnan	100

Consider, as an example, the above relation. It is assumed that:

1. A professor can work in more than one department
2. The percentage of the time he spends in each department is given.
3. Each department has only one Head of Department.

The relation diagram for the above relation is given as the following:

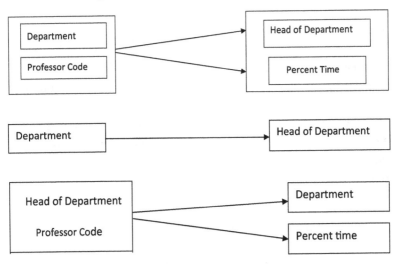

The given relation is in 3NF. Observe, however, that the names of Dept. and Head of Dept. are duplicated. Further, if Professor P2 resigns, rows 3 and 4 are deleted. We lose the information that Rao is the Head of Department of Chemistry. The normalization of the relation is done by creating a new relation for Dept. and Head of Dept. and deleting Head of Dept. form the given relation. The normalized relations are shown in the following.

Professor Code	Department	Percent Time
P1	Physics	50
P1	Mathematics	50
P2	Chemistry	25
P2	Physics	75
P3	Mathematics	100

Department	Head of Dept.
Physics	Ghosh
Mathematics	Krishnan
Chemistry	Rao

See the dependency diagrams for these new relations

5.5   FOURTH NORMAL FORM (4NF)

When attributes in a relation have multi-valued dependency, further Normalization to 4NF and 5NF are required. Let us first find out what multi-valued dependency is.

A **multi-valued dependency** is a typical kind of dependency in which each and every attribute within a relation depends upon the other, yet none of them is a unique primary key. We will illustrate this with an example. Consider a vendor supplying many items to many projects in an organization. The following are the assumptions:

1. A vendor is capable of supplying many items.
2. A project uses many items.
3. A vendor supplies to many projects.

4.   An item may be supplied by many vendors.

A multi valued dependency exists here because all the attributes depend upon the other and yet none of them is a primary key having unique value.

Vendor Code	Item Code	Project No.
V1	I1	P1
V1	I2	P1
V1	I1	P3
V1	I2	P3
V2	I2	P1
V2	I3	P1
V3	I1	P2
V3	I1	P3

The given relation has a number of problems. For example:

1.   If vendor V1 has to supply to project P2, but the item is not yet decided, then a row with a blank for item code has to be introduced.
2.   The information about item I1 is stored twice for vendor V3.

Observe that the relation given is in 3NF and also in BCNF. It still has the problem mentioned above. The problem is reduced by expressing this relation as two relations in the Fourth Normal Form (4NF). A relation is in 4NF if it has no more than one independent multi valued dependency or one independent multi valued dependency with a functional dependency. The table can be expressed as the two 4NF relations given as following. The fact that vendors are capable of supplying certain items and that they are assigned to supply for some projects in independently specified in the 4NF relation.

Vendor-Supply

Vendor Code	Item Code
V1	I1
V1	I2
V2	I2
V2	I3
V3	I1

Vendor-Project

Vendor Code	Project No
V1	P1
V1	P3
V2	P1
V3	P2

5.6   FIFTH NORMAL FORM (5NF)

These relations still have a problem. While defining the 4NF we mentioned that all the attributes depend upon each other. While creating the two tables in the 4NF, although we have preserved the dependencies between Vendor Code and Item code in the first table and Vendor Code and Item code in the second table, we have lost the relationship between Item Code and Project No. If there were a primary key then this loss of dependency would not have occurred. In order to revive this relationship we must add a new table like the following. Please note that during the entire process of normalization, this is the only step where a new table is created by joining two attributes, rather than splitting them into separate tables.

Project No.	Item Code
P1	11
P1	12
P2	11
P3	11
P3	13

Let us finally summarize the normalization steps we have discussed so far.

Input Relation	Transformation	Output Relation
All Relations	Eliminate variable length record. Remove multi-attribute lines in table.	1NF
1NF Relation	Remove dependency of non-key attributes on part of a multi-attribute key.	2NF
2NF	Remove dependency of non-key attributes on other non-key attributes.	3NF
3NF	Remove dependency of an attribute of a multi attribute key on an attribute of another (overlapping) multi-attribute key.	BCNF
BCNF	Remove more than one independent multi-valued dependency from relation by splitting relation.	4NF
4NF	Add one relation relating attributes with multi-valued dependency.	5NF

Chapter 6

Transactions Management

6.1 TRANSACTION

A transaction is an event which occurs on the database. Generally a transaction reads a value from the database or writes a value to the database. If you have any concept of Operating Systems, then we can say that a transaction is analogous to processes. A transaction is a logical unit of processing in a DBMS which entails one or more database access operation. In a nutshell, database transactions represent real-world events of any enterprise. All types of database access operation which are held between the beginning and end transaction statements are considered as a single logical transaction. During the transaction the database is inconsistent. Only once the database is committed the state is changed from one consistent state to another.

6.1.2 ACID Properties

A **transaction** is a single logical unit of work which accesses and possibly modifies the contents of a database. For maintaining the integrity of data, the DBMS system you have to ensure ACID properties. ACID stands for **A**tomicity, **C**onsistency, **I**solation, and **D**urability. Transactions access data using read and write operations. In order to maintain consistency in a database, before and after the transaction, certain properties are followed. These are called **ACID** properties.

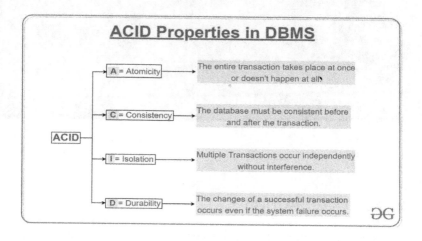

Atomicity

By this, we mean that either the entire transaction takes place at once or doesn't happen at all. There is no midway i.e. transactions do not occur partially. Each transaction is considered as one unit and either runs to completion or is not executed at all. It involves the following two operations.

Abort: If a transaction aborts, changes made to database are not visible.

Commit: If a transaction commits, changes made are visible. Atomicity is also known as the 'All or nothing rule'.

Consider the following transaction **T** consisting of **T1** and **T2**: Transfer of 100 from account **X** to account **Y**.

Before: X : 500	Y: 200
Transaction T	
T1	T2
Read (X)	Read (Y)
X: = X − 100	Y: = Y + 100
Write (X)	Write (Y)
After: X : 400	Y : 300

If the transaction fails after completion of **T1** but before completion of **T2**.(say, after **write(X)** but before **write(Y)**), then amount has been deducted from **X** but not added to **Y**. This results in an inconsistent database state. Therefore, the transaction must be executed in entirety in order to ensure correctness of database state.

Consistency

This means that integrity constraints must be maintained so that the database is consistent before and after the transaction. It refers to the correctness of a database. Referring to the example above, The total amount before and after the transaction must be maintained.

Total **before T** occurs = **500 + 200 = 700**. Total **after T occurs** = **400 + 300 = 700**.

Therefore, database is **consistent**. Inconsistency occurs in case **T1** completes but **T2** fails. As a result T is incomplete.

Isolation

This property ensures that multiple transactions can occur concurrently without leading to the inconsistency of database state. Transactions occur independently without interference. Changes occurring in a particular transaction will not be visible to any other transaction until that particular change in that transaction is written to memory or has been committed. This property ensures that the execution of transactions concurrently will result in a state that is equivalent to a state achieved these were executed serially in some order.

Let **X**= 500, **Y** = 500.

Consider two transactions **T** and **T"**.

T	T"
Read (X)	Read (X)
X: = X*100	Read (Y)
Write (X)	Z: = X + Y
Read (Y)	Write (Z)
Y: = Y − 50	
Write	

Suppose **T** has been executed till **Read (Y)** and then **T"** starts. As a result, interleaving of operations takes place due to which **T"** reads correct value of **X** but incorrect value of **Y** and sum computed by **T"**: **(X+Y = 50, 000+500=50, 500)** is thus not consistent with the sum at end of transaction: **T: (X+Y = 50, 000 + 450 = 50, 450)**. This results in database inconsistency, due to a loss of 50 units. Hence, transactions must take place in isolation and changes should be visible only after they have been made to the main memory.

Durability

This property ensures that once the transaction has completed execution, the updates and modifications to the database are stored in and written to disk and they persist even if a system failure occurs. These updates now become permanent and are stored in non-volatile memory. The effects of the transaction, thus, are never lost.

The **ACID** properties, in totality, provide a mechanism to ensure correctness and consistency of a database in a way such that each transaction is a group of operations that acts a single unit, produces consistent results, acts in isolation from other operations and updates that it makes are durably stored.

6.2   IMPLEMENTATION OF ATOMICITY

Let's assume that before the transaction take place the balances in the account is Rs. 50000/ – and that in the account SB2359 is Rs. 35000/-. Now suppose that during the execution of the transaction a failure(for example, a power failure) occurred that prevented the successful completion of the transaction. The failure occurred after the Write(CA2090); operation was executed, but before the execution of Write(SB2359); in this case the value of the accounts CA2090 and SB2359 are reflected in the database are Rs. 48, 000/ – and Rs. 35000/ – respectively. The Rs. 200/- that we have taken from the account is lost. Thus the failure has created a problem. The state of the database no longer reflects a real state of the world that the database is supposed to capture. Such a state is called an inconsistent state.

The database system should ensure that such inconsistencies are not visible in a database system. It should be noted that even during the successful execution of a transaction there exists points at which the system is in an inconsistent state. But the difference in the case of a successful transaction is that the period for which the database is in an inconsistent state is very short and once the transaction is over the system will be brought back to a consistent state. So if a transaction never started or is completed successfully, the inconsistent states would not be visible except during the execution of the transaction. This is the reason for the atomicity requirement.

If the atomicity property provided all actions of the transaction are reflected in the database of none are. The mechanism of maintaining atomicity is as follows The DBMS keeps tracks of the old values of any data on which a transaction performs a Write and if the transaction does not complete its execution, old values are restored o make it appear as though the transaction never took place. The transaction management component of the DBMS ensures the atomicity of each transaction.

6.3   IMPLEMENTATION OF CONSISTENCY

The consistency requirement in the above eg is that the sum of CA2090 and SB2359 be unchanged by the execution of the transaction. Before the execution of the transaction the amounts in the accounts in CA2090 and SB2359 are 50, 000 and 35, 000 respectively. After the execution the amounts become 48, 000 and 37, 000. In both cases the sum of the amounts is 85, 000 thus maintaining consistency. Ensuring the consistency for an individual transaction is the responsibility of the application programmer who codes the transaction. 2

6.4 IMPLEMENTION OF ISOLATION

Even if the atomicity and consistency properties are ensured for each transaction there can be problems if several transactions are executed concurrently. The different transactions interfere with one another and cause undesirable results. Suppose we are executing the above transaction Ti. We saw that the database is temporarily inconsistent while the transaction is being executed. Suppose that the transaction has performed the Write(CA2090) operation, during this time another transaction is reading the balances of different accounts. It checks the account CA2090 and finds the account balance at 48, 000. Suppose that it reads the account balance of the other account(account SB2359, before the first transaction has got a chance to update the account. So the account balance in the account Sb2359 is 35000. After the second transaction has read the account balances, the first transaction reads the account balance of the account SB2359 and updates it to 37000. But here we are left with a problem.

The first transaction has executed successfully and the database is back to a consistent state. But while it was in an inconsistent state, another transaction performed some operations(May be updated the total account balances). This has left the database in an inconsistent state even after both the transactions have been executed successfully. On solution to the situation(concurrent execution of transactions) is to execute the transactions serially – one after the other. This can create many problems. Suppose long transactions are being executed first. Then all other transactions will have to wait in the queue. There might be many transactions that are independent(or that do not interfere with one another). There is no need for such transactions to wait in the queue. Also concurrent executions of transactions have significant performance advantages.

So the DBMS have found solutions to allow multiple transactions to execute concurrency with out any problem. The isolation property of a transaction ensures that the concurrent execution of transactions result in a system state that is equivalent to a state that could have been obtained if the transactions were executed one after another. Ensuring isolation property is the responsibility of the concurrency-control component of the DBMS.

6.5 IMPLEMENTION OF DURABILITY

The durability property guarantees that, once a transaction completes successfully, all updates that it carried out on the database persist, even if there is a system failure after the transaction completes execution. We can guarantee durability by ensuring that either the updates carried out by the transaction have been written to the disk before the transaction completes or information about the updates that are carried out by the transaction and written to the disk are sufficient for the data base to reconstruct the updates when the data base is restarted after the failure. Ensuring durability is the responsibility of the recovery – management component of the DBMS.

6.6 TRANSACTION STATES

There are the following six states in which a transaction may exist

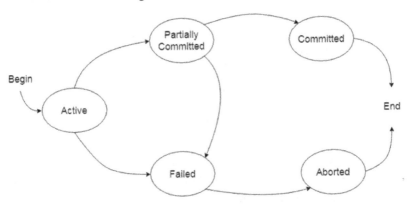

Active state

The active state is the first state of every transaction. In this state, the transaction is being executed. For example: Insertion or deletion or updating a record is done here. But all the records are still not saved to the database.

Partially Committed

In the partially committed state, a transaction executes its final operation, but the data is still not saved to the database. In the total mark calculation example, a final display of the total marks step is executed in this state.

Committed

A transaction is said to be in a committed state if it executes all its operations successfully. In this state, all the effects are now permanently saved on the database system.

Failed state

If any of the checks made by the database recovery system fails, then the transaction is said to be in the failed state. In the example of total mark calculation, if the database is not able to fire a query to fetch the marks, then the transaction will fail to execute.

Aborted

If any of the checks fail and the transaction has reached a failed state then the database recovery system will make sure that the database is in its previous consistent state. If not then it will abort or roll back the transaction to bring the database into a consistent state.

- ✧ If the transaction fails in the middle of the transaction then before executing the transaction, all the executed transactions are rolled back to its consistent state.
- ✧ After aborting the transaction, the database recovery module will select one of the two operations:

    1.   Re-start the transaction

    2.   Kill the transaction

6.7 SCHEDULE

The following sequence of operations is a schedule. Here we have two transactions T1 & T2 which are running concurrently.

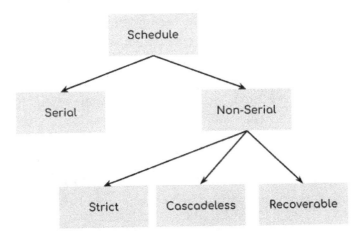

This schedule determines the exact order of operations that are going to be performed on database. In this example, all the instructions of transaction T1 are executed before the instructions of transaction T2, however this is not always necessary and we can have various types of schedules which we will discuss in this article.

T1	T2
R(X)	
W(X)	
R(Y)	
	R(Y)
	R(X)
	W(Y)

Types Of Schedules

We have various types of schedules in DBMS. Lets discuss them one by one. We have various types of schedules in DBMS. Lets discuss them one by one.

Serial Schedule

In **Serial schedule**, a transaction is executed completely before starting the execution of another transaction. In other words, you can say that in serial schedule, a transaction does not start execution until the currently running transaction finished execution. This type of execution of transaction is also known as **non-interleaved** execution. The example we have seen above is the serial schedule. Lets take another example.

Serial Schedule example Here R refers to the read operation and W refers to the write operation. In this example, the transaction T2 does not start execution until the transaction T1 is finished.

T1	T2
R(A)	
R(B)	
W(A)	
commit	
	R(B)
	R(A)
	W(B)
	commit

Strict Schedule

In Strict schedule, if the write operation of a transaction precedes a conflicting operation (Read or Write operation) of another transaction then the commit or abort operation of such transaction should also precede the conflicting operation of other transaction. Lets take an example.

Strict Schedule example

Lets say we have two transactions Ta and Tb. The write operation of transaction Ta precedes the read or write operation of transaction Tb, so the commit or abort operation of transaction Ta should also precede the read or write of Tb.

Ta	Tb
R(X)	
	R(X)
W(X)	
commit	
	W(X)
	R(X)
	Commit

Here the write operation W(X) of Ta precedes the conflicting operation (Read or Write operation) of Tb so the conflicting operation of Tb had to wait the commit operation of Ta.

Cascadeless Schedule

In Cascadeless Schedule, if a transaction is going to perform read operation on a value, it has to wait until the transaction who is performing write on that value commits.

Cascadeless Schedule Example

For example, lets say we have two transactions Ta and Tb. Tb is going to read the value X after the W(X) of Ta then Tb has to wait for the commit operation of transaction Ta before it reads the X.

Ta	Tb
R(X)	
W(X)	
	W(X)
commit	

Contd...

Ta	Tb
	R(X)
	W(X)
	Commit

Recoverable Schedule

In Recoverable schedule, if a transaction is reading a value which has been updated by some other transaction then this transaction can commit only after the commit of other transaction which is updating value.

Recoverable Schedule example

Here Tb is performing read operation on X after the Ta has made changes in X using W(X) so Tb can only commit after the commit operation of Ta.

Ta	Tb
R(X)	
W(X)	
	R(X)
	W(X)
	R(X)
commit	
	Commit

6.8   SERIALIZABILITY

When multiple transactions are running concurrently then there is a possibility that the database may be left in an inconsistent state. Serializability is a concept that helps us to check which schedules are serializable. A serializable schedule is the one that always leaves the database in consistent state.

What is a Serializable Schedule?

A serializable schedule always leaves the database in consistent state. A serial schedule is always a serializable schedule because in serial schedule, a transaction only starts when the other transaction finished execution. However a non-serial schedule needs to be checked for Serializability. A non-serial schedule of n number of transactions is said to be serializable schedule, if it is equivalent to the serial schedule of those n transactions. A serial schedule doesn't allow concurrency, only one transaction executes at a time and the other starts when the already running transaction finished.

Types of Serializability

There are two types of Serializability.

1. Conflict Serializability
2. View Serializability

1. Conflict Serializability

Conflict Serializability Two instructions of two different transactions may want to access the same data item in order to perform a read/write operation. Conflict Serializability deals with detecting whether the instructions are conflicting in any way, and specifying the order in which these two instructions will be executed in case there is any conflict. A conflict arises if at least one (or both) of the instructions is a write operation.

The following rules are important in Conflict Serializability:

1. If two instructions of the two concurrent transactions are both for read operation, then they are not in conflict, and can be allowed to take place in any order.
2. If one of the instructions wants to perform a read operation and the other instruction wants to perform a write operation, then they are in conflict, hence their ordering is important.

If the read instruction is performed first, then it reads the old value of the data item and after the reading is over, the new value of the data item is written. It the write instruction is performed first, then updates the data item with the new value and the read instruction reads the newly updated value. 3. If both the transactions are for write operation, then they are in conflict but can be allowed to take place in any order, because the transaction do not read the value updated by each other. However, the value that persists in the data item after the schedule is over is the one written by the instruction that performed the last write. It may happen that we may want to execute the same set of transaction in a different schedule on another day.

Keeping in mind these rules, we may sometimes alter parts of one schedule (S1) to create another schedule (S2) by swapping only the non-conflicting parts of the first schedule. The conflicting parts cannot be swapped in this way because the ordering of the conflicting instructions is important and cannot be changed in any other schedule that is derived from the first. If these two schedules are made of the same set of transactions, then both S1 and S2 would yield the same result if the conflict resolution rules are maintained while creating the new schedule. In that case the schedule S1 and S2 would be called **Conflict Equivalent**.

Let's see some examples to understand this:

Example 1: Operation W(X) of transaction T1 and operation R(X) of transaction T2 are conflicting operations, because they satisfy all the three conditions mentioned above. They belong to different transactions, they are working on same data item X, one of the operation in write operation.

Example 2: Similarly Operations W(X) of T1 and W(X) of T2 are conflicting operations.

Example 3: Operations W(X) of T1 and W(Y) of T2 are non-conflicting operations because both the write operations are not working on same data item so these operations don't satisfy the second condition.

Example 4: Similarly R(X) of T1 and R(X) of T2 are non-conflicting operations because none of them is write operation.

Example 5: Similarly W(X) of T1 and R(X) of T1 are non-conflicting operations because both the operations belong to same transaction T1.

Conflict Equivalent Schedules

Two schedules are said to be conflict Equivalent if one schedule can be converted into other schedule after swapping non-conflicting operations.

Conflict Serializable check

Let's check whether a schedule is conflict serializable or not. If a schedule is conflict Equivalent to its serial schedule then it is called Conflict Serializable schedule. Lets take few examples of schedules.

Example of Conflict Serializability

Let's consider this schedule:

T1	T2
R(A)	
R(B)	
	R(A)
	R(B)
	W(B)
W(A)	

To convert this schedule into a serial schedule we must have to swap the R(A) operation of transaction T2 with the W(A) operation of transaction T1. However we cannot swap these two operations because they are conflicting operations, thus we can say that this given schedule is **not Conflict Serializable**.

Let's take another example:

T1	T2
R(A)	
	R(A)
	R(B)
	W(B)
R(B)	
W(A)	

Let's **swap non-conflicting operations**:

After swapping R(A) of T1 and R(A) of T2 we get:

T1	T2
	R(A)
R(A)	
	R(B)
	W(B)
R(B)	
W(A)	

After swapping R(A) of T1 and R(B) of T2 we get:

T1	T2
	R(A)
	R(B)
R(A)	
	W(B)
R(B)	
W(A)	

After swapping R(A) of T1 and W(B) of T2 we get:

T1	T2
	R(A)
	R(B)
	W(B)
R(A)	
R(B)	
W(A)	

We finally got a serial schedule after swapping all the non-conflicting operations so we can say that the given schedule is **Conflict Serializable**.

2. View Serializability

This is another type of serializability that can be derived by creating another schedule out of an existing schedule, involving the same set of transactions. These two schedules would be called View Serializable if the following rules are followed while creating the second schedule out of the first. Let us consider that the transactions T1 and T2 are being serialized to create two different schedules S1 and S2 which we want to be View Equivalent and both T1 and T2 wants to access the same data item. 1.

If in S1, T1 reads the initial value of the data item, then in S2 also, T1 should read the initial value of that same data item. 2. If in S1, T1 writes a value in the data item which is read by T2, then in S2 also, T1 should write the value in the data item before T2 reads it. 3. If in S1, T1 performs the final write operation on that data item, then in S2 also, T1 should perform the final write operation on that data item. Except in these three cases, any alteration can be possible while creating S2 by modifying S1.

View Serializability is a process to find out that a given schedule is view serializable or not.

To check whether a given schedule is view serializable, we need to check whether the given schedule is **View Equivalent** to its serial schedule. Let's take an example to understand what I mean by that.

Given Schedule

T1	T2
R(X)	
W(X)	
	R(X)
	W(X)
R(Y)	
W(Y)	
	R(Y)
	W(Y)

Serial Schedule of the Above Given Schedule

As we know that in Serial schedule a transaction only starts when the current running transaction is finished. So the serial schedule of the above given schedule would look like this:

T1	T2
R(X)	
W(X)	
R(Y)	
W(Y)	
	R(X)
	W(X)
	R(Y)
	W(Y)

If we can prove that the given schedule is **View Equivalent** to its serial schedule then the given schedule is called **view Serializable**.

Why We Need View Serializability?

We know that a serial schedule never leaves the database in inconsistent state because there are no concurrent transactions execution. However a non-serial schedule can leave the database in inconsistent state because there are multiple transactions running concurrently. By checking that a given non-serial schedule is view serializable, we make sure that it is a consistent schedule. You may be wondering instead of checking that a non-serial schedule is serializable or not, can't we have serial schedule all the time? The answer is no, because concurrent execution of transactions fully utilize the system resources and are considerably faster compared to serial schedules.

View Equivalent

Let's learn how to check whether the two schedules are view equivalent.

Two schedules T1 and T2 are said to be view equivalent, if they satisfy all the following conditions:

- ✧ **Initial Read:** Initial read of each data item in transactions must match in both schedules. For example, if transaction T1 reads a data item X before transaction T2 in schedule S1 then in schedule S2, T1 should read X before T2.

- ✧ **Read vs Initial Read:** You may be confused by the term initial read. Here initial read means the first read operation on a data item, for example, a data item X can be read multiple times in a schedule but the first read operation on X is called the initial read. This will be more clear once we will get to the example in the next section of this same article.

- ✧ **Final Write:** Final write operations on each data item must match in both the schedules. For example, a data item X is last written by Transaction T1 in schedule S1 then in S2, the last write operation on X should be performed by the transaction T1.

✦ **Update Read:** If in schedule S1, the transaction T1 is reading a data item updated by T2 then in schedule S2, T1 should read the value after the write operation of T2 on same data item. For example, In schedule S1, T1 performs a read operation on X after the write operation on X by T2 then in S2, T1 should read the X after T2 performs write on X.

View Serializable

If a schedule is view equivalent to its serial schedule then the given schedule is said to be View Serializable. Lets take an example.

View Serializable Example

```
   Non-Serial              Serial
   -------------        ---------------      S2 is the serial
       S1                    S2              schedule of S1. If
   -------------        ---------------      we can prove that
   T1      T2           T1      T2           they are view
   -----   ------       -----   ------       equivalent then
   R(X)                 R(X)                 we we can say
   W(X)                 W(X)                 that given
           R(X)         R(Y)                 schedule S1 is
           W(X)         W(Y)                 view Serializable
   R(Y)                         R(X)
   W(Y)                         W(X)
           R(Y)                 R(Y)
           W(Y)                 W(Y)
```

Let's check the three conditions of view serializability:

Initial Read

In schedule S1, transaction T1 first reads the data item X. In S2 also transaction T1 first reads the data item X. Lets check for Y. In schedule S1, transaction T1 first reads the data item Y. In S2 also the first read operation on Y is performed by T1. We checked for both data items X & Y and the **initial read** condition is satisfied in S1 & S2.

Final Write

In schedule S1, the final write operation on X is done by transaction T2. In S2 also transaction T2 performs the final write on X. Let's check for Y. In schedule S1, the final write operation on Y is done by transaction T2. In schedule S2, final write on Y is done by T2. We checked for both data items X & Y and the **final write** condition is satisfied in S1 & S2.

Update Read

In S1, transaction T2 reads the value of X, written by T1. In S2, the same transaction T2 reads the X after it is written by T1. In S1, transaction T2 reads the value of Y, written by T1. In S2, the same transaction T2 reads the value of Y after it is updated by T1. The update read condition is also satisfied for both the schedules.

Result: Since all the three conditions that checks whether the two schedules are view equivalent are satisfied in this example, which means S1 and S2 are view equivalent. Also, as we know that the schedule S2 is the serial schedule of S1, thus we can say that the schedule S1 is view serializable schedule.

6.9   CONCURRENT EXECUTION

Concurrent Execution A schedule is a collection of many transactions which is implemented as a unit. Depending upon how these transactions are arranged in within a schedule, a schedule can be of two types:

Serial: The transactions are executed one after another, in a non-preemptive manner. Concurrent: The transactions are executed in a preemptive, time shared method.

In Serial schedule, there is no question of sharing a single data item among many transactions, because not more than a single transaction is executing at any point of time. However, a serial schedule is inefficient in the sense that the transactions suffer for having a longer waiting time and response time, as well as low amount of resource utilization. In concurrent schedule, CPU time is shared among two or more transactions in order to run them concurrently.

However, this creates the possibility that more than one transaction may need to access a single data item for read/write purpose and the database could contain inconsistent value if such accesses are not handled properly. Let us explain with the help of an example. Let us consider there are two transactions T1 and T2, whose instruction sets are given as following. T1 is the same as we have seen earlier, while T2 is a new transaction. T1 Read A; A = A − 100; Write A; Read B; B = B + 100; Write B; T2 Read A; Temp = A * 0.1; Read C; C = C + Temp; Write C;

6.10   RECOVERABILITY

As discussed, a transaction may not execute completely due to hardware failure, system crash or software issues. In that case, we have to roll back the failed transaction. But some other transaction may also have used values produced by the failed transaction. So we have to roll back those transactions as well.

Recoverable Schedules

⅄   Schedules in which transactions commit only after all transactions whose changes they read commit are called recoverable schedules. In other words, if some transaction T_j is reading value updated or written by some other transaction T_i, then the commit of T_j must occur after the commit of T_i.

Example 1

S1: R1(x), **W1(x)**, R2(x), R1(y), R2(y),

W2(x), W1(y), **C1, C2;**

Given schedule follows order of **Ti->Tj => C1->C2**. Transaction T1 is executed before T2 hence there is no chances of conflict occur. R1(x) appears before W1(x) and transaction T1 is committed before T2 i.e. completion of first transaction performed first update on data item x, hence given schedule is recoverable.

Example 2: Consider the following schedule involving two transactions T_1 and T_2.

T_1	T_2
R(A)	
W(A)	
	W(A)
	R(A)
Commit	
	commit

This is a recoverable schedule since T_1 commits before T_2, that makes the value read by T_2 correct.

Irrecoverable Schedule

⅄ The table below shows a schedule with two transactions, T1 reads and writes A and that value is read and written by T2. T2 commits. But later on, T1 fails. So we have to rollback T1. Since T2 has read the value written by T1, it should also be rollbacked. But we have already committed that. So this schedule is irrecoverable schedule. When Tj is reading the value updated by Ti and Tj is committed before committing of Ti, the schedule will be irrecoverable.

T1	T1's buffer space	T2	T2's Buffer Space	Database
				A=5000
R(A);	A=5000			A=5000
A=A-100;	A=4000			A=5000
W(A);	A=4000			A=4000
		R(A);	A=4000	A=4000
		A=A+500;	A=4500	A=4000
		W(A);	A=4500	A=4500
		Commit;		
Failure Point				
Commit;				

Recoverable with Cascading Rollback

⅄ The table below shows a schedule with two transactions, T1 reads and writes A and that value is read and written by T2. But later on, T1 fails. So we have to rollback T1. Since T2 has read the value written by T1, it should also be rollbacked. As it has not committed, we can rollback T2 as well. So it is recoverable with cascading rollback. Therefore, if Tj is reading value updated by Ti and commit of Tj is delayed till commit of Ti, the schedule is called recoverable with cascading rollback.

T1	T1's buffer space	T2	T2's Buffer Space	Database
				A=5000
R(A);	A=5000			A=5000
A=A-100;	A=4000			A=5000
W(A);	A=4000			A=4000
		R(A);	A=4000	A=4000
		A=A+500;	A=4500	A=4000
		W(A);	A=4500	A=4500
Failure Point				
Commit;				
		Commit;		

Cascadeless Recoverable Rollback

⋏   The table below shows a schedule with two transactions, T1 reads and writes A and commits and that value is read by T2. But if T1 fails before commit, no other transaction has read its value, so there is no need to rollback other transaction. So this is a Cascadeless recoverable schedule. So, if Tj reads value updated by Ti only after Ti is committed, the schedule will be cascadeless recoverable.

T1	T1's buffer space	T2	T2's Buffer Space	Database
				A=5000
R(A);	A=5000			A=5000
A=A-100;	A=4000			A=5000
W(A);	A=4000			A=4000
Commit;				
		R(A);	A=4000	A=4000
		A=A+500;	A=4500	A=4000
		W(A);	A=4500	A=4500
		Commit;		

Chapter 7

Concurrency Control

7.1 CONCURRENCY CONTROL

Concurrency control is the procedure in DBMS for managing simultaneous operations without conflicting with each another. Concurrent access is quite easy if all users are just reading data. There is no way they can interfere with one another. Though for any practical database, would have a mix of reading and WRITE operations and hence the concurrency is a challenge. Concurrency control is used to address such conflicts which mostly occur with a multi-user system. It helps you to make sure that database transactions are performed concurrently without violating the data integrity of respective databases.

Therefore, concurrency control is a most important element for the proper functioning of a system where two or multiple database transactions that require access to the same data, are executed simultaneously.

Why use Concurrency method?

Reasons for using Concurrency control method is DBMS:

- ✧ To apply Isolation through mutual exclusion between conflicting transactions
- ✧ To resolve read-write and write-write conflict issues

✧ To preserve database consistency through constantly preserving execution obstructions

✧ The system needs to control the interaction among the concurrent transactions. This control is achieved using concurrent-control schemes.

✧ Concurrency control helps to ensure serializability

Example

Assume that two people who go to electronic kiosks at the same time to buy a movie ticket for the same movie and the same show time.

However, there is only one seat left in for the movie show in that particular theatre. Without concurrency control, it is possible that both moviegoers will end up purchasing a ticket. However, concurrency control method does not allow this to happen. Both moviegoers can still access information written in the movie seating database. But concurrency control only provides a ticket to the buyer who has completed the transaction process first.

Concurrency Problems

When multiple transactions execute concurrently in an uncontrolled or unrestricted manner, then it might lead to several problems. These problems are commonly referred to as concurrency problems in database environment. The five concurrency problems that can occur in database are:

iii. Temporary Update Problem
iv. Incorrect Summary Problem
v. Lost Update Problem
vi. Unrepeatable Read Problem
vii. Phantom Read Problem

These are explained as following below.

1. Temporary Update Problem

Temporary update or dirty read problem occurs when one transaction updates an item and fails. But the updated item is used by another transaction before the item is changed or reverted back to its last value.

Example

T1	T2
read_item(X) X = X - N write_item(X)	
	read_item(X) X = X + M write_item(X)
read_item(Y)	

In the above example, if transaction 1 fails for some reason then X will revert back to its previous value. But transaction 2 has already read the incorrect value of X.

2. Incorrect Summary Problem

Consider a situation, where one transaction is applying the aggregate function on some records while another transaction is updating these records. The aggregate function may calculate some values before the values have been updated and others after they are updated.

Example

T1	T2
	sum = 0
	read_item(A)
	sum = sum + A
read_item(X)	
X = X - N	
write_item(X)	
	read_item(X)
	sum = sum + X
	read_item(Y)
	sum = sum + Y
read_item(Y)	
Y = Y + N	
write_item(Y)	

In the above example, transaction 2 is calculating the sum of some records while transaction 1 is updating them. Therefore the aggregate function may calculate some values before they have been updated and others after they have been updated.

3. Lost Update Problem

In the lost update problem, update done to a data item by a transaction is lost as it is overwritten by the update done by another transaction.

Example

T1	T2
read_item(X)	
X = X + N	
	X = X + 10
	write_item(X)

In the above example, transaction 1 changes the value of X but it gets overwritten by the update done by transaction 2 on X. Therefore, the update done by transaction 1 is lost.

4. Unrepeatable Read Problem

The unrepeatable problem occurs when two or more read operations of the same transaction read different values of the same variable.

Example

T1	T2
Read(X)	
	Read(X)
Write(X)	
	Read(X)

In the above example, once transaction 2 reads the variable X, a write operation in transaction 1 changes the value of the variable X. Thus, when another read operation is performed by transaction 2, it reads the new value of X which was updated by transaction 1.

5. Phantom Read Problem

The phantom read problem occurs when a transaction reads a variable once but when it tries to read that same variable again, an error occurs saying that the variable does not exist.

Example

T1	T2
Read(X)	
	Read(X)
Delete(X)	
	Read(X)

In the above example, once transaction 2 reads the variable X, transaction 1 deletes the variable X without transaction 1's knowledge. Thus, when transaction 2 tries to read X, it is not able to it.

7.2   LOCK BASED PROTOCOL

A lock is nothing but a mechanism that tells the DBMS whether a particular data item is being used by any transaction for read/write purpose. Since there are two types of operations, i.e. read and write, whose basic nature are different, the locks for read and write operation may behave differently.

Read operation performed by different transactions on the same data item poses less of a challenge. The value of the data item, if constant, can be read by any number of transactions at any given time.

Write operation is something different. When a transaction writes some value into a data item, the content of that data item remains in an inconsistent state, starting from the moment when the writing operation begins up to the moment the writing operation is over. If we allow any other transaction to read/write the value of the data item during the write operation, those transaction will read an inconsistent value or overwrite the value being written by the first transaction. In both the cases anomalies will creep into the database.

The simple rule for locking can be derived from here. If a transaction is reading the content of a sharable data item, then any number of other processes can be allowed to read the content of the same data item. But if any transaction is writing into a sharable data item, then no other transaction will be allowed to read or write that same data item.

Depending upon the rules we have found, we can classify the locks into two types.

Shared Lock: A transaction may acquire shared lock on a data item in order to read its content. The lock is shared in the sense that any other transaction can acquire the shared lock on thatsame data item for reading purpose.

Exclusive Lock: A transaction may acquire exclusive lock on a data item in order to both read/write into it. The lock is excusive in the sense that no other transaction can acquire any kind of lock (either shared or exclusive) on that same data item.

The relationship between Shared and Exclusive Lock can be represented by the following table which is known as **Lock Matrix**.

Locks already existing

	Shared	**Exclusive**
Shared	TRUE	FALSE
Exclusive	FALSE	FALSE

How Should Lock be Used?

In a transaction, a data item which we want to read/write should first be locked before the read/write is done. After the operation is over, the transaction should then unlock the data item so that other transaction can lock that same data item for their respective usage. In the earlier chapter we had seen a transaction to deposit Rs 100/

– from account A to account B. The transaction should now be written as the following:

Lock-X (A); (Exclusive Lock, we want to both read A's value and modify it)

Read A;

A = A – 100;

Write A;

Unlock (A); (Unlocking A after the modification is done)

Lock-X (B); (Exclusive Lock, we want to both read B's value and modify it)

Read B;

B = B + 100;

Write B;

Unlock (B); (Unlocking B after the modification is done)

And the transaction that deposits 10% amount of account A to account C should now be written as:

Lock-S (A); (Shared Lock, we only want to read A's value)

Read A;

Temp = A * 0.1;

Unlock (A); (Unlocking A)

Lock-X (C); (Exclusive Lock, we want to both read C's value and modify it)

Read C;

C = C + Temp;

Write C;

Unlock (C); (Unlocking C after the modification is done)

Let us see how these locking mechanisms help us to create error free schedules. You should remember that in the previous chapter we discussed an example of an erroneous schedule:

T1	T2
Read A;	
A = A – 100;	
	Read A;
	Temp = A * 0.1;
	Read C;
	C = C + Temp;
	Write C;
Write A;	
Read B;	
B = B + 100;	
Write B;	

We detected the error based on common sense only, that the Context Switching is being performed before the new value has been updated in A. T2 reads the old value of A, and thus deposits a wrong amount in C. Had we used the locking mechanism, this error could never have occurred. Let us rewrite the schedule using the locks.

T1	T2
Lock-X (A)	
Read A;	
A = A – 100;	
Write A;	
	Lock-S (A)

Contd...

T1	T2
	Read A;
	Temp = A * 0.1;
	Unlock (A)
	Lock-X(C)
	Read C;
	C = C + Temp;
	Write C;
	Unlock (C)
Write A;	
Unlock (A)	
Lock-X (B)	
Read B;	
B = B + 100;	
Write B;	
Unlock (B)	

We cannot prepare a schedule like the above even if we like, provided that we use the locks in the transactions. See the first statement in T2 that attempts to acquire a lock on A. This would be impossible because T1 has not released the excusive lock on A, and T2 just cannot get the shared lock it wants on A. It must wait until the exclusive lock on A is released by T1, and can begin its execution only after that. So the proper schedule would look like the following:

T1	T2
Lock-X (A)	
Read A;	
A = A – 100;	
Write A;	
Unlock (A)	
	Lock-S (A)
	Read A;

T1	T2
	Temp = A * 0.1;
	Unlock (A)
	Lock-X(C)
	Read C;
	C = C + Temp;
	Write C;
	Unlock (C)
Lock-X (B)	
Read B;	
B = B + 100;	
Write B;	
Unlock (B)	

And this automatically becomes a very correct schedule. We need not apply any manual effort to detect or correct the errors that may creep into the schedule if locks are not used in them.

7.2.1 Two Phase Locking Protocol

The use of locks has helped us to create neat and clean concurrent schedule. The Two Phase Locking Protocol defines the rules of how to acquire the locks on a data item and how to release the locks. The Two Phase Locking Protocol assumes that a transaction can only be in one of two phases.

Growing Phase

In this phase the transaction can only acquire locks, but cannot release any lock. The transaction enters the growing phase as soon as it acquires the first lock it wants. From now on it has no option but to keep acquiring all the locks it would need. It cannot release any lock at this phase even if it has finished working with a locked data item. Ultimately the transaction reaches a point where all the lock it may need has been acquired. This point is called **Lock Point**.

Shrinking Phase

After Lock Point has been reached, the transaction enters the shrinking phase. In this phase the transaction can only release locks, but cannot acquire any new lock. The transaction enters the shrinking phase as soon as it releases the first lock after crossing the Lock Point. From now on it has no option but to keep releasing all the acquired locks.

There are two different versions of the Two Phase Locking Protocol. One is called the Strict Two Phase Locking Protocol and the other one is called the Rigorous Two Phase Locking Protocol.

Strict Two Phase Locking Protocol

In this protocol, a transaction may release all the shared locks after the Lock Point has been reached, but it cannot release any of the exclusive locks until the transaction commits. This protocol helps in creating cascade less schedule. A **Cascading Schedule** is a typical problem faced while creating concurrent schedule. Consider the following schedule once again.

T1	T2
Lock-X (A)	
Read A;	
A = A – 100;	
Write A;	
Unlock (A)	
	Lock-S (A)
	Read A;
	Temp = A * 0.1;
	Unlock (A)
	Lock-X(C)
	Read C;
	C = C + Temp;

T1	T2
	Write C;
	Unlock (C)
Lock-X (B)	
Read B;	
B = B + 100;	
Write B;	
Unlock (B)	

The schedule is theoretically correct, but a very strange kind of problem may arise here. T1 releases the exclusive lock on A, and immediately after that the Context Switch is made. T2 acquires a shared lock on A to read its value, perform a calculation, update the content of account C and then issue COMMIT. However, T1 is not finished yet. What if the remaining portion of T1 encounters a problem (power failure, disc failure etc) and cannot be committed? In that case T1 should be rolled back and the old BFIM value of A should be restored. In such a case T2, which has read the updated (but not committed) value of A and calculated the value of C based on this value, must also have to be rolled back. We have to rollback T2 for no fault of T2 itself, but because we proceeded with T2 depending on a value which has not yet been committed. This phenomenon of rolling back a child transaction if the parent transaction is rolled back is called Cascading Rollback, which causes a tremendous loss of processing power and execution time.

Using Strict Two Phase Locking Protocol, Cascading Rollback can be prevented. In Strict Two Phase Locking Protocol a transaction cannot release any of its acquired exclusive locks until the transaction commits. In such a case, T1 would not release the exclusive lock on A until it finally commits, which makes it impossible for T2 to acquire the shared lock on A at a time when A's value has not been committed. This makes it impossible for a schedule to be cascading.

Rigorous Two Phase Locking Protocol

In Rigorous Two Phase Locking Protocol, a transaction is not allowed to release any lock (either shared or exclusive) until it commits. This means that until the transaction commits, other transaction might acquire a shared lock on a data item on which the uncommitted transaction has a shared lock; but cannot acquire any lock on a data item on which the uncommitted transaction has an exclusive lock.

7.3　TIMESTAMP ORDERING PROTOCOL

A **timestamp** is a tag that can be attached to any transaction or any data item, which denotes a specific time on which the transaction or data item had been activated in any way. We, who use computers, must all be familiar with the concepts of "Date Created" or "Last Modified" properties of files and folders. Well, timestamps are things like that. A timestamp can be implemented in two ways. The simplest one is to directly assign the current value of the clock to the transaction or the data item. The other policy is to attach the value of a logical counter that keeps incrementing as new timestamps are required. The timestamp of a transaction denotes the time when it was first activated. The timestamp of a data item can be of the following two types:

W-timestamp (Q): This means the latest time when the data item Q has been written into.

R-timestamp (Q): This means the latest time when the data item Q has been read from.

These two timestamps are updated each time a successful read/write operation is performed on the data item Q.

How Should Timestamps Be Used?

The timestamp ordering protocol ensures that any pair of conflicting read/write operations will be executed in their respective timestamp order. This is an alternative solution to using locks.

For Read Operations

⮞ **If TS (T) < W-timestamp (Q),** then the transaction T is trying to read a value of data item Q which has already been overwritten by some other transaction. Hence the value which T wanted to read from Q does not exist there anymore, and T would be rolled back.

⮞ **If TS (T) >= W-timestamp (Q),** then the transaction T is trying to read a value of data item Q which has been written and committed by some other transaction earlier. Hence T will be allowed to read the value of Q, and the R-timestamp of Q should be updated to TS (T).

For Write Operations

⮞ **If TS (T) < R-timestamp (Q),** then it means that the system has waited too long for transaction T to write its value, and the delay has become so great that it has allowed another transaction to read the old value of data item Q. In such a case T has lost its relevance and will be rolled back.

⮞ Else **if TS (T) < W-timestamp (Q),** then transaction T has delayed so much that the system has allowed another transaction to write into the data item Q. in such a case too, T has lost its relevance and will be rolled back.

⮞ Otherwise the system executes transaction T and updates the W-timestamp of Q to TS (T).

7.4   VALIDATION BASED PROTOCOL

Validation phase is also known as optimistic concurrency control technique. In the validation based protocol, the transaction is executed in the following three phases:

1. Read Phase

In this phase, the transaction T is read and executed. It is used to read the value of various data items and stores them in temporary local variables. It can perform all the write operations on temporary variables without an update to the actual database.

2. Validation Phase

In this phase, the temporary variable value will be validated against the actual data to see if it violates the serializability.

3. Write Phase

If the validation of the transaction is validated, then the temporary results are written to the database or system otherwise the transaction is rolled back.

Here each phase has the following different timestamps:

Start(Ti): It contains the time when Ti started its execution.

Validation (T_j): It contains the time when Ti finishes its read phase and starts its validation phase.

Finish(Ti): It contains the time when Ti finishes its write phase.

- ✧ This protocol is used to determine the time stamp for the transaction for serialization using the time stamp of the validation phase, as it is the actual phase which determines if the transaction will commit or rollback.
- ✧ Hence TS(T) = validation(T).
- ✧ The serializability is determined during the validation process. It can't be decided in advance.
- ✧ While executing the transaction, it ensures a greater degree of concurrency and also less number of conflicts.
- ✧ Thus it contains transactions which have less number of rollbacks.

Thomas write Rule

Thomas Write Rule provides the guarantee of serializability order for the protocol. It improves the Basic Timestamp Ordering Algorithm.

The basic Thomas write rules are as follows:

- **If TS(T) < R_TS(X)** then transaction T is aborted and rolled back, and operation is rejected.
- **If TS(T) < W_TS(X)** then don't execute the W_item(X) operation of the transaction and continue processing.
- If neither condition 1 nor condition 2 occurs, then allowed to execute the WRITE operation by transaction Ti and set W_TS(X) to TS(T).

If we use the Thomas write rule then some serializable schedule can be permitted that does not conflict serializable as illustrate by the schedule in a given figure:

T1	T2
R(A)	
	W(A)
	Commit
W(A)	
Commit	

Fig.7.1: A Serializable Schedule that is not Conflict Serializable

In the above fig.7.1, T1's read and precedes T1's write of the same data item. This schedule does not conflict serializable.

Thomas write rule checks that T2's write is never seen by any transaction. If we delete the write operation in transaction T2, then conflict serializable schedule can be obtained which is shown in below figure.

T1	T2
R(A)	Commit
W(A) Commit	

Fig.7.2: A Conflict Serializable Schedule

7.5 MULTIPLE GRANULARITY

Let's start by understanding the meaning of granularity.

Granularity: It is the size of data item allowed to lock.

Multiple Granularity

It can be defined as hierarchically breaking up the database into blocks which can be locked. The Multiple Granularity protocol enhances concurrency and reduces lock overhead. It maintains the track of what to lock and how to lock. It makes easy to decide either to lock a data item or to unlock a data item. This type of hierarchy can be graphically represented as a tree.

For example: Consider a tree which has four levels of nodes.

- ✧ The first level or higher level shows the entire database.
- ✧ The second level represents a node of type area. The higher level database consists of exactly these areas.

The area consists of children nodes which are known as files. No file can be present in more than one area. Finally, each file contains child nodes known as records. The file has exactly those records that are its child nodes. No records represent in more than one file.

Hence, the levels of the tree starting from the top level are as follows:

- ✦ Database
- ✦ Area
- ✦ File
- ✦ Record

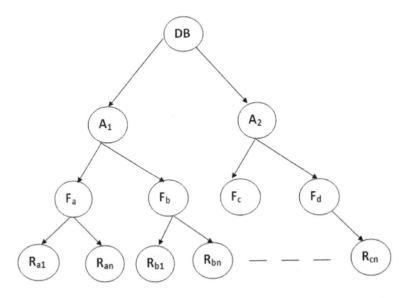

In this example, the highest level shows the entire database. The levels below are file, record, and fields.

There are three additional lock modes with multiple granularity:

Intention Mode Lock

Intention-Shared (IS)

It contains explicit locking at a lower level of the tree but only with shared locks.

Intention-Exclusive (IX)

It contains explicit locking at a lower level with exclusive or shared locks.

Shared & Intention-Exclusive (SIX):

In this lock, the node is locked in shared mode, and some node is locked in exclusive mode by the same transaction.

Compatibility Matrix with Intention Lock Modes: The below table describes the compatibility matrix for these lock modes:

	IS	IX	S	SIX	X
IS	✓	✓	✓	✓	X
IX	✓	✓	X	X	X
S	✓	X	✓	X	X
SIX	✓	X	X	X	X
X	X	X	X	X	X

It uses the intention lock modes to ensure serializability. It requires that if a transaction attempts to lock a node, then that node must follow these protocols:

Transaction T1 should follow the lock-compatibility matrix.

The multiple-granularity locking protocol uses the intention lock modes to ensure serializability. It requires that a transaction T_i that attempts to lock a node must follow these protocols:

1. Transaction T_i must follow the lock-compatibility matrix.
2. Transaction T_i must lock the root of the tree first, and it can lock it in any mode.
3. Transaction T_i can lock a node in S or IS mode only if T_i currently has the parent of the node locked in either IX or IS mode.
4. Transaction T_i can lock a node in X, SIX, or IX mode only if T_i currently has the parent of the node locked in either IX or SIX mode.
5. Transaction T_i can lock a node only if T_i has not previously unlocked any node (i.e., T_i is two phase).
6. Transaction T_i can unlock a node only if T_i currently has none of the children of the node locked.

Observe that the multiple-granularity protocol requires that locks be acquired in top-down (root-to-leaf) order, whereas locks must be released in bottom-up (leaf to-root) order.

As an illustration of the protocol, consider the tree given above and the transactions:

❖ Say transaction T_1 reads record R_{a2} in file F_a. Then, T_2 needs to lock the database, area A_1, and F_a in IS mode (and in that order), and finally to lock R_{a2} in S mode.

❖ Say transaction T_2 modifies record R_{a9} in file F_a. Then, T_2 needs to lock the database, area A_1, and file F_a (and in that order) in IX mode, and at last to lock R_{a9} in X mode.

❖ Say transaction T_3 reads all the records in file F_a. Then, T_3 needs to lock the database and area A_1 (and in that order) in IS mode, and at last to lock F_a in S mode.

❖ Say transaction T_4 reads the entire database. It can do so after locking the database in S mode.

Note that transactions T_1, T_3 and T_4 can access the database concurrently. Transaction T_2 can execute concurrently with T_1, but not with either T_3 or T_4.

This protocol enhances concurrency and reduces lock overhead. Deadlock are still possible in the multiple-granularity protocol, as it is in the two-phase locking protocol. These can be eliminated by using certain deadlock elimination techniques.

7.6 DEADLOCK

A **deadlock** is a condition wherein two or more tasks are waiting for each other in order to be finished but none of the task is willing to give up the resources that other task needs. In this situation no task ever gets finished and is in waiting state forever.

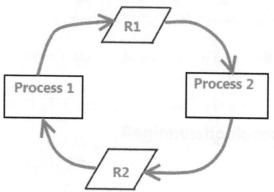

Process P1 holds resource R2 and requires R1 while
Process P2 holds resource R1 and requires R2.

Coffman Conditions

Coffman stated four conditions for a deadlock occurrence. A
deadlock may occur if all the following conditions holds true.

- ✦ **Mutual exclusion condition**: There must be at least one
  resource that cannot be used by more than one process
  at a time.
- ✦ **Hold and wait condition**: A process that is holding a
  resource can request for additional resources that are being
  held by other processes in the system.
- ✦ **No preemption condition**: A resource cannot be forcibly
  taken from a process. Only the process can release a resource
  that is being held by it.
- ✦ **Circular wait condition**: A condition where one process is
  waiting for a resource that is being held by second process
  and second process is waiting for third process .... so on and
  the last process is waiting for the first process. Thus making
  a circular chain of waiting.

7.6.1   Deadlock Handling

Ignore the Deadlock (Ostrich Algorithm)

Did that made you laugh? You may be wondering how ignoring a deadlock can come under deadlock handling. But to let you know that the windows you are using on your PC, uses this approach of deadlock handling and that is reason sometimes it hangs up and you have to reboot it to get it working. Not only Windows but UNIX also uses this approach.

The Question is Why? Why Instead of Dealing with a Deadlock They Ignore It and Why This is Being Called as Ostrich Algorithm?

Well! Let me answer the second question first, This is known as Ostrich algorithm because in this approach we ignore the deadlock and pretends that it would never occur, just like Ostrich behavior "to stick one's head in the sand and pretend there is no problem."

Let's discuss why we ignore it: When it is believed that deadlocks are very rare and cost of deadlock handling is higher, in that case ignoring is better solution than handling it. For example: Let's take the operating system example – If the time requires handling the deadlock is higher than the time requires rebooting the windows then rebooting would be a preferred choice considering that deadlocks are very rare in windows.

7.6.2   Deadlock Detection

Resource scheduler is one that keeps the track of resources allocated to and requested by processes. Thus, if there is a deadlock it is known to the resource scheduler. This is how a deadlock is detected.

Once a deadlock is detected it is being corrected by following methods:

⋏　**Terminating processes involved in deadlock:**

Terminating all the processes involved in deadlock or terminating process one by one until deadlock is resolved can be the solutions but both of these approaches are not good. Terminating all processes cost high and partial work done by processes gets lost. Terminating one by one takes lot of time because each time a process is terminated, it needs to check whether the deadlock is resolved or not. Thus, the best approach is considering process age and priority while terminating them during a deadlock condition.

⋏　**Resource Preemption:**

Another approach can be the preemption of resources and allocation of them to the other processes until the deadlock is resolved.

When a transaction waits indefinately to obtain a lock, The database managememt system should detect whether the transaction is involved in a deadlock or not.

Wait-for-graph is one of the methods for detecting the deadlock situation. This method is suitable for smaller database. In this method a graph is drawn based on the transaction and their lock on the resource. If the graph created has a closed loop or a cycle, then there is a deadlock.

For the above mentioned scenario the Wait-For graph is drawn below

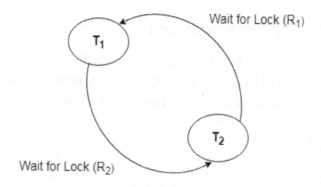

Wait for Lock (R$_1$)

T_1

T_2

Wait for Lock (R$_2$)

7.6.3 Deadlock Prevention

We have learnt that if all the four Coffman conditions hold true then a deadlock occurs so preventing one or more of them could prevent the deadlock.

⅄ **Removing mutual exclusion**

All resources must be sharable that means at a time more than one processes can get a hold of the resources. That approach is practically impossible.

⅄ **Removing hold and wait condition**

This can be removed if the process acquires all the resources that are needed before starting out. Another way to remove this to enforce a rule of requesting resource when there are none in held by the process.

⅄ **Preemption of resources**

Preemption of resources from a process can result in rollback and thus this needs to be avoided in order to maintain the consistency and stability of the system.

⅄ **Avoid circular wait condition**

This can be avoided if the resources are maintained in a hierarchy and process can hold the resources in increasing order of precedence. This avoid circular wait. Another way of doing this to force one resource per process rule – A process can request for a resource once it releases the resource currently being held by it. This avoids the circular wait.

In a database, a deadlock is an unwanted situation in which two or more transactions are waiting indefinitely for one another to give up locks. Deadlock is said to be one of the most feared complications in DBMS as it brings the whole system to a Halt.

Example

Let us understand the concept of Deadlock with an example:

Suppose, Transaction T1 holds a lock on some rows in the Students table and **needs to update** some rows in the Grades table. Simultaneously, Transaction **T2 holds** locks on those very rows (Which T1 needs to update) in the Grades table **but needs** to update the rows in the Student table **held by Transaction T1**.

Now, the main problem arises. Transaction T1 will wait for transaction T2 to give up lock, and similarly transaction T2 will wait for transaction T1 to give up lock. As a consequence, All activity comes to a halt and remains at a standstill forever unless the DBMS detects the deadlock and aborts one of the transactions.

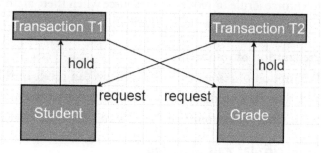

Fig.7.3: Deadlock in DBMS

For large database, deadlock prevention method is suitable. A deadlock can be prevented if the resources are allocated in such a way that deadlock never occur. The DBMS analyzes the operations whether they can create deadlock situation or not, If they do, that transaction is never allowed to be executed.

Deadlock prevention mechanism proposes two schemes:

⋏ **Wait-Die Scheme**

In this scheme, If a transaction request for a resource that is locked by other transaction, then the DBMS simply checks the timestamp of both transactions and allows the older transaction to wait until the resource is available for execution.

Suppose, there are two transactions T1 and T2 and Let timestamp of any transaction T be TS (T). Now, If there is a lock on T2 by some other transaction and T1 is requesting for resources held by T2, then DBMS performs following actions:

▲ Checks if TS (T1) < TS (T2) – if T1 is the older transaction and T2 has held some resource, then it allows T1 to wait until resource is available for execution. That means if a younger transaction has locked some resource and older transaction is waiting for it, then older transaction is allowed wait for it till it is available. If T1 is older transaction and has held some resource with it and if T2 is waiting for it, then T2 is killed and restarted latter with random delay but with the same timestamp. i.e. if the older transaction has held some resource and younger transaction waits for the resource, then younger transaction is killed and restarted with very minute delay with same timestamp.

This scheme allows the older transaction to wait but kills the younger one.

▲ **Wound Wait Scheme**

In this scheme, if an older transaction requests for a resource held by younger transaction, then older transaction forces younger transaction to kill the transaction and release the resource. The younger transaction is restarted with minute delay but with same timestamp. If the younger transaction is requesting a resource which is held by older one, then younger transaction is asked to wait till older releases it.

7.7 MULTIVERSION CONCURRENCY CONTROL TECHNIQUES (MVCC)

The aim of Multi-Version Concurrency is to avoid the problem of Writers blocking Readers and vice-versa, by making use of multiple versions of data. The problem of Writers blocking Readers can be avoided if Readers can obtain access to a previous version of the data that is locked by Writers for modification.

The problem of Readers blocking Writers can be avoided by ensuring that Readers do not obtain locks on data. Multi-Version Concurrency allows Readers to operate without acquiring any locks, by taking advantage of the fact that if a Writer has updated a particular record, its prior version can be used by the Reader without waiting for the Writer to Commit or Abort. In a Multi-version Concurrency solution, Readers do not block Writers, and vice versa. While Multi-version concurrency improves database concurrency, its impact on data consistency is more complex.

7.7.1 Requirements of Multi-Version Concurrency Systems

As its name implies, multi-version concurrency relies upon multiple versions of data to achieve higher levels of concurrency. Typically, a DBMS offering multi-version concurrency (MVDB), needs to provide the following features:

1.   The DBMS must be able to retrieve older versions of a row.
2.   The DBMS must have a mechanism to determine which version of a row is valid in the context of a transaction.

Usually, the DBMS will only consider a version that was committed prior to the start of the transaction that is running the query. In order to determine this, the DBMS must know which transaction created a particular version of a row, and whether this transaction committed prior to the starting of the current transaction.

7.7.2 Approaches to Multi-Version Concurrency

There are essentially two approaches to multi-version concurrency. The first approach is to store multiple versions of records in the database, and garbage collect records when they are no longer required. This is the approach adopted by PostgreSQL and Firebird/ Interbase. The second approach is to keep only the latest version of data in the database, as in SVDB implementations, but reconstruct older versions of data dynamically as required by exploiting information within the Write Ahead Log. This is the approach taken by Oracle and MySQL/InnoDb.

Chapter 8

Query Processing and Optimization

8.1 QUERY PROCESSING

The fundamental part of any DBMS is query processing and optimization. The results of queries must be available in the timeframe needed by the submitting user. Query Processing is a procedure of transforming a high-level query (such as SQL) into a correct and efficient execution plan expressed in low-level language. A query processing select a most appropriate plan that is used in responding to a database request. When a database system receives a query for update or retrieval of information, it goes through a series of compilation steps, called execution plan. In the first phase called syntax checking phase, the system parses the query and checks that it follows the syntax rules or not. It then matches the objects in the query syntax with the view tables and columns listed in the system table.

Finally it performs the appropriate query modification. During this phase the system validates the user privileges and that the query does not disobey any integrity rules. The execution plan is finally execute to generate a response. So query processing is a stepwise process. The user gives a query request, which may be in QBE or other form. This is first transformed into a standard high-level query language, such as SQL. This SQL query is read by syntax analyzer so that it can be check for correctness. At this step the syntax analyzer use the grammar of SQL as input and the parser portion of the query processor check the syntax and verify whether the relation and attributes of the requested query are defined in database.

At this stage the SQL query is translated in to an algebraic expression using various rules. So that the process of transforming a high-level SQL query into a relational algebraic form is called Query Decomposition. The relational algebraic expression now passes to the query optimizer. Here optimization is performed by substituting equivalent expression depends on the factors such that the existence of certain database structures, whether or not a given file is stored, the presence of different indexes & so on. Query optimization module work in tandem with the join manager module to improve the order in which joins are performed.

Query processing techniques based on multiple design dimensions can be classified as:

1. Query Model

Processing techniques are classified according to the query model they assume. Some techniques assume a selection query model, where scores are attached directly to base tuples. Other techniques assume a join query model, where scores are computed over join results. A third category assumes an aggregate query model, where we are interested in ranking groups of tuples.

2. Data Access Methods

Processing techniques are classified according to the data access methods they assume to be available in the underlying data sources. For example, some techniques assume the availability of random access, while others are restricted to only sorted access.

3. Implementation Level

Processing techniques are classified according to their level of integration with database systems. For example, some techniques are implemented in an application layer on top of the database system, while others are implemented as query operators.

4. Data and Query Uncertainty

Processing techniques are classified based on the uncertainty involved in their data and query models. Some techniques produce exact answers, while others allow for approximate answers, or deal with uncertain data.

5. Ranking Function

Processing techniques are classified based on the restrictions they impose on the underlying ranking (scoring) function. Most proposed techniques assume monotone scoring functions.

Query processing refers to the range of activities involved in extracting data from a database. The activities include translation of queries in high-level database languages into expressions that can be used at the physical level of the file system, a variety of query-optimizing transformations, and actual evaluation of queries. A database query is the vehicle for instructing a DBMS to update or retrieve specific data to/from the physically stored medium. The actual updating and retrieval of data is performed through various "low – level" operations. Examples of such operations for a relational DBMS can be relational algebra operations such as project, join, select, Cartesian product, etc. While the DBMS is designed to process these low – level operations efficiently, it can be quite the burden to a user to submit requests to the DBMS in these formats.

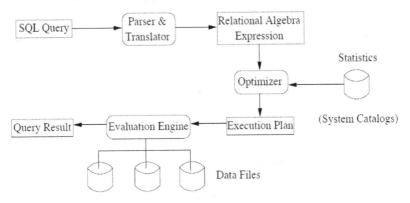

Fig.8.1: Steps in query processing

1. Parsing and Translating

Translate the query into its internal form (parse tree). This is then translated into an expression of the relational algebra. Parser checks syntax, validates relations, attributes and access permissions

2. Evaluation

The query execution engine takes a physical query plan (execution plan), executes the plan, and returns the result.

3. Optimization

Find the cheapest" execution plan for a query

8.1.1 Measures Of Query Cost

The cost of query evaluation can be measured in terms of a number of different resources, including disk accesses, CPU time to execute a query, and, in a distributed or parallel database system, the cost of communication. The response time for a query-evaluation plan, assuming no other activity is going on the computer, would account for all these costs, and could be used as a good measure of the cost of the plan. In large database systems, however, disk accesses are usually the most important cost, since disk accesses are slow compared to in-memory operations. Also CPU speeds have been improving much faster than have disk speeds.

Thus, it is likely that the time spent in disk activity will continue to dominate the total time to execute a query. Finally, estimating the CPU time is relatively hard, compared to estimating the disk-access cost. Therefore, most people consider the disk-access cost a reasonable measure of the cost of a query-evaluation plan.

8.2   QUERY ALGORITHMS

Queries are ultimately reduced to a number of file scan operations on the underlying physical file structures [3, 4]. For each relational operation, there can exist several different access paths to the particular records needed. The query execution engine can have a multitude of specialized algorithms designed to process particular relational operation and access path combinations.

A. Selection Algorithms

The Select operation must search through the data files for records meeting the selection criteria. Following are some examples of simple (one attribute) selection algorithms:

1. Linear Search

Every record from the file is read and compared to the selection criteria. The execution cost for searching on a non-key attribute is br, where br is the number of blocks in the file representing relation r. On a key attribute, the average cost is br/2, with a worst case of br.

2. Binary Search

A binary search, on equality, performed on a primary key attribute has a worst-case cost of [log (br)]. This can be considerably more efficient than the linear search, for a large number of records.

3. Search Using a Primary Index on Equality

With a B+-tree index, an equality comparison on a key attribute will have a worst – case cost of the height of the tree plus one to retrieve the record from the data file. An equality comparison on a non-key attribute will be the same except that multiple records may meet the condition, in which case, we add the number of blocks containing the records to the cost.

4. Search Using a Primary Index on Comparison

When the comparison operators (<, <=, >, >=) are used to retrieve multiple records from a file sorted by the search attribute, the first record satisfying the condition is located and the total blocks before (<, <=) or after (>, >=) is added to the cost of locating the first record.

5. Search Using a Secondary Index on Equality

Retrieve one record with an equality comparison on a key attribute; or retrieve a set of records on a non-key attribute. For a single record, the cost will be equal to the cost of locating the search key in the index file plus one for retrieving the data record. For multiple records, the cost will be equal to the cost of locating the search key in the index file plus one block access for each data record retrieval, since the data file is not ordered on the search attribute.

B. Join Algorithms

The join algorithm can be implemented in a different ways. In terms of disk accesses, the join operations can be very expensive, so implementing and utilizing efficient join algorithms is important in minimizing a query's execution time. The following are 4 well – known types of join algorithms:

1. Nested-Loop Join

It consists of a inner for loop nested within an outer for loo.

2. Index Nested-Loop Join

This algorithm is the same as the Nested-Loop Join, except an index file on the inner relation's join attribute is used versus a data-file scan on each index lookup in the inner loop is essentially an equality selection for utilizing one of the selection algorithms Let c be the cost for the lookup, then the worst – case cost for joining rand sis br + nr * c.

3. Sort –Merge Join

This algorithm can be used to perform natural joins and equi-joins and requires that each relation be sorted by the common attributes between them

4. Hash Join

The hash join algorithm can be used to perform natural joins and equi-joins. The hash join utilizes two hash table file structures (one for each relation) to partition each relation's records into sets containing identical hash values on the join attributes. Each relation is scanned and its corresponding hash table on the join attribute values is built.

C. Indexes Role

The execution time of various operations such as select and join can be reduced by using indexes. Let us review some of the types of index file structures and the roles they play in reducing execution time and overhead:

1. Dense Index

Data-file is ordered by the search key and every search key value has a separate index record. This structure requires only a single seek to find the first occurrence of a set of contiguous record s with the desired search value.

2. Sparse Index

Data-file is ordered by the index search key and only some of the search key values have corresponding index records. Each index record's data-file pointer points to the first data-file record with the search key value. While this structure can be less efficient than a dense index to find the desired records, it requires less storage space and less overhead during insertion and deletion operations.

3. Primary Index

The data file is ordered by the attribute that is also the search key in the index file. Primary indices can be dense or sparse. This is also referred to as an Index-Sequential File.

4. Secondary Index

The data file is ordered by an attribute that is different from the search key in the index file. Secondary indices must be dense.

5. Multi-Level Index

An index structure consisting of 2 or more tier s of records where an upper tier's records point to associated index records of the tier below. The bottom tier's index records contain the pointers to the data-file records. Multi-level indices can be used, for instance, to reduce the number of disk block reads needed during a binary search.

6. Clustering Index

A two-level index structure where the records in the first level contain the clustering field value in one field and a second field pointing to a block [of 2nd level records] in the second level. The records in the second level have one field that points to an actual data file record or to another 2nd level block.

7. B + – Tree Index

Multi – level index with a balanced-tree structure. Finding a search key value in a B+ – tree is. While this, onùlog(height)éproportional to the height of the tree maximum number of seeks required is average, is more than a single – level, dense index that requires only one seek, the B+ – tree structure has a distinct advantage in that it does not require reorganization, it is self-optimizing because the tree is kept balanced during insertions and deletions

8.3   QUERY OPTIMIZATION

The primary goal of query optimization is of choosing an efficient execution strategy for processing a query. The query optimizer attempts to minimize the use of certain resources (mainly the number of I/O and CPU time) by selecting a best execution plan (access plan). A query optimization start during the validation phase by the system to validate the user has appropriate privileges. Now an action plan is generate to perform the query. Relational algebra query tree generated by the query simplifier module of querydecomposer. Estimation formulas used to determine the cardinality of the intermediate result table. A cost ModelStatistical data from the database catalogue. The output of the query optimizer is the execution plan in form of optimized relational algebra query. The query optimizer uses these two techniques to determine which process or expression to consider for evaluating the query.

There are two methods of query optimization.

1. Cost based Optimization (Physical)

This is based on the cost of the query. The query can use different paths based on indexes, constraints, sorting methods etc. This method mainly uses the statistics like record size, number of records, number of records per block, number of blocks, table size, whether whole table fits in a block, organization of tables, uniqueness of column values, size of columns etc.

Suppose, we have series of table joined in a query.

T1 ∞ T2 ∞ T3 ∞ T4∞ T5 ∞ T6

For above query we can have any order of evaluation. We can start taking any two tables in any order and start evaluating the query. Ideally, we can have join combinations in $(2(n-1))! / (n-1)!$ ways. For example, suppose we have 5 tables involved in join, then we can have 8! / 4! = 1680 combinations. But when query optimizer runs, it does not evaluate in all these ways always. It uses dynamic programming where it generates the costs for join orders of any combination of tables. It is calculated and generated only once. This least cost for all the table combination is then stored in the database and is used for future use. i.e.; say we have a set of tables, T = {T1,

T2, T3.. Tn}, then it generates least cost combination for all the tables and stores it.

⅄ Dynamic Programming

As we learnt above, the least cost for the joins of any combination of table is generated here. These values are stored in the database and when those tables are used in the query, this combination is selected for evaluating the query.

While generating the cost, it follows below steps:

Suppose we have set of tables, T = {T1, T2, T3.. Tn}, in a DB. It picks the first table, and computes cost for joining with rest of the tables in set T. It calculates cost for each of the tables and then chooses the best cost. It continues doing the same with rest of the tables in set T. It will generate 2n – 1 cases and it selects the lowest cost and stores it. When a query uses those tables, it checks for the costs here and that combination is used to evaluate the query. This is called dynamic programming.

In this method, time required to find optimized query is in the order of 3n, where n is the number of tables. Suppose we have 5 tables, then time required in 35 = 243, which is lesser than finding all the combination of tables and then deciding the best combination (1680). Also, the space required for computing and storing the cost is also less and is in the order of 2n. In above example, it is 25 = 32.

⅄ Left Deep Trees

This is another method of determining the cost of the joins. Here, the tables and joins are represented in the form of trees. The joins always form the root of the tree and table is kept at the right side of the root. LHS of the root always point to the next join. Hence it gets deeper and deeper on LHS. Hence it is called as left deep tree.

Here instead of calculating the best join cost for set of tables, best join cost for joining with each table is calculated. In this method, time required to find optimized query is in the order of n2n, where n is the number of tables. Suppose we have 5 tables, then time required in 5*25 =160, which is lesser than dynamic programming. Also, the space required for computing storing the cost is also less and is in the order of 2n. In above example, it is 25 = 32, same as dynamic programming.

⋏ Interesting Sort Orders

This method is an enhancement to dynamic programming. Here, while calculating the best join order costs, it also considers the sorted tables. It assumes, calculating the join orders on sorted tables would be efficient. i.e.; suppose we have unsorted tables T1, T2, T3.. Tn and we have join on these tables.

$$(T1 \infty T2) \infty T3 \infty \ldots \infty Tn$$

This method uses hash join or merge join method to calculate the cost. Hash Join will simply join the tables. We get sorted output in merge join method, but it is costlier than hash join. Even though merge join is costlier at this stage, when it moves to join with third table, the join will have less effort to sort the tables.

This is because first table is the sorted result of first two tables. Hence it will reduce the total cost of the query. But the number of tables involved in the join would be relatively less and this cost/space difference will be hardly noticeable. All these cost based optimizations are expensive and are suitable for large number of data. There is another method of optimization called heuristic optimization, which is better compared to cost based optimization.

2. Heuristic Optimization (Logical)

This method is also known as rule based optimization. This is based on the equivalence rule on relational expressions; hence the number of combination of queries get reduces here. Hence the cost of the query too reduces. This method creates relational tree for the given query based on the equivalence rules. These equivalence rules by providing an alternative way of writing and evaluating the query, gives the better path to evaluate the query. This rule need not be true in all cases. It needs to be examined after applying those rules. The most important set of rules followed in this method is listed below:

✧ Perform all the selection operation as early as possible in the query. This should be first and foremost set of actions on the tables in the query. By performing the selection operation, we can reduce the number of records involved in the query, rather than using the whole tables throughout the query.

Suppose we have a query to retrieve the students with age 18 and studying in class DESIGN_01. We can get all the student details from STUDENT table, and class details from CLASS table. We can write this query in two different ways. Here both the queries will return same result. But when we observe them closely we can see that first query will join the two tables first and then applies the filters. That means, it traverses whole table to join, hence the number of records involved is more. But he second query, applies the filters on each table first. This reduces the number of records on each table (in class table, the number of record reduces to one in this case!). Then it joins these intermediary tables. Hence the cost in this case is comparatively less.

Instead of writing query the optimizer creates relational algebra and tree for above case.

✧ Perform all the projection as early as possible in the query. This is similar to selection but will reduce the number of columns in the query.

Suppose for example, we have to select only student name, address and class name of students with age 18 from STUDENT and CLASS tables.

Here again, both the queries look alike, results alike. But when we compare the number of records and attributes involved at each stage, second query uses less records and hence more efficient.

✧ Next step is to perform most restrictive joins and selection operations. When we say most restrictive joins and selection means, select those set of tables and views which will result in comparatively less number of records. Any query will have better performance when tables with few records are joined. Hence throughout heuristic method of optimization, the rules are formed to get less number of records at each stage, so that query performance is better. So is the case here too.

Suppose we have STUDENT, CLASS and TEACHER tables. Any student can attend only one class in an academic year and only one teacher takes a class. But a class can have more than 50 students. Now we have to retrieve STUDENT_NAME, ADDRESS, AGE, CLASS_NAME and TEACHER_NAME of each student in a school.

∏STD_NAME, ADDRESS, AGE, CLASS_NAME, TEACHER_NAME ((STUDENT ∞ CLASS_ID CLASS)∞ TECH_IDTEACHER)

Not So Efficient

∏STD_NAME, ADDRESS, AGE, CLASS_NAME, TEACHER_ NAME (STUDENT ∞ CLASS_ID (CLASS∞ TECH_ IDTEACHER))

Efficient

In the first query, it tries to select the records of students from each class. This will result in a very huge intermediary table. This table is then joined with another small table. Hence the traversing of number of records is also more. But in the second query, CLASS and TEACHER are joined first, which has one to one relation here. Hence the number of resulting record is STUDENT table give the final result. Hence this second method is more efficient.

❖ Sometimes we can combine above heuristic steps with cost based optimization technique to get better results.

All these methods need not be always true. It also depends on the table size, column size, type of selection, projection, join sort, constraints, indexes, statistics etc. Above optimization describes the best way of optimizing the queries.

To process the above query, two joins and two restrictions need to be performed. There are a number of different ways these may be performed including the following:

1. Join the relations student and enrolment, join the result with subject and then do the restrictions.
2. Join the relations student and enrolment, do the restrictions, join the result with subject
3. Do the restrictions, join the relations student and enrolment, join the result with subject
4. Join the relations enrolment and subject, join the result with student and then do the restrictions.

Here we are talking about the cost estimates. Before we attempt to compare the costs of the above four alternatives, it is necessary to understand that estimating the cost of a plan is often non – trivial. Since normally a database is disk-resident, often the cost of reading and writing to disk dominates the cost of processing a query. We would therefore estimate the cost of processing a query in terms of disk accesses or block accesses. Estimating the number of block accesses to process even a simple query is not necessarily straight forward since it would depend on how the data is stored and which, if any, indexes are available. In some database systems, relations are stored in packed form, that is, each block only has tuples of the same relation while other systems may store tuples from several relations in each block making it much more expensive to scan all of a relation.

Let us now compare the costs of the above four options. Since exact cost computations are difficult, we will use simple estimates of the cost. We consider a situation where the enrolment database consists of 10, 000 tuples in the relation student, 50, 000 in enrolment, and 1, 000 in the relation subject. For simplicity, let us assume that the relations student and subject have tuples of similar size of around 100 bytes each and therefore and we can accommodate 10 tuples per block if the block is assumed to be 1 Kbytes in size. For the relation enrolment, we assume a tuple size of 40 bytes and thus we use a figure of 25 tuples/block. In addition, let John Smith be enrolled in 10 subjects and let there be 20 subjects offered by Computer Science. We can now estimate the costs of the four plans listed above.

The cost of query plan (1) above may now be computed. Let the join be computed by reading a block of the first relation followed by a scan of the second relation to identify matching tuples (this method is called nested-scan and is not particularly efficient. We will discuss the issue of efficiency of algebraic operators in a later section). This is then followed by the reading of the second block of the first relation followed by a scan of the second relation and so on. The cost of R |X| S may therefore be estimated as the number of blocks in R times the number of blocks in S.

Since the number of blocks in student is 1000 and in enrolment 2, 000, the total number of blocks read in computing the join of student and enrolment is **1000X 2000=2, 000, 000** block accesses. The result of the join is 50, 000 tuples since each tuple from enrolment matches with a tuple from student. The joined tuples will be of size approximately 140 bytes since each tuple in the join is a tuple from student joined with another from enrolment. Given the tuple size of 140 bytes, we can only fit 7 tuples in a block and therefore we need about 7, 000 blocks to store all 50, 000 joined tuples. The cost of computing the join of this result with subject is **7000 X 100= 700, 00** block accesses. Therefore the total cost of plan (1) is approximately 2, 700, 000 block accesses.

To estimate the cost of plan (2), we know the cost of computing the join of student and enrolment has been estimated above as 2, 000, 000 block accesses. The result is 7000 blocks in size. Now the result of applying the restrictions to the result of the join reduces this result to about 5-10 tuples i.e. about 1-2 blocks. The cost of this restriction is about 7000 disk accesses. Also the result of applying the restriction to the relation subject reduces that relation to 20 tuples (2 blocks). The cost of this restriction is about 100 block accesses. The join now only requires about 4 block accesses. The total cost therefore is approximately 2, 004, 604.

To estimate the cost of plan (3), we need to estimate the size of the results of restrictions and their cost. The cost of the restrictions is reading the relations student and subject and writing the results. The reading costs are 1, 100 block accesses. The writing costs are very small since the size of the results is 1 tuple for student and 20 tuples for subject. The cost of computing the join of student and enrolment primarily involves the cost of reading enrolment. This is 2, 000 block accesses. The result is quite small in size and therefore the cost of writing the result back is small. The total cost of plan (3) is therefore 3, 100 block accesses.

Similar estimates may be obtained for processing plan (4). We will not estimate this cost, since the above estimates are sufficient to illustrate that brute force method of query processing is unlikely to be efficient. The cost can be significantly reduced if the query plan is optimized. The issue of optimization is of course much more complex than estimating the costs like we have done above since in the above estimation we did not consider the various alternative access paths that might be available to the system to access each relation.

The above cost estimates assumed that the secondary storage access costs dominate the query processing costs. This is often a reasonable assumption although the cost of communication is often quite important if we are dealing with a distributed system. The cost of storage can be important in large databases since some queries may require large intermediate results. The cost of CPU of course is always important and it is not uncommon for database applications to be CPU bound than I/O bound as is normally assumed.

In the present chapter we assume a centralized system where the cost of secondary storage access is assumed to dominate other costs although we recognize that this is not always true. For example, system R uses cost = page fetches + w cpu utilization When a query is specified to a DBMS, it must choose the best way to process it given the information it has about the database. The optimization part of query processing generally involves the following operations.

1. A suitable internal representation
2. Logical transformation of the query
3. Access path selection of the alternatives
4. Estimate costs and select best

We will discuss the above steps in detail.

8.3.1 Internal Representation

As noted earlier, a query posed in a query language like SQL must first be translated to a internal representation suitable for machine representation. Any internal query representation must be sufficiently powerful to represent all queries in the query language (e.g. SQL). The internal representation could be relational algebra or relational calculus since these languages are powerful enough (they have been shown to be relationally complete by E. F. Codd) although it will be necessary to modify them from what was discussed in an earlier chapter so that features like Group By and aggregations may be represented. A representation like relational algebra is procedural and therefore once the query is represented in that representation, a sequence of operations is clearly indicated. Other representations are possible. These include object graph, operator graph (or parse tree) and tableau. Further information about other representations is available in Jarke and Koch (1984) although some sort of tree representation appears to be most commonly used (why?). Our discussions will assume that a query tree representation is being used. In such a representation, the leaf nodes of the query tree are the base relations and the nodes correspond to relational operations.

8.3.2 Logical Transformations

At the beginning of this chapter we showed that the same query may be formulated in a number of different ways that are semantically equivalent. It is clearly desirable that all such queries be transformed into the same query representation. To do this, we need to translate each query to some canonical form and then simplify.

This involves transformations of the query and selection of an optimal sequence of operations. The transformations that we discuss in this section do not consider the physical representation of the database and are designed to improve the efficiency of query processing whatever access methods might be available. An example of such transformation has already been discussed in the examples given. If a query involves one or more joins and a restriction, it is always going to be more efficient to carry out the restriction first since that will reduce the size of one of the relations (assuming that the restriction applies to only one relation) and therefore the cost of the join, often quite significantly.

Heuristic Optimization — In the heuristic approach, the sequence of operations in a query is reorganized so that the query execution time improves.

Deterministic Optimization — In the deterministic approach, cost of all possible forms of a query are evaluated and the best one is selected.

Common Subexpression — In this technique, common subexpressions in the query, if any, are recognised so as to avoid executing the same sequence of operations more than once.

8.3.3 Heuristic in Query Optimization

Heuristic optimization often includes making transformations to the query tree by moving operators up and down the tree so that the transformed tree is equivalent to the tree before the transformations. Before we discuss these heuristics, it is necessary to discuss the following rules governing the manipulation of relational algebraic expressions:

1.   Joins and Products Are Commutative
Example

$$R \: X \: S = S \: X \: R$$

$$R \: |X| \: S = S \: |X| \: R$$

where |X| may be a join or a natural join. The order of attributes in the two products or joins may not be quite the same but the ordering of attributes is not considered significant in the relational model since the attributes are referred to by their name not by their position in the list of attributes.

2.   Restriction is Commutative
Example

$$\sigma_P(\sigma_q(R)) = \sigma_q(\sigma_P(R))$$

3.   Joins and Products Are Associative
Example

$$(R \: X \: S) \: X \: T = R \: X \: (S \: X \: T)$$

$$(R \: |X| \: S) \: |X| \: T = R \: |X| \: (S \: |X| \: T)$$

The associativity of the above operations guarantees that we will obtain the same results whatever be the ordering of computations of the operations product and join. Union and intersection are also associative.

4. Cascade of Projections
Example

$$\pi_A(\pi_B(R)) = \pi_A(R)$$

Where the attributes A is a subset of the attributes B. The above expression formalises the obvious that there is no need to take the projection with attributes B if there is going to be another projection which is a subset of B that follows it.

5. Cascade of Restrictions
Example

$$\sigma_p(\sigma_q(R)) = \sigma_{p \wedge q}(R)$$

The above expression also formalises the obvious that if there are two restrictions, one after the other, then there is no need to carry out the restrictions one at a time (since each will require processing a relation) and instead both restrictions could be combined.

6. Commuting Restrictions and Projections
Example

$$\sigma_p(\pi_A(R)) = \pi_A \sigma_p(R) \qquad \text{or}$$

$$\sigma_{p \wedge q}(R \times S) = \sigma_p(R) \times \sigma_q(S)$$

There is no difficulty in computing restriction with a projection since we are then doing the restriction before the projection. However if we wish to commute the projection and the restriction, that is possible only if the restriction used no attributes other than those that are in the projection.

7. **Commuting Restrictions with Cartesian Product. in Some Cases, It is Possible to Apply Commutative Law to Restrictions and a Product. for Example**

or

In the above expressions we have assumed that the predicate p has only attributes from R and the predicate q has attributes from S only.

8. **Commuting Restriction with a Union**

9. **Commuting Restriction with a Set Difference**

10. **Commuting Projection with a Cartesian Product or a Join — We Assume That the Projection Includes the Join Predicate Attributes**

11. **Commuting Projection with a Union**

We now use the above rules to transform the query tree to minimize the query cost. Since the cost is assumed to be closely related to the size of the relations on which the operation is being carried out, one of the primary aims of the transformations that we discuss is to reduce the size of intermediate relations.

The basic transformations include the following:

(a) Moving Restrictions Down the Tree as Far as Possible

The idea is to carry out restrictions as early as possible. If the query involves joins as well as restrictions, moving the restrictions down is likely to lead to substantial savings since the relations that are joined after restrictions are likely to be smaller (in some cases much smaller) than before restrictions. This is clearly shown by the example that we used earlier in this chapter to show that some query plans can be much more expensive than others. The query plans that cost the least were those in which the restriction was carried out first. There are of course situations where a restriction does not reduce the relation significantly, for example, a restriction selecting only women from a large relation of customers or clients.

(b) Projections Are Executed as Early as Possible

In real-life databases, a relation may have one hundred or more attributes and therefore the size of each tuple is relatively large. Some relations can even have attributes that are images making each tuple in such relations very large. In such situations, if a projection is executed early and it leads to elimination of many attributes so that the resulting relation has tuples of much smaller size, the amount of data that needs to be read in from the disk for the operations that follow could be reduced substantially leading to cost savings. It should be noted that only attributes that we need to retain from the relations are those that are either needed for the result or those that are to be used in one of the operations that is to be carried out on the relation.

(c) Optimal Ordering of the Joins

We have noted earlier that the join operator is associative and therefore when a query involves more than one join, it is necessary to find an efficient ordering for carrying out the joins. An ordering is likely to be efficient if we carry out those joins first that are likely to lead to small results rather than carrying out those joins that are likely to lead to large results.

(d) Cascading Restrictions and Projections

Sometimes it is convenient to carry out more than one operations together. When restrictions and projections have the same operand, the operations may be carried out together thereby saving the cost of scanning the relations more than once.

(e) Projections of projections are merged into one projection

Clearly, if more than one projection is to be carried out on the same operand relation, the projections should be merged and this could lead to substantial savings since no intermediate results need to be written on the disk and read from the disk.

(f) Combining certain restrictions and Cartesian Product to form a Join

A query may involve a cartesian product followed by a restriction rather than specifying a join. The optimizer should recognise this and execute a join which is usually much cheaper to perform.

(g) Sorting is deferred as much as possible

Sorting is normally a nlogn operation and by deferring sorting, we may need to sort a relation that is much smaller than it would have been if the sorting was carried out earlier.

(h) A set of operations is reorganised using commutativity and distribution if a reorganised form is more efficient.

8.4   BASIC ALGORITHMS FOR EXECUTING QUERY OPERATIONS

The efficiency of query processing in a relational database system depends on the efficiency of the relational operators. Even the simplest operations can often be executed in several different ways and the costs of the different ways could well be quite different. Although the join is a frequently used and the most costly operator and therefore worthy of detailed study, we also discuss other operators to show that careful thought is needed in efficiently carrying out the simpler operators as well.

Selection

Let us consider the following simple query:

SELECT A FROM R WHERE p

The above query may involve any of a number of types of predicates. The following list is presented by Selinger et al: [could have a query with specifying WHERE condition in different ways]

1. attribute = value
2. attribute1 = attribute2
3. attribute > value
4. attribute between value1 and value2
5. attribute IN (list of values)
6. attribute IN subquery
7. predicate expression OR predicate expression
8. predicate expression AND predicate expression

Even in the simple case of equality, two or three different approaches may be possible depending on how the relation has been stored. Traversing a file to find the information of interest is often called a file scan even if the whole file is not being scanned. For example, if the predicate involves an equality condition on a single attribute and there is an index on that attribute, it is most efficient to search that index and find the tuple where the attribute value is equal to the value given. That should be very efficient since it will only require accessing the index and then one block to access the tuple. Of course, it is possible that there is no index on the attribute of interest or the condition in the WHERE clause is not quite as simple as an equality condition on a single attribute. For example, the condition might be an inequality or specify a range. The index may still be useful if one exists but the usefulness would depend on the condition that is posed in the WHERE clause. In some situations it will be necessary to scan the whole relation R to find the tuples that satisfy the given condition. This may not be so expensive if the relation is not so large and the tuples are stored in packed form but could be very expensive if the relation is large and the tuples are stored such that each block has tuples from several different relations. Another possibility is of course that the relation R is stored as a hash file using the attribute of interest and then again one would be able to hash on the value specified and find the record very efficiently.

As noted above, often the condition may be a conjunction or disjunction of several different conditions i.e. it may be like **P$_1$ AND P$_2$** or **P$_1$ OR P$_2$**. Sometime such conjunctive queries can be efficiently processed if there is a composite index based on the attributes that are involved in the two conditions but this is an exception rather than a rule. Often however, it is necessary to assess which one of the two or more conditions can be processed efficiently. Perhaps one of the conditions can be processed using an index. As a first step then, those tuples that satisfy the condition that involves the most efficient search (or perhaps that which retrieves the smallest number of tuples) are retrived and the remaining conditions are then tested on the tuples that are retrieved. Processing disjunctive queries of course requires somewhat different techniques since in this case we are looking at a union of all tuples that satisfy any one of the conditions and therefore each condition will need to be processed separately. It is therefore going to be of little concern which of the conditions is satisfied first since all must be satisfied independently of the other. Of course, if any one of the conditions requires a scan of the whole relation then we can test all the conditions during the scan and retrieve all tuples that satisfy any one or more conditions.

Projection

A projection would of course require a scan of the whole relation but if the projection includes a candidate key of the relation then no duplicate removal is necessary since each tuple in the projection is then guaranteed to be unique. Of course, more often the projection would not include any candidate key and may then have duplicates. Although many database systems do not remove duplicates unless the user specifies so, duplicates may be removed by sorting the projected relation and then identifying the duplicates and eliminating them. It is also possible to use hashing which may be desirable if the relations are particularly large since hashing would hash identical tuples to the same bucket and would therefore only require sorting the relations in each bucket to find the duplicates if any.

Often of course one needs to compute a restriction and a join together. It is then often appropriate to compute the restriction first by using the best access paths available (e.g. an index).

Join

We assume that we wish to carry out an equi-join of two relations R and S that are to be joined on attributes a in R and b in S. Let the cardinality of R and S be m and n respectively. We do not count join output costs since these are identical for all methods. We assume $|R| <= |S|$. We further assume that all restrictions and projections of R and S have already been carried out and neither R nor S is ordered or indexed unless explicitly noted.

Because of the importance of the join operator in relational database systems and the fact that the join operator is considerably more expensive than operators like selection and projection, a number of algorithms have been suggested for processing the join. The more commonly used algorithms are:

1. The Nested Scan Method
2. The Sort-Merge algorithm
3. Hashing algorithm (hashing no good if not equi-join?)
4. Variants of hashing
5. Semi-joins
6. Filters
7. Links
8. Indexes
9. More recently, the concept of join indices has been proposed by Valduriez (1987). Hashing methods are not good when the join is not an equi-join.

8.4.1   Nested Iteration

Before discussing the methods listed above, we briefly discuss the naive nested iteration method that accesses every pair of tuples and concatenates them if the equi-join condition (or for that matter, any other condition) is satisfied. The cost of the naive algorithm is $O(mn)$ assuming that R and S both are not ordered. The cost obviously can be large when m and n are large.

We will assume that the relation R is the outer relation, that is, R is the relation whose tuples are retrieved first. The relation S is then the inner relation since in the nested iteration loop, tuples of S will only be retrieved when a tuple of R has been read. A predicate which related the join attributes is called the join predicate. The algorithm may be written as:

for i = 1 to m
do access ith tuple of R;

for j = 1 to n do

access jth tuple of S;

compare ith tuple of R and the jth tuple of S;

if equi-join condition is satisfied then concatenate and save;

end

end.

This method basically scans the outer relation (R) first and retrieves the first tuple. The entire inner relation S is then scanned and all the tuples of S that satisfy the join predicate with the first tuple of R are combined with that tuple of R and output as result. The process then continues with the next tuple of R until R is exhausted.

This has cost $(m + mn)$ which is order(mn). If the memory buffers can store two blocks, one from R and one from S, the cost will go down by a factor rs where r and s are the number of tuples per block in R and S respectively. The technique is sometimes called the nested block method. Some cost saving is achieved by reading the smaller relation in the outer block since this reduces $(m + mn)$. The cost of the method would of course be much higher if the relations are not stored in a packed form since then we might need to retrieve many more tuples. Efficiency of the nested iteration (or nested block iteration) would improve significantly if an index was available on one of the join attributes. If the average number of blocks of relation S accessed for each tuple of R was c then the cost of the join would be (m + mc) where **c< n**.

8.4.2 Using Indexes

The nested iteration method can be made more efficient if indexes are available on both join columns in the relations R and S.

Assume that we have available indexes on both join columns a and b in the relations R and S respectively. We may now scan both the indexes to determine whether a pair of tuples has the same value of the join attribute. If the value is the same, the tuple from R is selected and then all the tuples from S are selected that have the same join attribute value. This is done by scanning the index on the join attribute in S. The index on the join attribute in R is now scanned to check if there are more than the one tuple with the same value of the attribute. All the tuples of R that have the same join attribute value are then selected and combined with the tuples of S that have already been selected. The process then continues with the next value for which tuples are available in R and S.

Clearly this method requires substantial storage so that we may store all the attributes from R and S that have the same join attribute value. The cost of the join when the indexes are used may be estimated as follows. Let the cost of reading the indexes be aN_1 and BN_2, then the total cost is

$$aN_1 + BN_2 + N_1 + N_2$$

Cost savings by using indexes can be large enough to justify building an index when a join needs to be computed.

8.4.3 The Sort Merge Method

The nested scan technique is simple but involves matching each block of R with every block of S. This can be avoided if both relations were ordered on the join attribute. The sort-merge algorithm was introduced by Blasgen and Eswaran in 1977. It is a classical technique that has been the choice for joining relations that have no index on either of the two attributes.

This method involves sorting the relations R and S on the join attributes (if not already sorted), storing them as temporary lists and then scanning them block by block and merging those tuples that satisfy the join condition. The advantage of this scheme is that all of the inner relation (in the nested iteration) does not need to be read in for each tuple of the outer relation. This saving can be substantial if the outer relation is large.

Let the cost of sorting R and S be C_r and Cs and let the cost of reading the two relations in main memory be N_r and N_s respectively. The total cost of the join is then

$$C_r + Cs + N_r + N_s$$

If one or both the relations are already sorted on the join attribute then the cost of the join reduces.

The algorithm can be improved if we use Multiway Merge-Sort The cost of sorting is $n \log_n$.

8.4.4 Simple Hash Join Method

This method involves building a hash table of the smaller relation R by hashing each tuple on its hash attribute. Since we have assumed that the relation R is too large to fit in the main memory, the hash table would in general not fit into the main memory. The hash table therefore must be built in stages. A number of addresses of the hash table are first selected such that the tuples hashed to those addresses can be stored in the main memory. The tuples of R that do not hash to these addresses are written back to the disk. Let these tuples be relation **R'**. Now the algorithm works as follows:

(a) Scan Relation R and Hash Each Tuple on Its Join Attribute

If the hashed value is equal to one of the addresses that are in the main memory, store the tuple in the hash table. Otherwise write the tuple back to disk in a new relation **R'**.

(b) Scan the Relation S And Hash Each Tuple of S on Its Join Attribute. One of the Following Three Conditions Must Hold

1. The hashed value is equal to one of the selected values, and one or more tuple of R with same attribute value exists. We combine the tuples of R that match with the tuple of S and output as the next tuples in the join.

2. The hashed value is equal to one of the selected values, but there is no tuple in R with same join attribute value. These tuple of S are rejected.

3. The hashed value is not equal to one of the selected values. These tuples are written back to disk as a new relation S'.

The above step continues till S is finished.

(c) Repeat steps (a) and (b) until either relation **R'** or **S'** or both are exhausted.

8.4.5   Grace Hash-Join Method

This method is a modification of the Simple Hash Join method in that the partitioning of R is completed before S is scanned and partitioning of S is completed before the joining phase. The method consists of the following three phases:

1. **Partition R** – Since R is assumed to be too large to fit in the main memory, a hash table for it cannot be built in the main memory. The first phase of the algorithm involves partitioning the relation into n buckets, each

bucket corresponding to a hash table entry. The number of buckets n is chosen to be large enough so that each bucket will comfortably fit in the main memory.

2. **Partition S** – The second phase of the algorithm involves partitioning the relation S into the same number (n) of buckets, each bucket corresponding to a hash table entry. The same hashing function as for R is used.

3. **Compute the Join** – A bucket of R is read in and the corresponding bucket of S is read in. Matching tuples from the two buckets are combined and output as part of the join.

8.4.6 Hybrid Hash Join Method

The hybrid hash join algorithm is a modification of the Grace hash join method.

Aggregation

Aggregation is often found in queries given the frequency of requirements of finding an average, the maximum or how many times something happens. The functions supported in SQL are average, minimum, maximum, count, and sum. Aggregation can itself be of different types including aggregation that only requires one relation, for example finding the maximum mark in a subject, or it may involve a relation but require something like finding the number of students in each class. The latter aggregation would obviously require some grouping of the tuples in the relation before aggregation can be applied.

8.5   INTRODUCTION TO DATABASE TUNING

Database Tuning

In this section, we begin by discussing the physical design factors that affect the performance of applications and transactions, and then we comment on the specific guidelines for RDBMSs.

Factors That Influence Physical Database Design

Physical design is an activity where the goal is not only to create the appropriate structuring of data in storage, but also to do so in a way that guarantees good performance. For a given conceptual schema, there are many physical design alternatives in a given DBMS. It is not possible to make meaningful physical design decisions and performance analyses until the database designer knows the mix of queries, transactions, and applications that are expected to run on the database. This is called the **job mix** for the particular set of database system applications. The database administrators/ designers must analyze these applications, their expected frequencies of invocation, any timing constraints on their execution speed, the expected frequency of update operations, and any unique constraints on attributes. We discuss each of these factors next.

A. Analyzing the Database Queries and Transactions

Before undertaking the physical database design, we must have a good idea of the intended use of the database by defining in a high-level form the queries and transactions that are expected to run on the database. For each **retrieval query**, the following information about the query would be needed:

- ✧ The files that will be accessed by the query.
- ✧ The attributes on which any selection conditions for the query are specified.
- ✧ Whether the selection condition is an equality, inequality, or a range condi-tion.
- ✧ The attributes on which any join conditions or conditions to link multiple tables or objects for the query are specified.
- ✧ The attributes whose values will be retrieved by the query.

The attributes listed in items 2 and 4 above are candidates for the definition of access structures, such as indexes, hash keys, or sorting of the file.

For each **update operation** or **update transaction**, the following information would be needed:

✧ The files that will be updated.

✧ The type of operation on each file (insert, update, or delete).

✧ The attributes on which selection conditions for a delete or update are spec-ified.

✧ The attributes whose values will be changed by an update operation.

Again, the attributes listed in item 3 are candidates for access structures on the files, because they would be used to locate the records that will be updated or deleted. On the other hand, the attributes listed in item 4 are candidates for avoiding an access structure, since modifying them will require updating the access structures.

B. Analyzing the Expected Frequency of Invocation of Queries and Transactions.

Besides identifying the characteristics of expected retrieval queries and update transactions, we must consider their expected rates of invocation. This frequency information, along with the attribute information collected on each query and transaction, is used to compile a cumulative list of the expected fre-quency of use for all queries and transactions. This is expressed as the expected fre-quency of using each attribute in each file as a selection attribute or a join attribute, over all the queries and transactions. Generally, for large volumes of processing, the informal 80–20 rule can be used: approximately 80 percent of the processing is accounted for by only 20 percent of the queries and transactions. Therefore, in prac-tical situations, it is rarely necessary to collect exhaustive statistics and invocation rates on all the queries and transactions; it is sufficient to determine the 20 percent or so most important ones

❖ **Analyzing the Time Constraints of Queries and Transactions**

Some queries and transactions may have stringent performance constraints. For example, a transaction may have the constraint that it should terminate within 5 seconds on 95 percent of the occasions when it is invoked, and that it should never take more than 20 seconds. Such timing constraints place further priorities on the attributes that are candidates for access paths. The selection attributes used by queries and transactions with time constraints become higher-priority candidates for primary access structures for the files, because the primary access structures are generally the most efficient for locating records in a file.

❖ **Analyzing the Expected Frequencies of Update Operations**

A minimum number of access paths should be specified for a file that is frequently updated, because updating the access paths themselves slows down the update operations. For example, if a file that has frequent record insertions has 10 indexes on 10 different attributes, each of these indexes must be updated whenever a new record is inserted. The overhead for updating 10 indexes can slow down the insert operations.

❖ **Analyzing the Uniqueness Constraints on Attributes**

Access paths should be specified on all candidate key attributes—or sets of attributes—that are either the primary key of a file or unique attributes. The existence of an index (or other access path) makes it sufficient to only search the index when checking this uniqueness constraint, since all values of the attribute will exist in the leaf nodes of the index. For example, when inserting a new record, if a key attribute value of the new record already exists in the index, the insertion of the new record should be rejected, since it would violate the uniqueness constraint on the attribute.

Once the preceding information is compiled, it is possible to address the physical database design decisions, which consist mainly of deciding on the storage structures and access paths for the database files.

8.6   PHYSICAL DATABASE DESIGN DECISIONS

Most relational systems represent each base relation as a physical database file. The access path options include specifying the type of primary file organization for each relation and the attributes of which indexes that should be defined. At most, one of the indexes on each file may be a primary or a clustering index. Any number of additional secondary indexes can be created.

Design Decisions About Indexing

The attributes whose values are required in equality or range conditions (selection operation) are those that are keys or that participate in join conditions (join operation) requiring access paths, such as indexes. The performance of queries largely depends upon what indexes or hashing schemes exist to expedite the processing of selections and joins. On the other hand, during insert, delete, or update operations, the existence of indexes adds to the overhead. This overhead must be justified in terms of the gain in efficiency by expediting queries and transactions.

The physical design decisions for indexing fall into the following categories:

Whether to Index An Attribute

The general rules for creating an index on an attribute are that the attribute must either be a key (unique), or there must be some query that uses that attribute either in a selection condition (equal-ity or range of values) or in a join condition. One reason for creating multi-ple indexes is that some operations can be processed by just scanning the indexes, without having to access the actual data file.

What Attribute or Attributes to Index On

An index can be constructed on a single attribute, or on more than one attribute if it is a composite index. If multiple attributes from one relation are involved together in several queries, (for example, (Garment_style_#, Color) in a garment inventory database), a multiattribute (composite) index is warranted. The ordering of attributes within a multiattribute index must correspond to the queries. For instance, the above index assumes that queries would be based on an ordering of col-ors within a Garment_style_# rather than vice versa.

Whether to Set Up a Clustered Index

At most, one index per table can be a primary or clustering index, because this implies that the file be physically ordered on that attribute. In most RDBMSs, this is specified by the keyword CLUSTER. If a table requires several indexes, the decision about which one should be the primary or clustering index depends upon whether keeping the table ordered on that attribute is needed. Range queries benefit a great deal from clustering. If several attributes require range queries, relative benefits must be evaluated before deciding which attribute to cluster on. If a query is to be answered by doing an index search only (without retrieving data records), the corresponding index should not be clustered, since the main benefit of clustering is achieved when retrieving the records themselves. A clustering index may be set up as a multiattribute index if range retrieval by that composite key is useful in report creation (for example, an index on Zip_code, Store_id, and Product_id may be a clustering index for sales data).

Whether to Use a Hash Index Over a Tree Index

In general, RDBMSs use B⁺-trees for indexing. However, ISAM and hash indexes are also provided in some systems (see Chapter 18). B⁺-trees support both equality and range queries on the attribute used as the search key. Hash indexes work well with equality conditions, particularly during joins to find a matching record(s), but they do not support range queries.

Whether to Use Dynamic Hashing for the File

For files that are very volatile—that is, those that grow and shrink continuously—one of the dynamic hashing schemes discussed in Section 17.9 would be suitable. Currently, they are not offered by many commercial RDBMSs.

How to Create An Index

Many RDBMSs have a similar type of command for creating an index, although it is not part of the SQL standard. The general form of this command is:

CREATE [UNIQUE] INDEX <index name> ON <table name> (<column name> [<order>] {, <column name> [<order>]}) [CLUSTER];

The keywords UNIQUE and CLUSTER are optional. The keyword CLUSTER is used when the index to be created should also sort the data file records on the indexing attribute. Thus, specifying CLUSTER on a key (unique) attribute would create some variation of a primary index, whereas specifying CLUSTER on a nonkey (nonunique) attribute would create some variation of a clustering index. The value for <order> can be either ASC (ascending) or DESC (descending), and specifies whether the data file should be ordered in ascending or descending values of the indexing attribute. The default is ASC. For example, the following would create a clustering (ascending) index on the nonkey attribute Dno of the EMPLOYEE file:

CREATE INDEX DnoIndex ON EMPLOYEE (Dno) CLUSTER;

Denormalization as a Design Decision for Speeding Up Queries. The ulti-mate goal during normalization is to separate attributes into tables to minimize redundancy, and thereby avoid the update anomalies that lead to an extra processing overhead to maintain consistency in the database. The ideals that are typically followed are the third or Boyce-Codd normal forms

The above ideals are sometimes sacrificed in favor of faster execution of frequently occurring queries and transactions. This process of storing the logical database design (which may be in BCNF or 4NF) in a weaker normal form, say 2NF or 1NF, is called **denormalization**. Typically, the designer includes certain attributes from a table S into another table R. The reason is that the attributes from S that are included in R are frequently needed—along with other attributes in R—for answer-ing queries or producing reports. By including these attributes, a join of R with S is avoided for these frequently occurring queries and reports.

This reintroduces redundancy in the base tables by including the same attributes in both tables R and S. A partial functional dependency or a transitive dependency now exists in the table R, thereby creating the associated redundancy problems A tradeoff exists between the additional updating needed for maintaining consistency of redundant attributes versus the effort needed to perform a join to incorporate the additional attributes needed in the result. For example, consider the following relation:

ASSIGN (Emp_id, Proj_id, Emp_name, Emp_job_title, Percent_assigned, Proj_name, Proj_mgr_id, Proj_mgr_name), which corresponds exactly to the headers in a report called The Employee Assignment Roster. This relation is only in 1NF because of the following functional dependencies:

Proj_id → Proj_name, Proj_mgr_id

Proj_mgr_id → Proj_mgr_name

Emp_id → Emp_name, Emp_job_title

This relation may be preferred over the design in 2NF (and 3NF) consisting of the following three relations:

EMP (Emp_id, Emp_name, Emp_job_title)

PROJ (Proj_id, Proj_name, Proj_mgr_id)

EMP_PROJ (Emp_id, Proj_id, Percent_assigned)

This is because to produce the The Employee Assignment Roster report (with all fields shown in ASSIGN above), the latter multirelation design requires two NATURAL JOIN (indicated with *) operations (between EMP and EMP_PROJ, and between PROJ and EMP_PROJ), plus a final JOIN between PROJ and EMP to retrieve the Proj_mgr_name from the Proj_mgr_id. Thus the following JOINs would be needed (the final join would also require renaming (aliasing) of the last EMP table, which is not shown):

$$((EMP\_PROJ * EMP) * PROJ) \bowtie_{PROJ.Proj\_mgr\_id\,=\,EMP.Emp\_id} EMP$$

It is also possible to create a view for the ASSIGN table. This does not mean that the join operations will be avoided, but that the user need not specify the joins. If the view table is materialized, the joins would be avoided, but if the virtual view table is not stored as a materialized file, the join computations would still be necessary. Other forms of denormalization consist of storing extra tables to maintain original functional dependencies that are lost during BCNF decomposition. For example, the TEACH(Student, Course, Instructor) relation with the func-tional dependencies {{Student, Course} → Instructor, Instructor → Course}. A lossless decomposition of TEACH into T1(Student, Instructor) and T2(Instructor, Course) does not allow queries of the form *what course did student Smith take from instructor Navathe* to be answered without joining T1 and T2. Therefore, storing T1, T2, and TEACH may be a possible solution, which reduces the design from BCNF to 3NF. Here, TEACH is a materialized join of the other two tables, representing an extreme redundancy. Any updates to T1 and T2 would have to be applied to TEACH. An alter-nate strategy is to create T1 and T2 as updatable base tables, and to create TEACH as a view (virtual table) on T1 and T2 that can only be queried.

8.7   AN OVERVIEW OF DATABASE TUNING IN RELATIONAL SYSTEMS

After a database is deployed and is in operation, actual use of the applications, transactions, queries, and views reveals factors and problem areas that may not have been accounted for during the initial physical design. The inputs to physical design listed in Section 20.1.1 can be revised by gathering actual statistics about usage patterns. Resource utilization as well as internal DBMS processing—such as query optimiza-tion—can be monitored to reveal bottlenecks, such as contention for the same data or devices. Volumes of activity and sizes of data can be better estimated. Therefore, it is necessary to monitor and revise the physical database design constantly—an activ-ity referred to as **database tuning**. The goals of tuning are as follows:

- ✧ To make applications run faster.
- ✧ To improve (lower) the response time of queries and transactions.
- ✧ To improve the overall throughput of transactions.

The dividing line between physical design and tuning is very thin. The same design decisions are revisited during database tuning, which is a continual adjustment of the physical design. We give a brief overview of the tuning process below. The inputs to the tuning process include statistics related to the same factors. In particular, DBMSs can internally collect the following statistics:

✧ Sizes of individual tables.

✧ Number of distinct values in a column.

✧ The number of times a particular query or transaction is submitted and executed in an interval of time.

✧ The times required for different phases of query and transaction processing (for a given set of queries or transactions).

✧ These and other statistics create a profile of the contents and use of the database. Other information obtained from monitoring the database system activities and processes includes the following:

Storage Statistics

Data deals about allocation of storage into tablespaces, index-spaces, and buffer pools.

I/O and device performance statistics

Total read/write activity (paging) on disk extents and disk hot spots.

Query/transaction Processing Statistics

Execution times of queries and transactions, and optimization times during query optimization.

Locking/logging Related Statistics

Rates of issuing different types of locks, transaction throughput rates, and log records activity.

Index Statistics

Number of levels in an index, number of noncontiguous leaf pages, and so on.

Some of the above statistics relate to transactions, concurrency control, and recovery,. Tuning a database involves deal-ing with the following types of problems:

✧ How to avoid excessive lock contention, thereby increasing concurrency among transactions?

✧ How to minimize the overhead of logging and unnecessary dumping of data?

✧ How to optimize the buffer size and scheduling of processes?

✧ How to allocate resources such as disks, RAM, and processes for most efficient utilization?

Most of the previously mentioned problems can be solved by the DBA by setting appropriate physical DBMS parameters, changing configurations of devices, changing operating system parameters, and other similar activities. The solutions tend to be closely tied to specific systems. The DBAs are typically trained to handle these tuning problems for the specific DBMS. We briefly discuss the tuning of various physical database design decisions below.

1. Tuning Indexes

The initial choice of indexes may have to be revised for the following reasons:

✧ Certain queries may take too long to run for lack of an index.
✧ Certain indexes may not get utilized at all.
✧ Certain indexes may undergo too much updating because the index is on an attribute that undergoes frequent changes.

Most DBMSs have a command or trace facility, which can be used by the DBA to ask the system to show how a query was executed—what operations were performed in what order and what secondary access structures (indexes) were used. By analyzing these execution plans, it is possible to diagnose the causes of the above problems. Some indexes may be dropped and some new indexes may be created based on the tuning analysis.

The goal of tuning is to dynamically evaluate the requirements, which sometimes fluctuate seasonally or during different times of the month or week, and to reorganize the indexes and file organizations to yield the best overall performance. Dropping and building new indexes is an overhead that can be justified in terms of performance improvements. Updating of a table is generally suspended while an index is dropped or created; this loss of service must be accounted for. Besides drop-ping or creating indexes and changing from a nonclustered to a clustered index and vice versa, **rebuilding the index** may improve performance. Most RDBMSs use B⁺-trees for an index. If there are many deletions on the index key, index pages may contain wasted space, which can be claimed during a rebuild operation. Similarly, too many insertions may cause overflows in a clustered index that affect performance. Rebuilding a clustered index amounts to reorganizing the entire table ordered on that key.

The available options for indexing and the way they are defined, created, and reorganized varies from system to system. As an illustration, consider the sparse and dense indexes in Chapter 18. A sparse index such as a primary index (see Section 18.1) will have one index pointer for each page (disk block) in the data file; a dense index such as a unique secondary index will have an index pointer for each record. Sybase provides clustering indexes as sparse indexes in the form of B⁺-trees, whereas INGRES provides sparse clustering indexes as ISAM files and dense clustering indexes as B⁺-trees. In some versions of Oracle and DB2, the option of setting up a clustering index is limited to a dense index (with many more index entries), and the DBA has to work with this limitation.

2. Tuning the Database Design

If a given physical database design does not meet the expected objectives, the DBA may revert to the logical database design, make adjustments such as denormalizations to the logical schema, and remap it to a new set of physical tables and indexes. As discussed, the entire database design has to be driven by the processing requirements as much as by data requirements. If the processing requirements are dynamically changing, the design needs to respond by making changes to the conceptual schema if necessary and to reflect those changes into the logical schema and physical design.

These changes may be of the following nature:

Existing tables may be joined (denormalized) because certain attributes from two or more tables are frequently needed together: This reduces the normalization level from BCNF to 3NF, 2NF, or 1NF.

> ✧ For the given set of tables, there may be alternative design choices, all of which achieve 3NF or BCNF. We illustrated alternative equivalent designs in Chapter 16. One normalized design may be replaced by another.

A relation of the form R(K, A, B, C, D,...)—with K as a set of key attributes— that is in BCNF can be stored in multiple tables that are also in BCNF—for example, R1(K, A, B), R2(K, C, D,), R3(K,...)—by replicating the key K in each table. Such a process is known as **vertical partitioning**. Each table group sets of attributes that areaccessed together.

For Example, the ta ble EMPLOYEE(Ssn, Name, Phone, Grade, Salary) may be split into two tables:

EMP1(Ssn, Name, Phone) and EMP2(Ssn, Grade, Salary). If the original table has a large number of rows (say 100, 000) and queries about phone numbers and salary information are totally distinct and occur with very different fre-quencies, then this separation of tables may work better.

Attribute(s) from one table may be repeated in another even though this cre-ates redundancy and a potential anomaly. For example, Part_name may be replicated in tables wherever the Part# appears (as foreign key), but there may be one master table called PART_MASTER(Part#, Part_name,...) where the Partname is guaranteed to be up-to-date. Just as vertical partitioning splits a table vertically into multiple tables, **horizontal partitioning** takes horizontal slices of a table and stores them as distinct tables. For example, product sales data may be separated into ten tables based on ten product lines. Each table has the same set of columns (attributes) but contains a distinct set of products (tuples). If a query or transaction applies to all product data, it may have to run against all the tables and the results may have to be combined.

These types of adjustments designed to meet the high volume of queries or transac-tions, with or without sacrificing the normal forms, are commonplace in practice.

3. Tuning Queries

We already discussed how query performance is dependent upon the appropriate selection of indexes, and how indexes may have to be tuned after analyzing queries that give poor performance by using the commands in the RDBMS that show the execution plan of the query. There are mainly two indications that suggest that query tuning may be needed:

❖ A query issues too many disk accesses (for example, an exact match query scans an entire table).

❖ The query plan shows that relevant indexes are not being used.

Some typical instances of situations prompting query tuning include the following:

Many query optimizers do not use indexes in the presence of arithmetic expressions (such as Salary/365 > 10.50), numerical comparisons of attrib-utes of different sizes and precision (such as Aqty = Bqty where Aqty is of type INTEGER and Bqty is of type SMALLINTEGER), NULL comparisons (such as Bdate IS NULL), and substring comparisons (such as Lname LIKE '%mann').

Indexes are often not used for nested queries using IN; for example, the following query:

SELECT Ssn FROM EMPLOYEE WHERE Dno IN (SELECT Dnumber FROM DEPARTMENT WHERE Mgr_ssn = '333445555');

May not use the index on Dno in EMPLOYEE, whereas using Dno = Dnumber in the WHERE-clause with a single block query may cause the index to be used. Some DISTINCTs may be redundant and can be avoided without changing the result. A DISTINCT often causes a sort operation and must be avoided as much as possible. Unnecessary use of temporary result tables can be avoided by collapsing multiple queries into a single query unless the temporary relation is needed for some intermediate processing. In some situations involving the use of correlated queries, temporaries are useful. Consider the following query, which retrieves the highest paid employee in each department:

SELECT Ssn FROM EMPLOYEE E WHERE Salary = SELECT MAX (Salary) FROM EMPLOYEE AS M WHERE M.Dno = E.Dno;

This has the potential danger of searching all of the inner EMPLOYEE table M for each tuple from the outer EMPLOYEE table E. To make the execution more efficient, the process can be broken into two queries, where the first query just computes the maximum salary in each department as follows:

SELECT MAX (Salary) AS High_salary, Dno INTO TEMP FROM EMPLOYEE GROUP BY Dno;

SELECT EMPLOYEE.Ssn FROM EMPLOYEE, TEMPWHERE EMPLOYEE.Salary = TEMP.High_salary AND EMPLOYEE.Dno = TEMP.Dno;

If multiple options for a join condition are possible, choose one that uses a clustering index and avoid those that contain string comparisons. For exam-ple, assuming that the Name attribute is a candidate key in EMPLOYEE and STUDENT, it is better to EMPLOYEE.Ssn = STUDENT.Ssn as a join condi-tion rather than EMPLOYEE.Name = STUDENT.Name if Ssn has a clustering index in one or both tables. Some query optimizers perform worse on nested queries compared to their equivalent unnested counterparts. There are four types of nested queries:

- ✧ Uncorrelated subqueries with aggregates in an inner query.
- ✧ Uncorrelated subqueries without aggregates.
- ✧ Correlated subqueries with aggregates in an inner query.
- ✧ Correlated subqueries without aggregates.

Of the four types above, the first one typically presents no problem, since most query optimizers evaluate the inner query once. However, for a query of the second type, such as the example in item 2, most query optimizers may not use an index on Dno in EMPLOYEE. However, the same optimizers may do so if the query is written as an unnested query. Transformation of correlated subqueries may involve setting temporary tables. Detailed exam-ples are outside our scope here.

Finally, many applications are based on views that define the data of interest to those applications. Sometimes, these views become overkill, because a query may be posed directly against a base table, rather than going through a view that is defined by a JOIN.

4. Additional Query Tuning Guidelines

Additional techniques for improving queries apply in certain situations as follows:

A query with multiple selection conditions that are connected via OR may not be prompting the query optimizer to use any index. Such a query may be split up and expressed as a union of queries, each with a condition on an attribute that causes an index to be used. For example,

SELECT Fname, Lname, Salary, Age FROM EMPLOYEE WHERE Age > 45 OR Salary < 50000;

May be executed using sequential scan giving poor performance. Splitting it up as

SELECT Fname, Lname, Salary, Age FROM EMPLOYEE WHERE Age > 45 UNION SELECT Fname, Lname, Salary, Age FROM EMPLOYEE WHERE Salary < 50000;

May utilize indexes on Age as well as on Salary. To help expedite a query, the following transformations may be tried:

- ✧ NOT condition may be transformed into a positive expression.
- ✧ Embedded SELECT blocks using IN, = ALL, = ANY, and = SOME may be replaced by joins.

If an equality join is set up between two tables, the range predicate (selec-tion condition) on the joining attribute set up in one table may be repeated for the other table.

3. WHERE conditions may be rewritten to utilize the indexes on multiple columns. For example,

SELECT Region#, Prod_type, Month, Sales FROM SALES_ STATISTICS WHERE Region# = 3 AND ((Prod_type BETWEEN 1 AND 3) OR (Prod_type BETWEEN 8 AND 10));

May use an index only on Region# and search through all leaf pages of the index for a match on Prod_type. Instead, using

SELECT Region#, Prod_type, Month, Sales FROM SALES_ STATISTICS WHERE (Region# = 3 AND (Prod_type BETWEEN 1 AND 3)) OR (Region# = 3 AND (Prod_type BETWEEN 8 AND 10));

May use a composite index on (Region#, Prod_type) and work much more efficiently.

In this section, we have covered many of the common instances where the inefficiency of a query may be fixed by some simple corrective action such as using a temporary table, avoiding certain types of query constructs, or avoiding the use of views. The goal is to have the RDBMS use existing single attribute or composite attribute indexes as much as possible. This avoids full scans of data blocks or entire scanning of index leaf nodes. Redundant processes like sorting must be avoided at any cost. The problems and the remedies will depend upon the workings of a query optimizer within an RDBMS. Detailed literature exists in database tuning guidelines for database administration by the RDBMS vendors. Major relational DBMS vendors like Oracle, IBM and Microsoft encourage their large customers to share ideas of tuning at the annual expos and other forums so that the entire industry benefits by using performance enhancement techniques. These techniques are typically available in trade literature and on various Web sites.

Recovery System

A computer system is an electrochemical device subject to failures of various types. The reliability of the database system is linked to the reliability of the computer system on which it runs. In this unit we will discuss recovery of the data contained in a database system following failure of various types and present the different approaches to database recovery. The types of failures that the computer system is likely to be subjected to include failures of components or subsystems, software failures, power outages, accidents, unforeseen situations and natural or man-made disasters. Database recovery techniques are methods of making the database fault tolerant. The aim of recovery scheme is to allow database operations to be resumed after a failure with minimum loss of information at an economically justifiable cost.

"Database security" is protection of the information contained in the database against unauthorized access, modification or destruction.

"Database integrity" is the mechanism that is applied to ensure that the data in the database is correct and consistent.

Database security and integrity have been discussed in this unit.

9.1   OBJECTIVES

At the end of this unit, you should be able to:

- ✧ describe the term RECOVERY and INTEGRITY
- ✧ describe Recovery Techniques

✧ define Error and Error detection techniques
✧ describe types of Authorization

9.2   WHAT IS RECOVERY?

In practice several things might happen to prevent a transaction from completing. Recovery techniques are used to bring database, which does not satisfy consistency requirements, into a consistent state. The inconsistencies may arise due to dissatisfaction of the semantic integrity constraints specified in the schema or may be due to violation of certain implicit constraints that are expected to hold for a database. In other words, if a transaction completes normally then all the changes that it performs on the database are permanently committed. But, if transaction does not complete normally then none of its changes are committed. An abnormal termination may be due to several reasons including:

  a.   user may decide to abort his transaction
  b.   there might be a deadlock
  c.   there might be a system failure.

So the recovery mechanisms must make sure that a consistent state of database can be restored under all circumstances. In case of transaction abort or deadlock the system remains in control but incase of failure the system loses control because computer itself fails or some critical data are lost.

9.2.1   Kinds of Failures

When a transaction/program is made to be executed, a number of difficulties can arise, which leads to its abnormal termination. The failures are mainly of two types:

  1.   **Soft failures:** In such cases, a CPU or memory or software error abruptly stops the execution of the current transaction

(or all transactions), thus lead to losing the state of program execution and the state/contents of the buffers. These can further be subdivided into two types:

a.   Statement failure
b.   Program failure

A Statement of program may cause to abnormal termination if it does not execute completely. If during the execution of a statement, an integrity constraints get violated it leads to abnormal termination of program due to which any updates made already may not got reflected in the database leaving it in an inconsistent state.

A failure of program can occur if some code in a program leads to its abnormal termination. E.g., a program which goes into an infinite loop. In such case the only way to break the loop is to abort the program. Thus part of program, which is executed before abortion from program may cause some updates in database, and hence the database is, updated only partially which leads to an inconsistent state of database. Also in case of deadlock i.e. if one program enters into a deadlock with some other program, then this program has to be restarted to get out of deadlock and thus the partial updates made by this program in the database makes the database in an inconsistent state.

Thus soft failures can be occurred due to either of statement failure or failure of program.

2.   **Hard failure:** Hard failures are those failures when some data on disk get damaged and cannot be read anymore. This may be due to many reasons e.g. a voltage fluctuation in the power supply to the computer makes it go off or some bad sectors may come on disk or there

is a disk crash. In all these cases, the database gets into an inconsistent state.

In practice soft failures are more common than hard failures. Fortunately, recovery from soft failures is much quicker.

9.2.2　Failure Controlling Methods

Although failures can be controlled and removed/handled using different recovery techniques to be discussed later, but they are quite expensive both in case of time and in memory space. In such a case it is more beneficial to better avoid the failure by some checks instead of deploying recovery technique to make database consistent. Also recovery from failure involves manpower, which can be used in some other productive work, if failure can be avoided. It is therefore, important to find out ways and means by which failures could be controlled.

Different methods/techniques can be adopted to control different types of failures. For e.g. consider a hard failure i.e. system crashing. The cause of system shutdown could be a failure in power supply unit or loss of power, due to which information stored on the storage medium can be lost. One method to avoid loss of data stored on disk due to power failure is to provide an uninterruptable power source by using voltage stabilizers or batteries or transformers. Also since recovery from soft failures is quicker, so it is hard failure, which, as far as possible, should be controlled by taking some preventive measures. In case of failure of system software, it can be controlled by ensuring that all the functions as well as statements used in the program have been placed in right positions and debugging is done prior to its execution so that appropriate solution can be applied thus avoiding inconsistency in database. Soft failure can also be controlled by checking the integrity constraints used in program prior to its execution or by checking the preconditions to be satisfied by a statement so that program won't go into an infinite loop thus causing abnormal termination and hence leaving database in a corrupt state. If all such precautions are taken in advance then no extra effort has to be done in recovering erroneous data on the database.

9.3 FAILURE CLASSIFICATION

To find that where the problem has occurred, we generalize a failure into the following categories:

1. Transaction failure
2. System crash
3. Disk failure

1. Transaction Failure

The transaction failure occurs when it fails to execute or when it reaches a point from where it can't go any further. If a few transaction or process is hurt, then this is called as transaction failure.

Reasons for a transaction failure could be –

- **Logical errors:** If a transaction cannot complete due to some code error or an internal error condition, then the logical error occurs.
- **Syntax error:** It occurs where the DBMS itself terminates an active transaction because the database system is not able to execute it. **For example,** The system aborts an active transaction, in case of deadlock or resource unavailability.

2. System Crash

⅄   System failure can occur due to power failure or other hardware or software failure. **Example:** Operating system error.

Fail-stop assumption: In the system crash, non-volatile storage is assumed not to be corrupted.

3. Disk Failure

▲   It occurs where hard-disk drives or storage drives used to fail frequently. It was a common problem in the early days of technology evolution.

▲   Disk failure occurs due to the formation of bad sectors, disk head crash, and unreachability to the disk or any other failure, which destroy all or part of disk storage.

9.4   STORAGE STRUCTURE

Storage media canbe distinguished by their relative speed, capacity, and resilience to failure, and classified as volatile storage or nonvolatile storage. We review these terms, and introduce another class of storage, called stable storage

Volatile Storage

Information residing in volatile storage does not usually survive system crashes. Examples of such storage are main memory and cache memory. Access to volatile storage is extremely fast, both because of the speed of the memory accessit self, and becausei t is possible to accessa ny data item in volatile storage directlY.

Nonvolatile Storage

Information residing in nonvolatile storage survives system crashes. Examples of such storage are disk and magnetic tapes, Disks are used for on line storage, whereas tapes are used for archival storage. Both, howevel, are subject to failure (for example, head crash), which may result in loss of information. At the current state of technology, nonvolatile storage is slower than volatile storage by several orders of magnitude. This isbecaused isk and tape devices are electromechanical, r ather than based entirely on chips, as is volatile storage. In database systems, disks are used for most nonvolatile storage. Other nonvolatile media are normally used only for backup data. Flash storage though nonvolatile, has insufficient capacity for most database systems.

Stablestorage

Information residing in stablestorage is never lost(never should be taken with a grain of salt, since theoretically neaerc arrrrobt e guaranteed for example, it is possible, although extremelyunlikely, that a biick hole may envelop the earth and permanently destroy all datal). Although stable storage is theoretically impossible to obtain, it can be closely approximated by techniques that make data loss extremely unlikely.

The distinctions among the various storage types are often less clear in practice than in our presentation. Certain systems provide battery backup, so that some main memory can survive system crashes and power failures. Alternative forms of nonvolatile storage, such as optical media, provide an even higher degree of reliability than do disks.

Stable-Storage Implementation

To implement stable storage, we need to replicate the needed information in several nonvolatile storage media (usually disk) with independent failure modes, and to update the information in a controlled manner to ensure that failure during data transfer does not damage the needed information.

Block transfer between memory and disk storage can result in

Successful Completion

The transferred information arrived safely at its destination.

Partial Failure

A failure occurred in the midst of transfer, and the destination block has incorrect information.

Total Failure

The failure occurred sufficiently early during the transfer that the destination block remains intact

9.5   LOG BASED RECOVERY

Atomicity property of DBMS states that either all the operations of transactions must be performed or none. The modifications done by an aborted transaction should not be visible to database and the modifications done by committed transaction should be visible. To achieve our goal of atomicity, user must first output to stable storage information describing the modifications, without modifying the database itself. This information can help us ensure that all modifications performed by committed transactions are reflected in the database. This information can also help us ensure that no modifications made by an aborted transaction persist in the database.

Log and Log Records

The log is a sequence of log records, recording all the update activities in the database. In a stable storage, logs for each transaction are maintained. Any operation which is performed on the database is recorded is on the log. Prior to performing any modification to database, an update log record is created to reflect that modification.

An update log record represented as: <Ti, Xj, V1, V2> has these fields:

1. **Transaction identifier:** Unique Identifier of the transaction that performed the write operation.
2. **Data item:** Unique identifier of the data item written.
3. **Old value:** Value of data item prior to write.
4. **New value:** Value of data item after write operation.

Other type of log records are:

1. **<Ti start>**: It contains information about when a transaction Ti starts.
2. **<Ti commit>**: It contains information about when a transaction Ti commits.
3. **<Ti abort>**: It contains information about when a transaction Ti aborts.

Undo and Redo Operations

Because all database modifications must be preceded by creation of log record, the system has available both the old value prior to modification of data item and new value that is to be written for data item. This allows system to perform redo and undo operations as appropriate:

1. **Undo:** using a log record sets the data item specified in log record to old value.
2. **Redo:** using a log record sets the data item specified in log record to new value.

The Database Can Be Modified Using Two Approaches

1. **Deferred Modification Technique:** If the transaction does not modify the database until it has partially committed, it is said to use deferred modification technique.
2. **Immediate Modification Technique:** If database modification occur while transaction is still active, it is said to use immediate modification technique.

Recovery Using Log Records

After a system crash has occurred, the system consults the log to determine which transactions need to be redone and which need to be undone.

1.   Transaction Ti needs to be undone if the log contains the record <Ti start> but does not contain either the record <Ti commit> or the record <Ti abort>.

2.   Transaction Ti needs to be redone if log contains record <Ti start> and either the record <Ti commit> or the record <Ti abort>.

Use of Checkpoints

When a system crash occurs, user must consult the log. In principle, that need to search the entire log to determine this information. There are two major difficulties with this approach:

1.   The search process is time-consuming.

2.   Most of the transactions that, according to our algorithm, need to be redone have already written their updates into the database. Although redoing them will cause no harm, it will cause recovery to take longer.

To reduce these types of overhead, user introduce checkpoints. A log record of the form <checkpoint L> is used to represent a checkpoint in log where L is a list of transactions active at the time of the checkpoint. When a checkpoint log record is added to log all the transactions that have committed before this checkpoint have <Ti commit> log record before the checkpoint record. Any database modifications made by Ti is written to the database either prior to the checkpoint or as part of the checkpoint itself. Thus, at recovery time, there is no need to perform a redo operation on Ti.

After a system crash has occurred, the system examines the log to find the last <checkpoint L> record. The redo or undo operations need to be applied only to transactions in L, and to all transactions that started execution after the record was written to the log. Let us denote this set of transactions as T. Same rules of undo and redo are applicable on T as mentioned in Recovery using Log records part.

Note that user need to only examine the part of the log starting with the last checkpoint log record to find the set of transactions T, and to find out whether a commit or abort record occurs in the log for each transaction in T. For example, consider the set of transactions {T0, T1,..., T100}. Suppose that the most recent checkpoint took place during the execution of transaction T67 and T69, while T68 and all transactions with subscripts lower than 67 completed before the checkpoint. Thus, only transactions T67, T69,..., T100 need to be considered during the recovery scheme. Each of them needs to be redone if it has completed (that is, either committed or aborted); otherwise, it was incomplete, and needs to be undone

9.6 * CATEGORIZATION OF RECOVERY ALGORITHMS

Recovery from transaction failures usually means that the database is restored to the most recent consistent state just before the time of failure. To do this, the system must keep information about the changes that were applied to data items by the various transactions. This information is typically kept in the system log. A typical strategy for recovery may be summarized informally as follows:

1. If there is extensive damage to a wide portion of the database due to catastrophic failure, such as a disk crash, the recovery method restores a past copy of the database that was backed up to archival storage (typically tape) and reconstructs a more current state by reapplying or redoing the operations of committed transactions from the backed up log, up to the time of failure.

2. When the database is not physically damaged but has become inconsistent due to non catastrophic failures of types as we discussed in the previous chapter, the strategy is to reverse any changes that caused the inconsistency by undoing some operations. It may also be necessary to redo

some operations in order to restore a consistent state of the database, as we shall see. In this case we do not need a complete archival copy of the database. Rather, the entries kept in the online system log are consulted during recovery.

Conceptually, we can distinguish two main techniques for recovery from non catastrophic transaction failures:

1. deferred update and
2. immediate update.

The deferred update techniques do not physically update the database on disk until after a transaction reaches its commit point; then the updates are recorded in the database. Before reaching commit, all transaction updates are recorded in the local transaction workspace (or buffers). During commit, the updates are first recorded persistently in the log and then written to the database. If a transaction fails before reaching its commit point, it will not have changed the database in any way, so UNDO is not needed. It may be necessary to REDO the effect of the operations of a committed transaction from the log, because their effect may not yet have been recorded in the database. Hence, deferred update is also known as the NO-UNDO/ REDO algorithm.

In the immediate update techniques, the database may be updated by some operations of a transaction before the transaction reaches its commit point. However, these operations are typically recorded in the log on disk by force writing before they are applied to the database making recovery still possible. If a transaction fails after recording some changes in the database but before reaching its commit point, the effect of its operations on the database must be undone; that is, the transaction must be rolled back. In the general case of immediate update, both undo and redo may be required during recovery. This technique, known as the UNDO/REDO algorithm, requires both operations, and is used most often in practice. A variation of the algorithm where all updates are recorded in the database before a transaction commits requires undo only, so it is known as the UNDO/NO-REDO algorithm.

9.6.1 Caching (Buffering) of Disk Blocks

The recovery process is often closely intertwined with operating system functions-in particular, the buffering and caching of disk pages in main memory. Typically, one or more diskpages that include the data items to be updated are cached into main memory buffers and then updated in memory before being written back to disk. The caching of disk pages is traditionally an operating system function, but because of its importance to the efficiency of recovery procedures, it is handled by the DBMS by calling low-level perating systems routines. In general, it is convenient to consider recovery in terms of the database disk pages (blocks). Typically a collection of in-memory buffers, called the DBMS cache, is kept under the control of the DBMS for the purpose of holding these buffers.

A directory for the cache is used to keep track of which database items are in the buffers.' This can be a table of <disk page address, buffer location> entries. When the DBMS requests action on some item, it first checks the cache directory to determine whether the disk page containing the item is in the cache. If it is not, then the item must be located on disk, and the appropriate disk pages are copied into the cache. It may be necessary to replace (or flush) some of the cache buffers to make space available for the new item. Some page-replacement strategy from operating systems, such as least recently used (LRU) or first-in-first-out (FIFO), can be used to select the buffers for replacement. Associated with each buffer in the cache is a dirty bit, which can be included in the directory entry, to indicate whether or not the buffer has been modified.

When a page is first read from the database disk into a cache buffer, the cache directory is updated with the new disk page address, and the dirty bit is set to a (zero). As soon as the buffer is modified, the dirty bit for the corresponding directory entry is set to 1 (one). When the buffer contents are replaced (flushed) from the cache, the contents must first be written back to the corresponding disk page only if its dirty bit is 1. Another bit, called the pin-unpin bit, is also needed-a page in the cache is pinned (bit value 1 (one» if it cannot be written back to disk as yet. Two main strategies can be employed when flushing a modified buffer back to disk. The first strategy, known as in-place updating, writes the buffer back to the same original disk location, thus overwriting the old value of any changed data items on disk, Hence, a single copy of each database disk block is maintained. The second strategy, known as shadowing, writes an updated buffer at a different disk location, so multiple versions of data items can be maintained. In general, the old value of the data item before updating is called the before image (BFIM), and the new value after updating is called the after image (AFIM). In shadowing, both the BFIM and the AFIM can be kept on disk; hence, it is not strictly necessary to maintain a log for recovering.

9.6.2 Write-Ahead Logging, Steal/No-Steal, and Force/No-Force

When in-place updating is used, it is necessary to use a log for recovery. In this case, the recovery mechanism must ensure that the BFIM of the data item is recorded in the appropriate log entry and that the log entry is flushed to disk before the BFIM is overwritten with the AFIM in the database on disk. This process is generally known as write-ahead logging. Before we can describe a protocol for write-ahead logging, we need to distinguish between two types of log entry information included for a write command:

1. The information needed for UNDO and
2. That needed for REDO.

A REDO type log entry includes the new value (AFIM) of the item written by the operation since this is needed to redo the effect of the operation from the log (by setting the item value in the database to its AFIM). The UNDO-type log entries include the old value (BFIM) of the item since this is needed to undo the effect of the operation from the log (by setting the item value in the database back to its BFIM). In an UNDO/REDO algorithm, both types of log entries are combined. In addition, when cascading rollback is possible, read_item entries in the log are considered to be UNDO-type entries.

As mentioned, the DBMS cache holds the cached database disk blocks, which include not only data blocks but also index blocks and log blocks from the disk. When a log record is written, it is stored in the current log block in the DBMS cache. The log is simply a sequential (append-only) disk file and the DBMS cache may contain several log blocks (for example, the last n log blocks) that will be written to disk. When an update to a data block-stored in the DBMS cache-is made, an associated log record is written to the last log block in the DBMS cache.

With the write-ahead logging approach, the log blocks that contain the associated log records for a particular data block update must first be written to disk before the data block itself can be written back to disk. Standard DBMS recovery terminology includes the terms steal/no-steal and force/no force, which specify when a page from the database can be written to disk from the cache:

1. If a cache page updated by a transaction cannot be written to disk before the transaction commits, this is called a no-steal approach. The pin-unpin bit indicates if a page cannot be written back to disk. Otherwise, if the protocol allows writing an updated buffer before the transaction commits, it is called steal. Steal is used when the DBMS cache (buffer) manager needs a buffer frame for another transaction and the buffer manager replaces an existing page that had been updated but whose transaction has not committed.

2. If all pages updated by a transaction are immediately written to disk when the transaction commits, this is called a force approach. Otherwise, it is called no-force. The deferred update recovery scheme in Section 8.3 follows a no-steal approach.

However, typical database systems employ a steal/no-force strategy. The advantage of steal is that it avoids the need for a very large buffer space to store all updated pages in memory. The advantage of no-force is that an updated page of a committed transaction may still be in the buffer when another transaction needs to update it, thus eliminating the I/O cost to read that page again from disk. This may provide a substantial saving in the number of I/O operations when a specific page is updated heavily by multiple transactions. To permit recovery when in-place updating is used, the appropriate entries required for recovery must be permanently recorded in the logon disk before changes are applied to the database.

For example, consider the following write-ahead logging (WAL) protocol for a recovery algorithm that requires both UNDO and REDO:

1. The before image of an item cannot be overwritten by its after image in the database on disk until all UNDO-type log records for the updating transaction-up to this point in time-have been force-written to disk.
2. The commit operation of a transaction cannot be completed until all the REDO-type and UNDO-type log records for that transaction have been force-written to disk. To facilitate the recovery process, the DBMS recovery subsystem may need to maintain a number of lists related to the transactions being processed in the system. These include a list for active transactions that have started but not committed as yet, and it may also include lists of all committed

and aborted transactions since the last checkpoint (see next section). Maintaining these lists makes the recovery process more efficient.

9.6.3 Checkpoints in the System Log and Fuzzy Checkpointing

Another type of entry in the log is called a checkpoint. A [checkpoint] record is written into the log periodically at that point when the system writes out to the database on disk all DBMS buffers that have been modified. As a consequence of this, all transactions that have their [commit, T] entries in the log before a [checkpoint] entry do not need to have their WRITE operations redone in case of a system crash, since all their updates will be recorded in the database on disk during check pointing.

The recovery manager of a DBMS must decide at what intervals to take a checkpoint. The interval may be measured in time-say, every m minutes-or in the number t of committed transactions since the last checkpoint, where the values of m or t are system parameters. Taking a checkpoint consists of the following actions:

1. Suspend execution of transactions temporarily.
2. Force-write all main memory buffers that have been modified to disk.
3. Write a [checkpoint] record to the log, and force-write the log to disk.
4. Resume executing transactions.

As a consequence of step 2, a checkpoint record in the log may also include additional information, such as a list of active transaction ids, and the locations (addresses) of the first and most recent (last) records in the log for each active transaction. This can facilitate undoing transaction operations in the event that a transaction must be rolled back.

The time needed to force-write all modified memory buffers may delay transaction processing because of step 1. To reduce this delay, it is common to use a technique called fuzzy checkpointing in practice. In this technique, the system can resume transaction processing after the [checkpoint] record is written to the log without having to wait for step 2 to finish. However, until step 2 is completed, the previous [checkpoint] record should remain valid. To accomplish this, the system maintains a pointer to the valid checkpoint, which continues to point to the previous [checkpoint] record in the log. Once step 2 is concluded, that pointer is changed to point to the new checkpoint in the log.

9.6.4 Transaction Rollback

If a transaction fails for whatever reason after updating the database, it may be necessary to roll back the transaction. If any data item values have been changed by the transaction and written to the database, they must be restored to their previous values (BFIMs). The undotype log entries are used to restore the old values of data items that must be rolled back. If a transaction T is rolled back, any transaction S that has, in the interim, read the value of some data item X written by T must also be rolled back. Similarly, once S is rolled back, any transaction R that has read the value of some data item Y written by S must also be rolled back; and so on. This phenomenon is called cascading rollback, and can occur when the recovery protocol ensures recoverable schedules but does not ensure strict or cascadeless schedules. Cascading rollback, understandably, can be quite complex and time-consuming. That is why almost all recovery mechanisms are designed such that cascading rollback is never required.

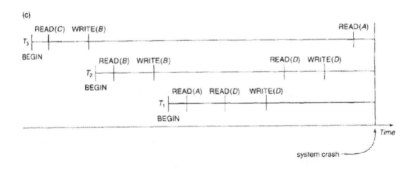

(a)

T_1	T_2	T_3
read_item(A)	read_item(B)	read_item(C)
read_item(D)	write_item(B)	write_item(B)
write_item(D)	read_item(D)	read_item(A)
	write_item(D)	write_item(A)

(b)

	A	B	C	D
	30	15	40	20
[start_transaction, T_3]				
[read_item, T_3,C]				
• [write_item, T_3,B,15,12]		12		
[start_transaction, T_2]				
[read_item, T_2,B]				
•• [write_item, T_2,B,12,18]		18		
[start_transaction, T_1]				
[read_item, T_1,A]				
[read_item, T_1,D]				
[write_item, T_1,D,20,25]				25
[read_item, T_2,D]				
•• [write_item, T_2,D,25,26]				26
[read_item, T_3,A]				

← system crash

•T_3 is rolled back because it did not reach its commit point.
••T_2 is rolled back because it reads the value of item B written by T_3.

(c)

FIG.9.1: shows an example where cascading rollback is required. The read and write operations of three individual transactions are shown in Figure 8.1a. Figure 8.1b shows the system log at the point of a system crash for a particular execution schedule of these transactions.

The values of data items A, B, C, and 0, which are used by the transactions, are shown to the right of the system log entries. We assume that the original item values, shown in the first line, are A = 30, B = 15, C = 40, and 0 = 20. At the point of system failure, transaction T_3 has not reached its conclusion and must be rolled back. The WRITE operations of T_3, marked by a single * in Figure 8.1b, are the T_3 operations that are undone during transaction rollback. Figure 8.1c graphically shows the operations of the different transactions along the time axis.

We must now check for cascading rollback. From Figure 8.1c we see that transaction T_2 reads the value of item B that was written by transaction T_3; this can also be determined by examining the log. Because T_3 is rolled back, T_2 must now be rolled back, too. The WRITE operations of T_2, marked by ** in the log, are the ones that are undone. Note that only write_item operations need to be undone during transaction rollback; read_item operations are recorded in the log only to determine whether cascading rollback of additional transactions is necessary.

In practice, cascading rollback of transactions is never required because practical recovery methods guarantee cascadeless or strict schedules. Hence, there is also no need to record any read_item operations in the log, because these are needed only for determining cascading rollback.

9.7   RECOVERY TECHNIQUES BASED ON DEFERRED UPDATE

The idea behind deferred update techniques is to defer or postpone any actual updates to the database until the transaction completes its execution successfully and reaches its commit point. During transaction execution, the updates are recorded only in the log and in the cache buffers. After the transaction reaches its commit point and the log is force-written to disk, the updates are recorded in the database. If a transaction fails before reaching its commit point, there is no need to undo any operations, because the transaction has not affected the database on disk in any way. Although this may simplify recovery, it cannot be used in practice unless transactions are short and each transaction changes few items. For other types of transactions, there is the potential for running out of buffer space because transaction changes must be held in the cache buffers until the commit point.

We can state a typical deferred update protocol as follows:

1. A transaction cannot change the database on disk until it reaches its commit point.

2. A transaction does not reach its commit point until all its update operations are recorded in the log and the log is force-written to disk.

   Notice that step of this protocol is a restatement of the write-ahead logging (WAL) protocol. Because the database is never updated on disk until after the transaction commits, there is never a need to UNDO any operations. Hence, this is known as the **NO UNDO/ REDO recovery algorithm.** REDO is needed in case the system fails after a transaction commits but before all its changes are recorded in the database on disk. In this case, the transaction operations are redone from the log entries.

   Usually, the method of recovery from failure is closely related to the concurrency control method in multi user systems. First we discuss recovery in single-user systems, where no concurrency control is needed, so that we can understand the recovery process independently of any concurrency control method. We then discuss how concurrency control may affect the recovery process.

9.7.1   Recovery Using Deferred Update in a Single-User Environment

In such an environment, the recovery algorithm can be rather simple. The algorithm RDU_S (Recovery using Deferred Update in a Single-user environment) uses a REDO procedure, given subsequently, for redoing certain write_item operations; it works as follows:

PROCEDURE RDU_S: Use two lists of transactions: the committed transactions since the last checkpoint, and the active transactions (at most one transaction will fall in this category, because the system is single-user). Apply the REDO operation to all the WRITE_ITEM operations of the committed transactions from the log in the order in which they were written to the log. Restart the active transactions.

The REDO procedure is defined as follows:

REDO(WRITE_OP): Redoing a write_item operation WRITE_OP consists of examining its log entry [write_item, T, X, new_value] and setting the value of item X in the database to new_val ue, which is the after image (AFIM).

The REDO operation is required to be idempotent-that is, executing it over and over is equivalent to executing it just once. In fact, the whole recovery process should be idempotent. This is so because, if the system were to fail during the recovery process, the next recovery attempt might REDO certain write_item operations that had already been redone during the first recovery process. The result of recovery from a system crash during recovery should be the same as the result of recovering when there is no crash during recovery Notice that the only transaction in the active list will have had no effect on the database because of the deferred update protocol, and it is ignored completely by the recovery process because none of its operations were reflected in the database on disk. However, this transaction must now be restarted, either automatically by the recovery process or manually by the user.

Figure 9.2 shows an example of recovery in a single-user environment, where the first failure occurs during execution of transaction Tv as shown in Figure 8.2b. The recovery process will redo the [write_item, T1, D, 20] entry in the log by resetting the value of item D to 20 (its new value). The [write, T2,...] entries in the log are ignored by the recovery process because T2 is not committed. If a second failure occurs during recovery from the first failure, the same recovery process is repeated from start to finish, with identical results.

(a)
$$T_1 \qquad\qquad T_2$$

T_1	T_2
read_item(A)	read_item(B)
read_item(D)	write_item(B)
write_item(D)	read_item(D)
	write_item(D)

(b) [start_transaction, T_1]
[write_item, T_1, D,20]
[commit, T_1]
[start_transaction, T_2]
[write_item, T_2, B,10]
[write_item, T_2, D,25] ← system crash

The [write_item,...] operations of T_1 are redone.
T_2 log entries are ignored by the recovery process.

Fig.9.2: An example of recovery using deferred update in a single-user environment. (a) The READ and WRITE operations of two transactions. (b) The system log at the point of crash.

9.7.2 Deferred Update with Concurrent Execution in a Multi User Environment

For multi user systems with concurrency control, the recovery process may be more complex, depending on the protocols used for concurrency control. In many cases, the concurrency control and recovery processes are interrelated. In general, the greater the degree of concurrency we wish to achieve, the more time consuming the task of recovery becomes.

Consider a system in which concurrency control uses strict two-phase locking, so the locks on items remain in effect until the transaction reaches its commit point. After that, the locks can be released. This ensures strict and serializable schedules. Assuming that [checkpoint] entries are included in the log, a possible recovery algorithm for this case, which we call RDU_M (Recovery using Deferred Update in a Multi user environment), is given next. This procedure uses the REDO procedure defined earlier.

Procedure RDU_M (With Checkpoints)

Use two lists of transactions maintained by the system: the committed transactions T since the last checkpoint (commit list), and the active transactions T' (active list). REDO all the WRITE operations of the committed transactions from the log, in the order in which they were written into the log. The transactions that are active and did not commit are effectively canceled and must be resubmitted.

Figure 9.3 shows a possible schedule of executing transactions. When the checkpoint was taken at time t), transaction T) had committed, whereas transactions T_3 and T_4 had not. Before the system crash at time t_2, T_3 and T_2 were committed but not T_4 and T_5. According to the RDU_M method, there is no need to redo the write_ item operations of transaction T_1-or any transactions committed before the last checkpoint time t). Write_item operations of T_2 and T_3 must be redone, however, because both transactions reached

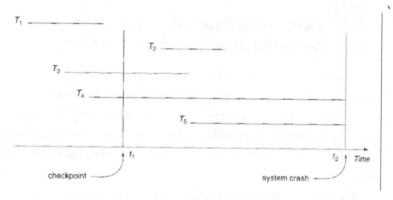

Fig.9.3: An example of recovery in a multiuser environment. their commit points after the last checkpoint.

Recall that the log is force-written before committing a transaction. Transactions T_4 and T_5 are ignored: They are effectively canceled or rolled back because none of their write_item operations were recorded in the database under the deferred update protocol. We will refer to Figure 9.3 later to illustrate other recovery protocols. We can make the NO-UNDO/REDO recovery algorithm more efficient by noting that, if a data item X has been updated-as indicated in the log entries-more than once by committed transactions since the last checkpoint, it is only necessary to REDO the last update of X from the log during recovery.

The other updates would be overwritten by this last REDO in any case. In this case, we start from the end of the log; then, whenever an item is redone, it is added to a list of redone items. Before REDO is applied to an item, the list is checked; if the item appears on the list, it is not redone again, since its last value has already been recovered. If a transaction is aborted for any reason (say, by the deadlock detection method), it is simply resubmitted, since it has not changed the database on disk. A drawback of the method described here is that it limits the concurrent execution of transactions because all items remain locked until the transaction reaches its commit point. In addition, it may require excessive buffer space to hold all updated items until the transactions commit. The method's main benefit is that transaction operations never need to be undone, for two reasons:

1. A transaction does not record any changes in the database on disk until after it reaches its commit point-that is, until it completes its execution successfully. Hence, a transaction is never rolled back because of failure during transaction execution.

2. A transaction will never read the value of an item that is written by an uncommitted transaction, because items

remain locked until a transaction reaches its commit point. Hence, no cascading rollback will occur. Figure 8.4 shows an example of recovery for a multi user system that utilizes the recovery and concurrency control method just described.

9.7.3 Transaction Actions That Do Not Affect the Database

In general, a transaction will have actions that do not affect the database, such as generating and printing messages or reports from information retrieved from the database. If a transaction fails before completion, we may not want the user to get these reports, since the transaction has failed to complete. If such erroneous reports are produced, part of the recovery process would have to inform the user that these reports are wrong, since the user may take an action based on these reports that affects the database. Hence, such reports should be generated only after the transaction reaches its commit point. A common method of dealing with such actions is to issue the commands that generate the reports but keep them as batch jobs, which are executed only after the transaction reaches its commit point. If the transaction fails, the batch jobs are canceled.

	T_1	T_2	T_3	T_4
(a)	read_item(A)	read_item(B)	read_item(A)	read_item(B)
	read_item(D)	write_item(B)	write_item(A)	write_item(B)
	write_item(D)	read_item(D)	read_item(C)	read_item(A)
		write_item(D)	write_item(C)	write_item(A)

(b) [start_transaction, T_1]
  [write_item, T_1, D, 20]
  [commit, T_1]
  [checkpoint]
  [start_transaction, T_4]
  [write_item, T_4, B, 15]
  [write_item, T_4, A, 20]
  [commit, T_4]
  [start_transaction, T_2]
  [write_item, T_2, B, 12]
  [start_transaction, T_3]
  [write_item, T_3, A, 30]
  [write_item, T_2, D, 25] ← system crash

T_2 and T_3 are ignored because they did not reach their commit points.
T_4 is redone because its commit point is after the last system checkpoint.

Fig.9.4: An example of recovery using deferred update with concurrent transactions. (a) The READ and WRITE operations of four transactions. (b) System log at the point of crash.

9.8   RECOVERY TECHNIQUES BASED ON IMMEDIATE UPDATE

In these techniques, when a transaction issues an update command, the database can be updated "immediately," without any need to wait for the transaction to reach its commit point. In these techniques, however, an update operation must still be recorded in the log (on disk) before it is applied to the database-using the write-ahead logging protocol-so that we can recover in case of failure.

Provisions must be made for undoing the effect of update operations that have been applied to the database by a failed transaction. This is accomplished by rolling back the transaction and undoing the effect of the transaction's write_item operations. Theoretically, we can distinguish two main categories of immediate update algorithms. If the recovery technique ensures that all updates of a transaction are recorded in the database on disk before the transaction commits, there is never a need to REDO any operations of committed transactions.

This is called the UNDO/NO-REDO recovery algorithm. On the other hand, if the transaction is allowed to commit before all its changes are written to the database, we have the most general case, known as the UNDO/REDO recovery algorithm. This is also the most complex technique. Next, we discuss two examples of UNDO/REDO algorithms and leave it as an exercise for the reader to develop the UNDO/NO-REDO variation.

9.8.1 UNDO/REDO Recovery Based on Immediate Update in a Single-User Environment

In a single-user system, if a failure occurs, the executing (active) transaction at the time of failure may have recorded some changes in the database. The effect of all such operations must be undone. The recovery algorithm RIU_S (Recovery using Immediate Update in a Single-user environment) uses the REDO procedure defined earlier, as well as the UNDO procedure defined below.

PROCEDURE RIU_S

1. Use two lists of transactions maintained by the system: the committed transactions since the last checkpoint and the active transactions (at most one transaction will fall in this category, because the system is single-user).
2. Undo all the write_item operations of the active transaction from the log, using the UNDO procedure described below.

3. Redo the write_item operations of the committed transactions from the log, in the order in which they were written in the log, using the REDO procedure described earlier.

The UNDO procedure is defined as follows:

UNDO(WRITE_OP): Undoing a write_item operation write_op consists of examining its log entry [write_item, T, X, old_value, new_value] and setting the value of item X in the database to old_value which is the before image (BFIM). Undoing a number of write_item operations from one or more transactions from the log must proceed in the reverse order from the order in which the operations were written in the log.

9.8.2 UNDO/REDO Recovery Based on Immediate Update with Concurrent Execution

When concurrent execution is permitted, the recovery process again depends on the protocols used for concurrency control. The procedure RIU_M (Recovery using Immediate Updates for a Multi user environment) outlines a recovery algorithm for concurrent transactions with immediate update. Assume that the log includes checkpoints and that the concurrency control protocol produces strict schedules-as, for example, the strict two phase locking protocol does. Recall that a strict schedule does not allow a transaction to read or write an item unless the transaction that last wrote the item has committed (or aborted and rolled back). However, deadlocks can occur in strict two-phase locking, thus requiring abort and UNDO of transactions. For a strict schedule, UNDO of an operation requires changing the item back to its old value (BFIM). PROCEDURE RIU_M

1. Use two lists of transactions maintained by the system: the committed transactions since the last checkpoint and the active transactions.

2. Undo all the wri te_item operations of the active (uncommitted) transactions, using the UNDO procedure. The operations should be undone in the reverse of the order in which they were written into the log.

3. Redo all the wri te_item operations of the committed transactions from the log, in the order in which they were written into the log.

More efficiently done by starting from the end of the log and redoing only the last update of each item X. Whenever an item is redone, it is added to a list of redone items and is not redone again. A similar procedure can be devised to improve the efficiency of step 2.

9.9   SHADOW PAGING

This recovery scheme does not require the use of a log in a single-user environment. In a multiuser environment, a log may be needed for the concurrency control method. Shadow paging considers the database to be made up of a number of fixed-size disk pages (or disk blocks)-say, n-for recovery purposes. A directory with n entries' is constructed, where the ith entry points to the ith database page on disk. The directory is kept in main memory if it is not too large, and all references-reads or writes-to database pages on disk go through it.

When a transaction begins executing, the current directory-whose entries point to the most recent or current database pages on disk-is copied into a shadow directory. The shadow directory is then saved on disk while the current directory is used by the transaction. During transaction execution, the shadow directory is never modified. When a write_ item operation is performed, a new copy of the modified database page is created, but the old copy of that page is not overwritten. Instead, the new page is written elsewhere-on some previously unused disk block. The current directory entry is modified to point to the new disk block, whereas the shadow directory is not modified and continues to point to the old unmodified disk block.

database disk blocks (pages)

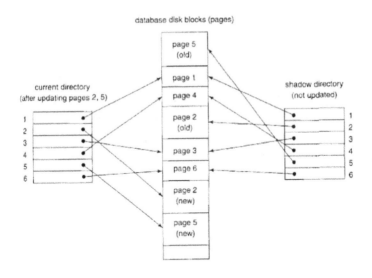

Fig.9.5: An example of shadow paging.

Fig.9.5illustrates the concepts of shadow and current directories. For pages updated by the transaction, two versions are kept. The old version is referenced by the shadow directory, and the new version by the current directory. To recover from a failure during transaction execution, it is sufficient to free the modified database pages and to discard the current directory. The state of the database before transaction execution is available through the shadow directory, and that state is recovered by reinstating the shadow directory. The database thus is returned to its state prior to the transaction that was executing when the crash occurred, and any modified pages are discarded.

Committing a transaction corresponds to discarding the previous shadow directory. Since recovery involves neither undoing nor redoing data items, this technique can be categorized as a NO-UNDO/NO-REDO technique for recovery. In a multiuser environment with concurrent transactions, logs and checkpoints must be incorporated into the shadow paging technique. One disadvantage of shadow paging is that the updated database pages change location on disk. This makes it difficult to keep related database pages close together on disk without complex storage management strategies.

Furthermore, if the directory is large, the overhead of writing shadow directories to disk as transactions commit is significant. A further complication is how to handle garbage collection when a transaction commits. The old pages referenced by the shadow directory that have been updated must be released and added to a list of free pages for future use. These pages are no longer needed after the transaction commits. Another issue is that the operation to migrate between current and shadow directories must be implemented as an atomic operation.

9.10   DATABASE BACKUP AND RECOVERY FROM CATASTROPHIC FAILURES

So far, all the techniques we have discussed apply to non catastrophic failures. A key assumption has been that the system log is maintained on the disk and is not lost as a result of the failure. Similarly, the shadow directory must be stored on disk to allow recovery when shadow paging is used. The recovery techniques we have discussed use the entries in the system log or the shadow directory to recover from failure by bringing the database back to a consistent state.

The recovery manager of a DBMS must also be equipped to handle more catastrophic failures such as disk crashes. The main technique used to handle such crashes is that of database backup. The whole database and the log are periodically copied onto a cheap storage medium such as magnetic tapes. In case of a catastrophic system failure, the latest backup copy can be reloaded from the tape to the disk, and the system can be restarted. To avoid losing all the effects of transactions that have been executed since the last backup, it is customary to back up the system log at more frequent intervals than full database backup by periodically copying it to magnetic tape. The system log is usually substantially smaller than the database itself and hence can be backed up more frequently. Thus users do not lose all transactions they have performed since the last database backup.

All committed transactions recorded in the portion of the system log that has been backed up to tape can have their effect on the database redone. A new log is started after each database backup. Hence, to recover from disk failure, the database is first recreated on disk from its latest backup copy on tape. Following that, the effects of all the committed transactions whose operations have been recorded in the backed-up copies of the system log are reconstructed.

Overview of Storage and Indexing

10.1 DATA ON EXTERNAL STORAGE

A DBMS stores vast quantities of data, and the data must persist across program executions. Therefore, data is stored on external storage devices such as disks and tapes, and fetched into main memory as needed for processing. The unit of information read from or written to disk is a page. The size of a page is a DBMS parameter, and typical values are 4KB or 8KB. The cost of page I/O (input from disk to main Inemory and output from memory to disk) dominates the cost of typical database operations, and databa, '>e systems are carefully optimized to rninimize this cost. While the details of how files of records are physically stored on disk and how main memory is utilized the following points are important to keep in mind:

* Disks are the most important external storage devices. They allow us to retrieve any page at a (more or less) fixed cost per page. However, if we read several pages in the order that they are stored physically, the cost can be much less than the cost of reading the same pages in a random order.
* Tapes are sequential access devices and force us to read data one page after the other. They are mostly used to archive data that is not needed on a regular basis.
* Each record in a file has a unique identifier called a record id, or **rid** for short. An rid ha.'3 the property that we can

identify the disk address of the page containing the record by using the rid.

Data is read into memory for processing, and written to disk for persistent storage, by a layer of software called the buffer manager. When the files and access methods layer (which we often refer to as just the file layer) needs to process a page, it asks the buffer manager to fetch the page, specifying the page's rid. The buffer manager fetches the page from disk if it is not already in memory. Space on disk is managed by the disk space manager, according to the DBMS software architecture. When the files and access methods layer needs additional space to hold new records in a file, it asks the disk space manager to allocate an additional disk page for the file; it also informs the disk space manager when it no longer needs one of its disk pages. The disk space manager keeps track of the pages in use by the file layer; if a page is freed by the file layer, the space rnanager tracks this, and reuses the space if the file layer requests a new page later on.

10.2 SECONDARY STORAGE DEVICES

In this section we describe some characteristics of magnetic disk and magnetic tape storage devices. Readers who have already studied these devices may simply browse through this section.

1. Hardware Description of Disk Devices

Magnetic disks are used for storing large amounts of data. The most basic unit of data on the disk is a single **bit** of information. By magnetizing an area on disk in certain ways, one can make it represent a bit value of either 0 (zero) or 1 (one). To code information, bits are grouped into **bytes** (or **characters**). Byte sizes are typically 4 to 8 bits, depending on the computer and the device. We assume that one character is stored in a single byte, and we use the terms byte and character interchangeably. The **capacity** of a disk is the number of bytes it can store, which is usually very large. Small floppy disks used with microcomputers typically hold from 400 KB to 1.5 MB; they are rapidly going out of circulation. Hard disks for personal computers typically hold from several hundred MB up to tens of GB; and large disk packs used with servers and mainframes have capacities of hundreds of GB. Disk capacities continue to grow as technology improves.

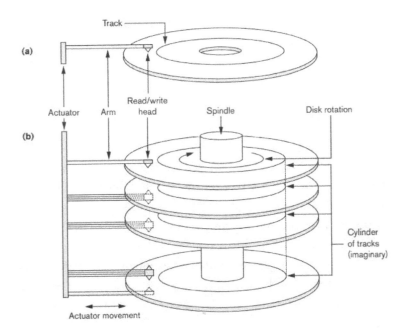

Fig. 10.1: (a) A single sided disk with read / write hardware, (b) A disk pack with read / write hardware

Whatever their capacity, all disks are made of magnetic material shaped as a thin circular disk, as shown in Fig. 10.1(a), and protected by a plastic or acrylic cover. A disk is **single-sided** if it stores information on one of its surfaces only and **double-sided** if both surfaces are used. To increase storage capacity, disks are assembled into a **disk pack**, as shown in Fig.10.1 (b), which may include many disks and there-fore many surfaces. Information is stored on a disk surface in concentric circles of small width, each having a distinct diameter. Each circle is called a **track**. In disk packs, tracks with the same diameter on the various surfaces are called a **cylinder** because of the shape they would form if connected in space. The concept of a cylinder is important because data stored on one cylinder can be retrieved much faster than if it were distributed among different cylinders.

The number of tracks on a disk ranges from a few hundred to a few thousand, and the capacity of each track typically ranges from tens of Kbytes to 150 Kbytes. Because a track usually contains a large amount of information, it is divided into smaller blocks or sectors. The division of a track into **sectors** is hard-coded on the disk surface and cannot be changed. One type of sector organization, as shown in Figure 17.2(a), calls a portion of a track that subtends a fixed angle at the center a sector. Several other sector organizations are possible, one of which is to have the sectors subtend smaller angles at the center as one moves away, thus maintaining a uniform density of recording, as shown in Figure 17.2(b).

A technique called ZBR (Zone Bit Recording) allows a range of cylinders to have the same number of sectors per arc. For example, cylinders 0–99 may have one sector per track, 100–199 may have two per track, and so on. Not all disks have their tracks divided into sectors.

The division of a track into equal-sized **disk blocks** (or **pages**) is set by the operating system during disk **formatting** (or **initialization**). Block size is fixed during initialization and cannot be changed dynamically. Typical disk block sizes range from 512 to 8192 bytes. A disk with hard-coded sectors often has the sectors subdivided into blocks during initialization. Blocks are separated by fixed-size **interblock gaps**, which include specially coded control information written during disk initialization.

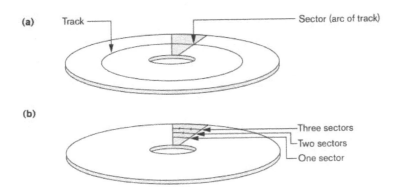

Fig.10.2 Different sector organization on disk (a) sectors subtending a fixed angle (b) sectors maintaining a uniform recording density

This information is used to determine which block on the track follows each interblock gap. Fig.10.3 illustrates the specifications of typical disks used on large servers in industry. The 10K and 15K prefixes on disk names refer to the rotational speeds in rpm (revolutions per minute). There is continuous improvement in the storage capacity and transfer rates associated with disks; they are also progressively getting cheaper—currently costing only a fraction of a dollar per megabyte of disk storage. Costs are going down so rapidly that costs as low 0.025 cent/MB—which translates to $0.25/GB and $250/TB—are already here.

A disk is a random access addressable device. Transfer of data between main memory and disk takes place in units of disk blocks. The **hardware address** of a block—a combination of a cylinder number, track number (surface number within the cylinder on which the track is located), and block number (within the track) is supplied to the disk I/O (input/output) hardware. In many modern disk drives, a single number called LBA (Logical Block Address), which is a number between 0 and n (assuming the total capacity of the disk is n + 1 blocks), is mapped automatically to the right block by the disk drive controller. The address of a **buffer**—a contiguous reserved area in main storage that holds one disk block—is also provided. For a **read** command, the disk block is copied into the buffer; whereas for a **write** command, the contents of the buffer are copied into the disk block. Sometimes several contiguous blocks, called a **cluster**, may be transferred as a unit. In this case, the buffer size is adjusted to match the number of bytes in the cluster.

Description	Cheetah 15K.6	Cheetah NS 10K
Model Number	ST3450856SS/FC	ST3400755FC
Height	25.4 mm	26.11 mm
Width	101.6 mm	101.85 mm
Length	146.05 mm	147 mm
Weight	0.709 kg	0.771 kg
Capacity		
Formatted Capacity	450 Gbytes	400 Gbytes
Configuration		
Number of disks (physical)	4	4
Number of heads (physical)	8	8
Performance		
Transfer Rates		
Internal Transfer Rate (min)	1051 Mb/sec	
Internal Transfer Rate (max)	2225 Mb/sec	1211 Mb/sec
Mean Time Between Failure (MTBF)		1.4 M hours
Seek Times		
Avg. Seek Time (Read)	3.4 ms (typical)	3.9 ms (typical)
Avg. Seek Time (Write)	3.9 ms (typical)	4.2 ms (typical)
Track-to-track, Seek, Read	0.2 ms (typical)	0.35 ms (typical)
Track-to-track, Seek, Write	0.4 ms (typical)	0.35 ms (typical)
Average Latency	2 ms	2.98 msec

Fig.10.3 specifications of Typical High-End Cheetah Disks from seagate

The actual hardware mechanism that reads or writes a block is the disk **read/write head**, which is part of a system called a **disk drive**. A disk or disk pack is mounted in the disk drive, which includes a motor that rotates the disks. A read/write head includes an electronic component attached to a **mechanical arm**. Disk packs with multiple surfaces are controlled by several read/write heads—one for each surface, as shown in Figure 10.1(b). All arms are connected to an **actuator** attached to another electrical motor, which moves the read/write heads in unison and positions them precisely over the cylinder of tracks specified in a block address.

Disk drives for hard disks rotate the disk pack continuously at a constant speed (typically ranging between 5, 400 and 15, 000 rpm). Once the read/write head is positioned on the right track and the block specified in the block address moves under the read/write head, the electronic component of the read/write head is activated to transfer the data. Some disk units have fixed read/write heads, with as many heads as there are tracks. These are called **fixed-head** disks, whereas disk units with an actuator are called **movable-head disks**.

For fixed-head disks, a track or cylinder is selected by electronically switching to the appropriate read/write head rather than by actual mechanical movement; consequently, it is much faster. However, the cost of the additional read/write heads is quite high, so fixed-head disks are not commonly used.

A **disk controller**, typically embedded in the disk drive, controls the disk drive and interfaces it to the computer system. One of the standard interfaces used today for disk drives on PCs and workstations is called **SCSI** (Small Computer System Interface). The controller accepts high-level I/O commands and takes appropriate action to position the arm and causes the read/write action to take place. To transfer a disk block, given its address, the disk controller must first mechanically position the read/write head on the correct track. The time required to do this is called the **seek time**. Typical seek times are 5 to 10 msec on desktops and 3 to 8 msecs on servers. Following that, there is another delay—called the **rotational delay** or **latency**—while the beginning of the desired block rotates into position under the read/write head. It depends on the rpm of the disk. For example, at 15, 000 rpm, the time per rotation is 4 msec and the average rotational delay is the time per half rev-olution, or 2 msec. At 10, 000 rpm the average rotational delay increases to 3 msec. Finally, some additional time is needed to transfer the data; this is called the **block transfer time**.

Hence, the total time needed to locate and transfer an arbitrary block, given its address, is the sum of the seek time, rotational delay, and block transfer time. The seek time and rotational delay are usually much larger than the block transfer time. To make the transfer of multiple blocks more efficient, it is common to transfer several consecutive blocks on the same track or cylinder. This eliminates the seek time and rotational delay for all but the first block and can result in a substantial saving of time when numerous contiguous blocks are transferred. Usually, the disk manufacturer provides a **bulk transfer rate** for calculating the time required to transfer consecutive blocks. Appendix B contains a discussion of these and other disk parameters.

The time needed to locate and transfer a disk block is in the order of milliseconds, usually ranging from 9 to 60 msec. For contiguous blocks, locating the first block takes from 9 to 60 msec, but transferring subsequent blocks may take only 0.4 to 2 msec each. Many search techniques take advantage of consecutive retrieval of blocks when searching for data on disk. In any case, a transfer time in the order of millisec-onds is considered quite high compared with the time required to process data in main memory by current CPUs. Hence, locating data on disk is a major bottleneck in database applications. The file structures we discuss here and in Chapter 18 attempt to minimize the number of block transfers needed to locate and transfer the required data from disk to main memory. Placing "related information" on contiguous blocks is the basic goal of any storage organization on disk.

2. Magnetic Tape Storage Devices

Disks are **random access** secondary storage devices because an arbitrary disk block may be accessed at random once we specify its address. Magnetic tapes are sequential access devices; to access the nth block on tape, first we must scan the preceding n − 1 blocks. Data is stored on reels of high-capacity magnetic tape, somewhat similar to audiotapes or videotapes. A tape drive is required to read the data from or write the data to a **tape reel**. Usually, each group of bits that forms a byte is stored across the tape, and the bytes themselves are stored consecutively on the tape.

A read/write head is used to read or write data on tape. Data records on tape are also stored in blocks—although the blocks may be substantially larger than those for disks, and interblock gaps are also quite large. With typical tape densities of 1600 to 6250 bytes per inch, a typical interblock gap of 0.6 inch corresponds to 960 to 3750 bytes of wasted storage space. It is customary to group many records together in one block for better space utilization.

The main characteristic of a tape is its requirement that we access the data blocks in **sequential order**. To get to a block in the middle of a reel of tape, the tape is mounted and then scanned until the required block gets under the read/write head. For this reason, tape access can be slow and tapes are not used to store online data, except for some specialized applications. However, tapes serve a very important function—**backing up** the database. One reason for backup is to keep copies of disk files in case the data is lost due to a disk crash, which can happen if the disk read/write head touches the disk surface because of mechanical malfunction. For this reason, disk files are copied periodically to tape. For many online critical applications, such as airline reservation systems, to avoid any downtime, mirrored systems are used to keep three sets of identical disks—two in online operation and one as backup. Here, offline disks become a backup device.

The three are rotated so that they can be switched in case there is a failure on one of the live disk drives. Tapes can also be used to store excessively large database files. Database files that are seldom used or are outdated but required for historical record keeping can be **archived** on tape. Originally, half-inch reel tape drives were used for data storage employing the so-called 9 track tapes. Later, smaller 8-mm magnetic tapes (similar to those used in camcorders) that can store up to 50 GB, as well as 4-mm helical scan data cartridges and writable CDs and DVDs, became popular media for backing up data files from PCs and workstations. They are also used for storing images and system libraries.

Backing up enterprise databases so that no transaction information is lost is a major undertaking. Currently, tape libraries with slots for several hundred cartridges are used with Digital and Superdigital Linear Tapes (DLTs and SDLTs) having capacities in hundreds of gigabytes that record data on linear tracks. Robotic arms are used to write on multiple cartridges in parallel using multiple tape drives with automatic labeling software to identify the backup cartridges. An example of a giant library is the SL8500 model of Sun Storage Technology that can store up to 70 petabytes (petabyte = 1000 TB) of data using up to 448 drives with a maximum throughput rate of 193.2 TB/hour. We defer the discussion of disk storage technology called RAID, and of storage area networks, network-attached storage, and iSCSI storage systems to the end of the chapter.

10.3   OPERATIONS ON FILES

Operations on files are usually grouped into **retrieval operations** and **update operations**. The former do not change any data in the file, but only locate certain records so that their field values can be examined and processed. The latter change the file by insertion or deletion of records or by modification of field values. In either case, we may have to **select** one or more records for retrieval, deletion, or modification based on a **selection condition** (or **filtering condition**), which specifies criteria that the desired record or records must satisfy.

Consider an EMPLOYEE file with fields Name, Ssn, Salary, Job_code, and Department. A **simple selection condition** may involve an equality comparison on some field value—for example, (Ssn = '123456789') or (Department = 'Research'). More com-plex conditions can involve other types of comparison operators, such as > or ≥; an example is (Salary ≥ 30000). The general case is to have an arbitrary Boolean expres-sion on the fields of the file as the selection condition.

Search operations on files are generally based on simple selection conditions. A complex condition must be decomposed by the DBMS (or the programmer) to extract a simple condition that can be used to locate the records on disk. Each located record is then checked to determine whether it satisfies the full selection condition. For example, we may extract the simple condition (Department = 'Research') from the complex condition ((Salary ≥ 30000) AND (Department = 'Research')); each record satisfying (Department = 'Research') is located and then tested to see if it also satisfies (Salary ≥ 30000).

When several file records satisfy a search condition, the first record—with respect to the physical sequence of file records—is initially located and designated the **current record**. Subsequent search operations commence from this record and locate the next record in the file that satisfies the condition.

Actual operations for locating and accessing file records vary from system to system. Below, we present a set of representative operations. Typically, high-level programs, such as DBMS software programs, access records by using these commands, so we sometimes refer to **program variables** in the following descriptions:

1. Open

Prepares the file for reading or writing, Allocates appropriate buffers (typically at least two) to hold file blocks from disk, and retrieves the file header, Sets the file pointer to the beginning of the file.

2. Reset

Sets the file pointer of an open file to the beginning of the file

3. Find (or Locate)

Searches for the first record that satisfies a search condition, Transfers the block containing that record into a main memory buffer (if it is not already there). The file pointer points to the record in the buffer and it becomes the current record. Sometimes, different verbs are used to indicate whether the located record is to be retrieved or updated.

4. Read (or Get)

Copies the current record from the buffer to a program variable in the user program, This command may also advance the current record pointer to the next record in the file, which may necessitate reading the next file block from disk.

5. FindNext

Searches for the next record in the file that satisfies the search condition, Transfers the block containing that record into a main memory buffer (if it is not already there). The record is located in the buffer and becomes the current record. Various forms of FindNext (for example, Find Next record within a current parent record, Find Next record of a given type, or Find Next record where a complex condition is met) are available in legacy DBMSs based on the hierarchical and network models.

6. Delete

Deletes the current record and (eventually) updates the file on disk to reflect the deletion.

7. Modify

Modifies some field values for the current record and (eventually) updates the file on disk to reflect the modification.

8. Insert

Inserts a new record in the file by locating the block where the record is to be inserted, transferring that block into a main memory buffer (if it is not already there), writing the record into the buffer, and (eventually) writ-ing the buffer to disk to reflect the insertion.

9. Close

Completes the file access by releasing the buffers and performing any other needed cleanup operations

The preceding (except for Open and Close) are called **record-at-a-time** operations because each operation applies to a single record. It is possible to streamline the operations Find, FindNext, and Read into a single operation, Scan, whose description is as follows:

Scan

If the file has just been opened or reset, Scan returns the first record; otherwise it returns the next record. If a condition is specified with the oper-ation, the returned record is the first or next record satisfying the condition.

In database systems, additional **set-at-a-time** higher-level operations may be applied to a file. Examples of these are as follows:

FindAll

Locates all the records in the file that satisfy a search condition.

Find (or Locate) n

Searches for the first record that satisfies a search condition and then continues to locate the next n − 1 records satisfying the same condition. Transfers the blocks containing the n records to the main memory buffer (if not already there).

FindOrdered

Retrieves all the records in the file in some specified order.

Reorganize

Starts the reorganization process. As we shall see, some file organizations require periodic reorganization. An example is to reorder the file records by sorting them on a specified field.

At this point, it is worthwhile to note the difference between the terms file organization and access method. A **file organization** refers to the organization of the data of a file into records, blocks, and access structures; this includes the way records and blocks are placed on the storage medium and interlinked. An **access method**, on the other hand, provides a group of operations—such as those listed earlier—that can be applied to a file. In general, it is possible to apply several access methods to a file organization. Some access methods, though, can be applied only to files organized in certain ways. For example, we cannot apply an indexed access method to a file without an index

Usually, we expect to use some search conditions more than others. Some files may be **static**, meaning that update operations are rarely performed; other, more **dynamic** files may change frequently, so update operations are constantly applied to them. A successful file organization should perform as efficiently as possible the operations we expect to apply frequently to the file. For example, consider the EMPLOYEE file, as shown in Figure 17.5(a), which stores the records for current employees in a company. We expect to insert records (when employees are hired), delete records (when employees leave the company), and modify records (for exam-ple, when an employee's salary or job is changed). Deleting or modifying a record requires a selection condition to identify a particular record or set of records. Retrieving one or more records also requires a selection condition.

If users expect mainly to apply a search condition based on Ssn, the designer must choose a file organization that facilitates locating a record given its Ssn value. This may involve physically ordering the records by Ssn value or defining an index on Ssn (see Chapter 18). Suppose that a second application uses the file to generate employees' paychecks and requires that paychecks are grouped by department. For this application, it is best to order employee records by department and then by name within each department.

The clustering of records into blocks and the organ-ization of blocks on cylinders would now be different than before. However, this arrangement conflicts with ordering the records by Ssn values. If both applications are important, the designer should choose an organization that allows both operations to be done efficiently. Unfortunately, in many cases a single organization does not allow all needed operations on a file to be implemented efficiently. This requires that a compromise must be chosen that takes into account the expected importance and mix of retrieval and update operations.

10.4 FILE ORGANIZATION

The **File** is a collection of records. Using the primary key, we can access the records. The type and frequency of access can be determined by the type of file organization which was used for a given set of records. File organization is a logical relationship among various records. This method defines how file records are mapped onto disk blocks. File organization is used to describe the way in which the records are stored in terms of blocks, and the blocks are placed on the storage medium. The first approach to map the database to the file is to use the several files and store only one fixed length record in any given file. An alternative approach is to structure our files so that we can contain multiple lengths for records. Files of fixed length records are easier to implement than the files of variable length records.

10.4.1 Objective of file organization

⌖ It contains an optimal selection of records, i.e., records can be selected as fast as possible.

⌖ To perform insert, delete or update transaction on the records should be quick and easy.

▲ The duplicate records cannot be induced as a result of insert, update or delete.

▲ For the minimal cost of storage, records should be stored efficiently.

10.4.2   Types of file organization

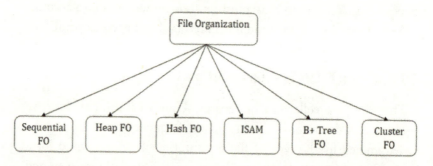

File organization contains various methods. These particular methods have pros and cons on the basis of access or selection. In the file organization, the programmer decides the best-suited file organization method according to his requirement.

Types of file organization are as follows:

1.   Sequential file organization
2.   Heap file organization
3.   Hash file organization
4.   B+ file organization
5.   Indexed sequential access method (ISAM)
6.   Cluster file organization

1. Sequential File Organization

This method is the easiest method for file organization. In this method, files are stored sequentially. This method can be implemented in two ways:

a. Pile File Method

It is a quite simple method. In this method, we store the record in a sequence, i.e., one after another. Here, the record will be inserted in the order in which they are inserted into tables. In case of updating or deleting of any record, the record will be searched in the memory blocks. When it is found, then it will be marked for deleting, and the new record is inserted.

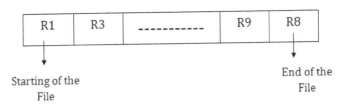

Insertion of the new record

Suppose we have four records R1, R3 and so on upto R9 and R8 in a sequence. Hence, records are nothing but a row in the table. Suppose we want to insert a new record R2 in the sequence, then it will be placed at the end of the file. Here, records are nothing but a row in any table.

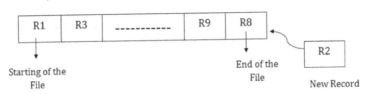

b. Sorted File Method

In this method, the new record is always inserted at the file's end, and then it will sort the sequence in ascending or descending order. Sorting of records is based on any primary key or any other key. In the case of modification of any record, it will update the record and then sort the file, and lastly, the updated record is placed in the right place.

Insertion of the new record

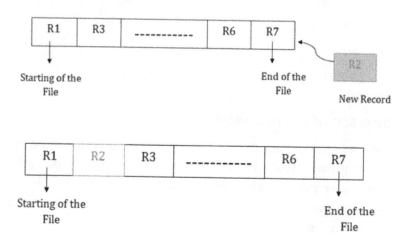

Suppose there is a preexisting sorted sequence of four records R1, R3 and so on upto R6 and R7. Suppose a new record R2 has to be inserted in the sequence, then it will be inserted at the end of the file, and then it will sort the sequence.

Pros of sequential file organization

➤ It contains a fast and efficient method for the huge amount of data.

➤ In this method, files can be easily stored in cheaper storage mechanism like magnetic tapes.

➤ It is simple in design. It requires no much effort to store the data.

➤   This method is used when most of the records have to be accessed like grade calculation of a student, generating the salary slip, etc.

➤   This method is used for report generation or statistical calculations.

Cons of sequential file organization

➤   It will waste time as we cannot jump on a particular record that is required but we have to move sequentially which takes our time.

➤   Sorted file method takes more time and space for sorting the records.

2. Heap file organization

It is the simplest and most basic type of organization. It works with data blocks. In heap file organization, the records are inserted at the file's end. When the records are inserted, it doesn't require the sorting and ordering of records. When the data block is full, the new record is stored in some other block. This new data block need not to be the very next data block, but it can select any data block in the memory to store new records. The heap file is also known as an unordered file. In the file, every record has a unique id, and every page in a file is of the same size. It is the DBMS responsibility to store and manage the new records.

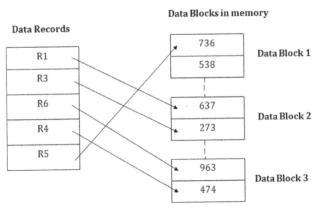

Insertion of a new record

Suppose we have five records R1, R3, R6, R4 and R5 in a heap and suppose we want to insert a new record R2 in a heap. If the data block 3 is full then it will be inserted in any of the database selected by the DBMS, let's say data block 1.

If we want to search, update or delete the data in heap file organization, then we need to traverse the data from staring of the file till we get the requested record. If the database is very large then searching, updating or deleting of record will be time-consuming because there is no sorting or ordering of records. In the heap file organization, we need to check all the data until we get the requested record

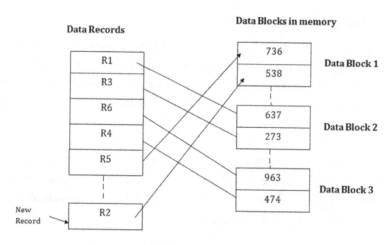

Pros of Heap file organization

⋏   It is a very good method of file organization for bulk insertion. If there is a large number of data which needs to load into the database at a time, then this method is best suited.

⋏   In case of a small database, fetching and retrieving of records is faster than the sequential record.

Cons of Heap file organization

➤ This method is inefficient for the large database because it takes time to search or modify the record.

➤ This method is inefficient for large databases.

3. Hash File Organization

Hash File Organization uses the computation of hash function on some fields of the records. The hash function's output determines the location of disk block where the records are to be placed. When a record has to be received using the hash key columns, then the address is generated, and the whole record is retrieved using that address. In the same way, when a new record has to be inserted, then the address is generated using the hash key and record is directly inserted. The same process is applied in the case of delete and update.

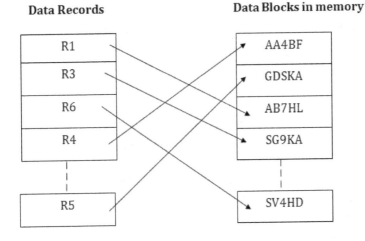

In this method, there is no effort for searching and sorting the entire file. In this method, each record will be stored randomly in the memory.

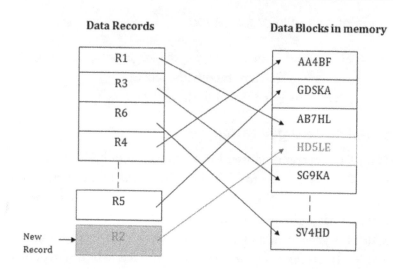

10.5 INDEXING

Indexing is defined as a data structure technique which allows you to quickly retrieve records from a database file. It is based on the same attributes on which the Indices has been done.

An index

* Takes a search key as input
* Efficiently returns a collection of matching records.

An Index is a small table having only two columns. The first column comprises a copy of the primary or candidate key of a table. Its second column contains a set of pointers for holding the address of the disk block where that specific key value stored.

Types of Indexing

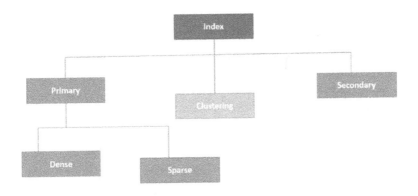

Type of Indexes

Database Indexing is defined based on its indexing attributes. Two main types of indexing methods are:

- ✧ Primary Indexing
- ✧ Secondary Indexing

Primary Indexing

Primary Index is an ordered file which is fixed length size with two fields. The first field is the same a primary key and second, filed is pointed to that specific data block. In the primary Index, there is always one to one relationship between the entries in the index table.

The primary Indexing is also further divided into two types.

- ✧ Dense Index
- ✧ Sparse Index

Dense Index

In a dense index, a record is created for every search key valued in the database. This helps you to search faster but needs more space to store index records. In this Indexing, method records contain search key value and points to the real record on the disk.

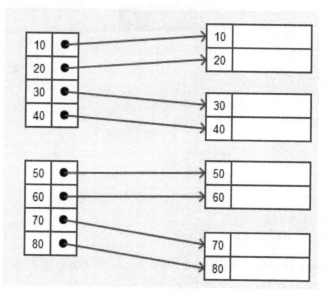

Sparse Index

It is an index record that appears for only some of the values in the file. Sparse Index helps you to resolve the issues of dense Indexing. In this method of indexing technique, a range of index columns stores the same data block address, and when data needs to be retrieved, the block address will be fetched.

However, sparse Index stores index records for only some search-key values. It needs less space, less maintenance overhead for insertion, and deletions but It is slower compared to the dense Index for locating records.

Example of Sparse Index

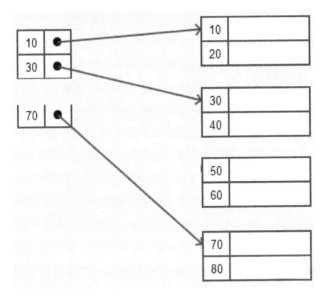

Secondary Index

The secondary Index can be generated by a field which has a unique value for each record, and it should be a candidate key. It is also known as a non-clustering index.

This two-level database indexing technique is used to reduce the mapping size of the first level. For the first level, a large range of numbers is selected because of this; the mapping size always remains small.

Example of secondary Indexing

In a bank account database, data is stored sequentially by acc_no; you may want to find all accounts in of a specific branch of ABC bank.

Here, you can have a secondary index for every search-key. Index record is a record point to a bucket that contains pointers to all the records with their specific search-key value.

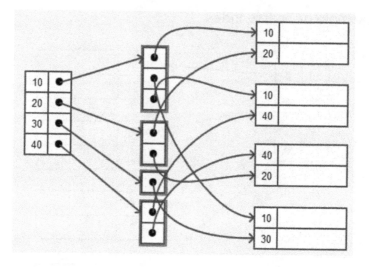

Clustering Index

In a clustered index, records themselves are stored in the Index and not pointers. Sometimes the Index is created on non-primary key columns which might not be unique for each record. In such a situation, you can group two or more columns to get the unique values and create an index which is called clustered Index. This also helps you to identify the record faster.

Example

Let's assume that a company recruited many employees in various departments. In this case, clustering indexing should be created for all employees who belong to the same dept.

It is considered in a single cluster, and index points point to the cluster as a whole. Here, Department _no is a non-unique key.

What is Multilevel Index?

Multilevel Indexing is created when a primary index does not fit in memory. In this type of indexing method, you can reduce the number of disk accesses to short any record and kept on a disk as a sequential file and create a sparse base on that file.

B-Tree Index

B-tree index is the widely used data structures for Indexing. It is a multilevel index format technique which is balanced binary search trees. All leaf nodes of the B tree signify actual data pointers.

Moreover, all leaf nodes are interlinked with a link list, which a llows a B tree to support both random and sequential access.

Advantages of Indexing

Important pros/ advantage of Indexing are:

* It helps you to reduce the total number of I/O operations needed to retrieve that data, so you don't need to access a row in the database from an index structure.
* Offers Faster search and retrieval of data to users.
* Indexing also helps you to reduce tablespace as you don't need to link to a row in a table, as there is no need to store the ROWID in the Index. Thus you will able to reduce the tablespace.
* You can't sort data in the lead nodes as the value of the primary key classifies it.

Disadvantages of Indexing

Important drawbacks/cons of Indexing are:

* To perform the indexing database management system, you need a primary key on the table with a unique value.
* You can't perform any other indexes on the Indexed data.
* You are not allowed to partition an index-organized table.

✧ SQL Indexing Decrease performance in INSERT, DELETE, and UPDATE query.

10.6   TREE BASED INDEXING

The data entries are arranged in sorted orderꬃ by search key value. A hierarchical search data structure (tree) is maintained that directs searches to the correct page of data entries. Tree-structured indexing techniques supportꬃ both range searches and equality searches.

10.6.1   INDEXED SEQUENTIAL ACCESS METHOD (ISAM)

This is an advanced sequential file organization method. Here records are stored in order of primary key in the file. Using the primary key, the records are sorted. For each primary key, an index value is generated and mapped with the record. This index is nothing but the address of record in the file.

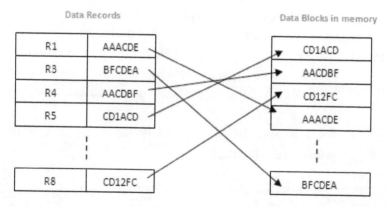

In this method, if any record has to be retrieved, based on its index value, the data block address is fetched and the record is retrieved from memory.

Advantages of ISAM

⅄ Since each record has its data block address, searching for a record in larger database is easy and quick. There is no extra effort to search records. But proper primary key has to be selected to make ISAM efficient.

⅄ This method gives flexibility of using any column as key field and index will be generated based on that. In addition to the primary key and its index, we can have index generated for other fields too. Hence searching becomes more efficient, if there is search based on columns other than primary key.

⅄ It supports range retrieval, partial retrieval of records. Since the index is based on the key value, we can retrieve the data for the given range of values. In the same way, when a partial key value is provided, say student names starting with 'JA' can also be searched easily.

Disadvantages of ISAM

⅄ An extra cost to maintain index has to be afforded. i.e.; we need to have extra space in the disk to store this index value. When there is multiple key-index combinations, the disk space will also increase.

As the new records are inserted, these files have to be restructured to maintain the sequence. Similarly, when the record is deleted, the space used by it needs to be released. Else, the performance of the database will slow down

10.6.2 B+ TREES

B Trees

B Trees are multi-way trees. That is each node contains a set of keys and pointers. A B Tree with four keys and five pointers represents the minimum size of a B Tree node. A B Tree contains only data pages. B Trees are dynamic. That is, the height of the tree grows and contracts as records are added and deleted.

B+ Trees

A B+ Tree combines features of ISAM and B Trees. It contains index pages and data pages. The data pages always appear as leaf nodes in the tree. The root node and intermediate nodes are always index pages. These features are similar to ISAM. Unlike ISAM, overflow pages are not used in B+ trees. The index pages in a B+ tree are constructed through the process of inserting and deleting records. Thus, B+ trees grow and contract like their B Tree counterparts. The contents and the number of index pages reflects this growth and shrinkage.

B+ Trees and B Trees use a "fill factor" to control the growth and the shrinkage. A 50% fill factor would be the minimum for any B+ or B tree. As our example we use the smallest page structure. This means that our B+ tree conforms to the following guidelines.

Number of Keys/page	4
Number of Pointers/page	5
Fill Factor	50%
Minimum Keys in each page	2

As this table indicates each page must have a minimum of two keys. The root page may violate this rule. The following table shows a B+ tree. As the example illustrates this tree does not have a full index page. (We have room for one more key and pointer in the root page.) In addition, one of the data pages contains empty slots.

B+ Tree with Four Keys

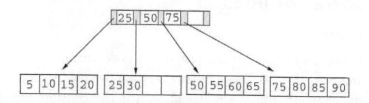

Adding Records to a B+ Tree

The key value determines a record's placement in a B+ tree. The leaf pages are maintained in sequential order AND a doubly linked list (not shown) connects each leaf page with its sibling page(s). This doubly linked list speeds data movement as the pages grow and contract. We must consider three scenarios when we add a record to a B+ tree. Each scenario causes a different action in the insert algorithm. The scenarios are:

The Insert Algorithm For B+ Trees

Leaf Page Full	Index Page FULL	Action
NO	NO	Place the record in sorted position in the appropriate leaf page
YES	NO	1. Split the leaf page 2. Place Middle Key in the index page in sorted order. 3. Left leaf page contains records with keys below the middle key. 4. Right leaf page contains records with keys equal to or greater than the middle key.

Contd...

Leaf Page Full	Index Page FULL	Action
YES	YES	1. Split the leaf page. 2. Records with keys < middle key go to the left leaf page. 3. Records with keys >= middle key go to the right leaf page. 4. Split the index page. 5. Keys < middle key go to the left index page. 6. Keys > middle key go to the right index page. 7. The middle key goes to the next (higher level) index. IF the next level index page is full, continue splitting the index pages.

Illustrations of the insert algorithm

The following examples illlustrate each of the **insert** scenarios. We begin with the simplest scenario: inserting a record into a leaf page that is not full. Since only the leaf node containing 25 and 30 contains expansion room, we're going to insert a record with a key value of 28 into the B+ tree. The following figures shows the result of this addition.

Add Record with Key 28

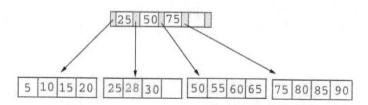

Adding a record when the leaf page is full but the index page is not

Next, we're going to insert a record with a key value of 70 into our B+ tree. This record should go in the leaf page containing 50, 55, 60, and 65. Unfortunately this page is full. This means that we must split the page as follows:

Left Leaf Page	Right Leaf Page
50 55	60 65 70

The middle key of 60 is placed in the index page between 50 and 75. The following table shows the B+ tree after the addition of 70.

Add Record with Key 70

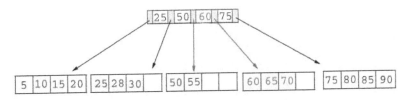

Adding a record when both the leaf page and the index page are full

As our last example, we're going to add a record containing a key value of 95 to our B+ tree. This record belongs in the page containing 75, 80, 85, and 90. Since this page is full we split it into two pages:

Left Leaf Page	Right Leaf Page
75 80	85 90 95

The middle key, 85, rises to the index page. Unfortunately, the index page is also full, so we split the index page:

Left Index Page	Right Index Page	New Index Page
25 50	75 85	60

The following table illustrates the addition of the record containing 95 to the B+ tree.

Add Record with Key 95

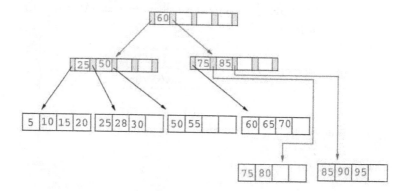

Rotation

B+ trees can incorporate rotation to reduce the number of page splits. A rotation occurs when a leaf page is full, but one of its sibling pages is not full. Rather than splitting the leaf page, we move a record to its sibling, adjusting the indices as necessary. Typically, the left sibling is checked first (if it exists) and then the right sibling.

As an example, consider the B+ tree before the addition of the record containing a key of 70. As previously stated this record belongs in the leaf node containing 50 55 60 65. Notice that this node is full, but its left sibling is not.

Add Record with Key 28

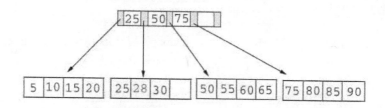

Using rotation we shift the record with the lowest key to its sibling. Since this key appeared in the index page we also modify the index page. The new B+ tree appears in the following table.

Illustration of Rotation

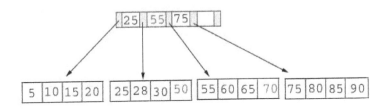

Deleting Keys from a B+ Tree

We must consider three scenarios when we delete a record from a B+ tree. Each scenario causes a different action in the delete algorithm. The scenarios are:

The delete algorithm for B+ Trees		
Leaf Page Below Fill Factor	Index Page Below Fill Factor	Action
NO	NO	Delete the record from the leaf page. Arrange keys in ascending order to fill void. If the key of the deleted record appears in the index page, use the next key to replace it.
YES	NO	Combine the leaf page and its sibling. Change the index page to reflect the change.

Contd...

The delete algorithm for B+ Trees		
Leaf Page Below Fill Factor	**Index Page Below Fill Factor**	**Action**
YES	YES	1. Combine the leaf page and its sibling. 2. Adjust the index page to reflect the change. 3. Combine the index page with its sibling. Continue combining index pages until you reach a page with the correct fill factor or you reach the root page.

As our example, we consider the B+ tree after we added 95 as a key. As a refresher this tree is printed in the following table.

Add Record with Key 95

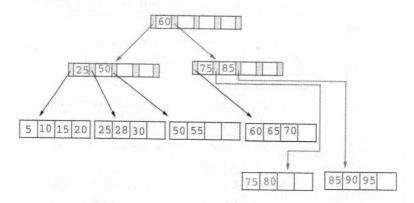

Delete 70 from the B+ Tree

We begin by deleting the record with key 70 from the B+ tree. This record is in a leaf page containing 60, 65 and 70. This page will contain 2 records after the deletion. Since our fill factor is 50% or (2 records) we simply delete 70 from the leaf node. The following table shows the B+ tree after the deletion.

Delete Record with Key 70

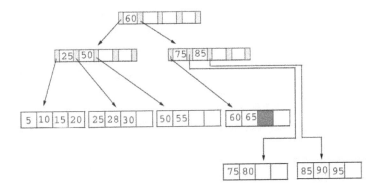

Delete 25 from the B+ tree

Next, we delete the record containing 25 from the B+ tree. This record is found in the leaf node containing 25, 28, and 30. The fill factor will be 50% after the deletion; however, 25 appears in the index page. Thus, when we delete 25 we must replace it with 28 in the index page. The following table shows the B+ tree after this deletion.

Delete Record with Key 25

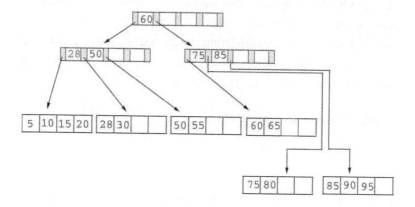

Delete 60 from the B+ tree

As our last example, we're going to delete 60 from the B+ tree. This deletion is interesting for several reasons:

1. The leaf page containing 60 (60 65) will be below the fill factor after the deletion. Thus, we must combine leaf pages.

2. With recombined pages, the index page will be reduced by one key. Hence, it will also fall below the fill factor. Thus, we must combine index pages.

3. Sixty appears as the only key in the root index page. Obviously, it will be removed with the deletion.

The following table shows the B+ tree after the deletion of 60. Notice that the tree contains a single index page.

Delete Record with Key 60

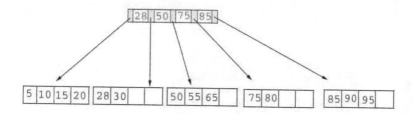

10.7 HASHING

Hashing is an efficient technique to directly search the location of desired data on the disk without using index structure. Data is stored at the data blocks whose address is generated by using hash function. The memory location where these records are stored is called as data block or data bucket.

Hash File Organization

- **⅄** **Data bucket** – Data buckets are the memory locations where the records are stored. These buckets are also considered as Unit Of Storage.
- **⅄** **Hash Function** – Hash function is a mapping function that maps all the set of search keys to actual record address. Generally, hash function uses primary key to generate the hash index – address of the data block. Hash function can be simple mathematical function to any complex mathematical function.
- **⅄** **Hash Index**-The prefix of an entire hash value is taken as a hash index. Every hash index has a depth value to signify how many bits are used for computing a hash function. These bits can address 2n buckets. When all these bits are consumed? then the depth value is increased linearly and twice the buckets are allocated.

Below given diagram clearly depicts how hash function work:

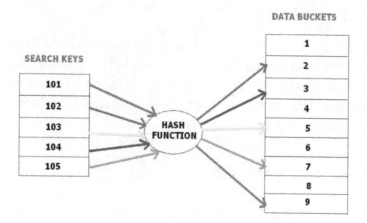

Hashing is further divided into two sub categories:

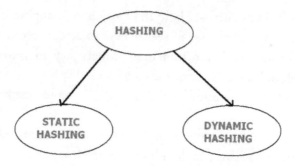

Static Hashing

In static hashing, when a search-key value is provided, the hash function always computes the same address. For example, if we want to generate address for STUDENT_ID = 76 using mod (5) hash function, it always result in the same bucket address 4. There will not be any changes to the bucket address here. Hence number of data buckets in the memory for this static hashing remains constant throughout.

Operations

➤ **Insertion** – When a new record is inserted into the table, The hash function h generate a bucket address for the new record based on its hash key K. Bucket address = h(K)

➤ **Searching** – When a record needs to be searched, The same hash function is used to retrieve the bucket address for the record. For Example, if we want to retrieve whole record for ID 76, and if the hash function is mod (5) on that ID, the bucket address generated would be 4. Then we will directly got to address 4 and retrieve the whole record for ID 104. Here ID acts as a hash key.

➤ **Deletion** – If we want to delete a record, Using the hash function we will first fetch the record which is supposed to be deleted. Then we will remove the records for that address in memory.

➤ **Updation** – The data record that needs to be updated is first searched using hash function, and then the data record is updated.

Now, If we want to insert some new records into the file But the data bucket address generated by the hash function is not empty or the data already exists in that address. This becomes a critical situation to handle. This situation in the static hashing is called **bucket overflow**. How will we insert data in this case? There are several methods provided to overcome this situation. Some commonly used methods are discussed below:

1. Open Hashing

In Open hashing method, next available data block is used to enter the new record, instead of overwriting older one. This method is also called linear probing.

For example, D3 is a new record which needs to be inserted, the hash function generates address as 105. But it is already full.

So the system searches next available data bucket, 123 and assigns D3 to it.

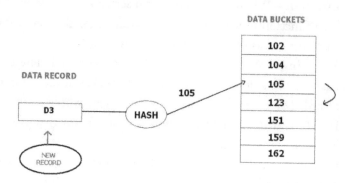

2. Closed hashing

In Closed hashing method, a new data bucket is allocated with same address and is linked it after the full data bucket. This method is also known as overflow chaining.

For example, we have to insert a new record D3 into the tables. The static hash function generates the data bucket address as 105. But this bucket is full to store the new data. In this case is a new data bucket is added at the end of 105 data bucket and is linked to it. Then new record D3 is inserted into the new bucket.

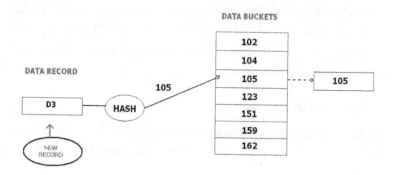

⅄ **Quadratic probing:**

Quadratic probing is very much similar to open hashing or linear probing. Here, The only difference between old and new bucket is linear. Quadratic function is used to determine the new bucket address.

⅄ **Double Hashing:**

Double Hashing is another method similar to linear probing. Here the difference is fixed as in linear probing, but this fixed difference is calculated by using another hash function. That's why the name is double hashing.

Dynamic Hashing

The drawback of static hashing is that that it does not expand or shrink dynamically as the size of the database grows or shrinks. In Dynamic hashing, data buckets grows or shrinks (added or removed dynamically) as the records increases or decreases. Dynamic hashing is also known as extended hashing.

In dynamic hashing, the hash function is made to produce a large number of values. For Example, there are three data records D1, D2 and D3. The hash function generates three addresses 1001, 0101 and 1010 respectively. This method of storing considers only part of this address – especially only first one bit to store the data. So it tries to load three of them at address 0 and 1.

10.8 EXTENDIBLE HASHING

Extendible Hashing is a dynamic hashing method wherein directories, and buckets are used to hash data. It is an aggressively flexible method in which the hash function also experiences dynamic changes.

Main features of Extendible Hashing:

The main features in this hashing technique are:

- ✧ **Directories:** The directories store addresses of the buckets in pointers. An id is assigned to each directory which may change each time when Directory Expansion takes place.
- ✧ **Buckets:** The buckets are used to hash the actual data.

Frequently used terms in Extendible Hashing:

- ▲ **Directories:** These containers store pointers to buckets. Each directory is given a unique id which may change each time when expansion takes place. The hash function returns this directory id which is used to navigate to the appropriate bucket. Number of Directories = 2^Global Depth.

- ▲ **Buckets:** They store the hashed keys. Directories point to buckets. A bucket may contain more than one pointers to it if its local depth is less than the global depth.

- ▲ **Global Depth:** It is associated with the Directories. They denote the number of bits which are used by the hash function to categorize the keys. Global Depth = Number of bits in directory id.

- ▲ **Local Depth:** It is the same as that of Global Depth except for the fact that Local Depth is associated with the buckets and not the directories. Local depth in accordance with the global depth is used to decide the action that to be performed in case an overflow occurs. Local Depth is always less than or equal to the Global Depth.

  - ✧ **Bucket Splitting:** When the number of elements in a bucket exceeds a particular size, then the bucket is split into two parts.
  - ✧ **Directory Expansion:** Directory Expansion Takes place when a bucket overflows. Directory Expansion is performed when the local depth of the overflowing bucket is equal to the global depth.

Basic structure of Extendible Hashing

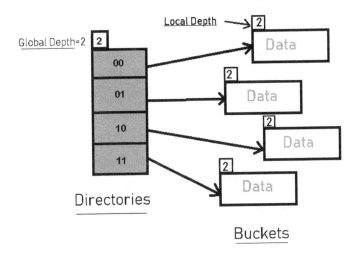

Extendible Hashing

Basic structure of Extendible Hashing

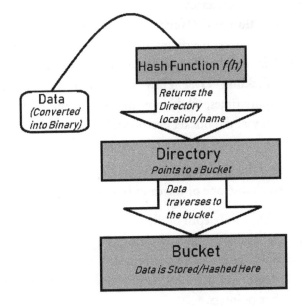

▲ **Step 1 – Analyze Data Elements:** Data elements may exist in various forms eg. Integer, String, Float, etc.. Currently, let us consider data elements of type integer. eg: 49.

▲ **Step 2 – Convert into binary format:** Convert the data element in Binary form. For string elements, consider the ASCII equivalent integer of the starting character and then convert the integer into binary form. Since we have 49 as our data element, its binary form is 110001.

▲ **Step 3 – Check Global Depth of the directory.** Suppose the global depth of the Hash-directory is 3.

▲ **Step 4 – Identify the Directory:** Consider the 'Global-Depth' number of LSBs in the binary number and match it to the directory id.

Eg. The binary obtained is: 110001 and the global-depth is 3. So, the hash function will return 3 LSBs of 110**001** viz. 001.

▲ **Step 5 – Navigation:** Now, navigate to the bucket pointed by the directory with directory-id 001.

▲ **Step 6 – Insertion and Overflow Check:** Insert the element and check if the bucket overflows. If an overflow is encountered, go to **step 7** followed by **Step 8**, otherwise, go to **step 9**.

▲ **Step 7 – Tackling Over Flow Condition during Data Insertion:** Many times, while inserting data in the buckets, it might happen that the Bucket overflows. In such cases, we need to follow an appropriate procedure to avoid mishandling of data.

First, Check if the local depth is less than or equal to the global depth. Then choose one of the cases below.

   ❖ **Case1:** If the local depth of the overflowing Bucket is equal to the global depth, then Directory Expansion, as well as Bucket Split, needs to be performed. Then increment the vglobal depth and the local depth value by 1. And, assign appropriate pointers.

Directory expansion will double the number of directories present in the hash structure.

✧ **Case2:** In case the local depth is less than the global depth, then only Bucket Split takes place. Then increment only the local depth value by 1. And, assign appropriatepointers.

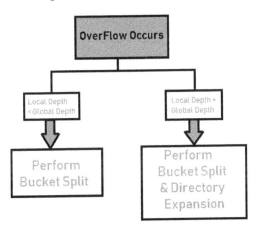

⮝ **Step 8 – Rehashing of Split Bucket Elements:** The Elements present in the overflowing bucket that is split are rehashed w.r.t the new global depth of the directory.

⮝ **Step 9 –** The element is successfully hashed.

Example based on Extendible Hashing

Now, let us consider a prominent example of hashing the following elements: **16, 4, 6, 22, 24, 10, 31, 7, 9, 20, 26. Bucket Size: 3** (Assume) **Hash Function:** Suppose the global depth is X. Then the Hash Function returns X LSBs.

⮝ **Solution:** First, calculate the binary forms of each of the given numbers.

16-10000

4-00100

6-00110

22-10110

24-11000

10-01010

31-11111

7-00111

9-01001

20-10100

26 – 01101

⅄ Initially, the global-depth and local-depth is always 1. Thus, the hashing frame looks like this:

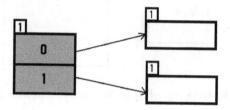

⅄ **Inserting 16**

The binary format of 16 is 10000 and global-depth is 1. The hash function returns 1 LSB of 10000 which is 0. Hence, 16 is mapped to the directory with id=0.

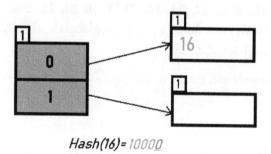

Hash(16)= 10000

⋏ **Inserting 4 and 6:**

Both 4(100) and 6(110) have 0 in their LSB. Hence, they are hashed as follows:

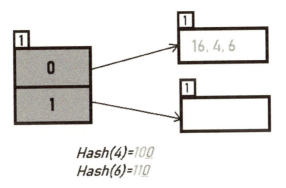

Hash(4)=100
Hash(6)=110

⋏ Inserting 22

The binary form of 22 is 10110. Its LSB is 0. The bucket pointed by directory 0 is already full. Hence, Over Flow occurs.

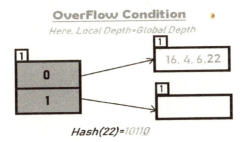

Hash(22)=10110

⋏ As directed by **Step 7-Case 1**, Since Local Depth = Global Depth, the bucket splits and directory expansion takes place. Also, rehashing of numbers present in the overflowing bucket takes place after the split. And, since the global depth is incremented by 1, now, the global depth is 2. Hence, 16, 4, 6, 22 are now rehashed w.r.t 2 LSBs.[16(100**00**), 4(1**00**), 6(1**10**), 22(101**10**)]

After Bucket Split and Directory Expansion

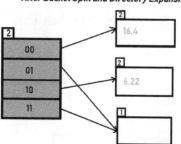

▲   *Notice that the bucket which was underflow has remained untouched. But, since the number of directories has doubled, we now have 2 directories 01 and 11 pointing to the same bucket. This is because the local-depth of the bucket has remained 1. And, any bucket having a local depth less than the global depth is pointed-to by more than one directories.

▲   Inserting 24 and 10

24(11**00**) and 10 (10**10**) can be hashed based on directories with id 00 and 10. Here, we encounter no overflow condition.

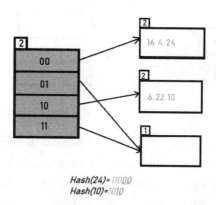

Hash(24)= 11000
Hash(10)=1010

▲   Inserting 31, 7, 9:

All of these elements[31(111**11**), 7(1**11**), 9(10**01**)] have either 01 or 11 in their LSBs. Hence, they are mapped on the bucket pointed out by 01 and 11. We do We do not encounter any overflow condition here.

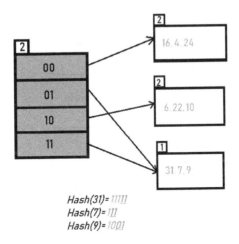

A   **Inserting 20**

Insertion of data element 20 (101**00**) will again cause the overflow problem.

OverFlow, Local Depth= Global Depth

A   20 is inserted in bucket pointed out by 00. As directed by **Step 7-Case 1**, since the **local depth of the bucket = global-depth**, directory expansion (doubling) takes place along with bucket splitting. Elements present in overflowing bucket are rehashed with the new global depth. Now, the new Hash table looks like this:

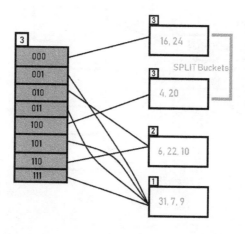

⅄ Inserting 26:

Global depth is 3. Hence, 3 LSBs of 26(11**010**) are considered. Therefore 26 best fits in the bucket pointed out by directory 010.

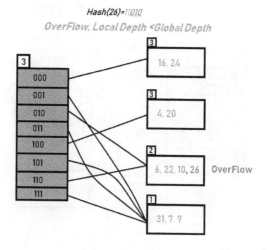

⅄ The bucket overflows, and, as directed by **Step 7-Case 2,** since the **local depth of bucket < Global depth (2<3),** directories are not doubled but, only the bucket is split and elements are rehashed.

⅄ Finally, the output of hashing the given list of numbers is obtained.

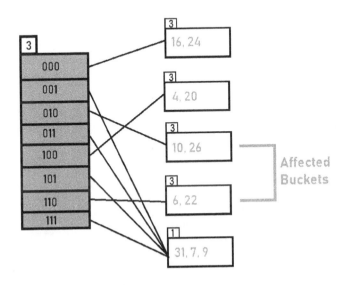

⅄ **Hashing of 11 Numbers is Thus Completed**

Key Observations

1. A Bucket will have more than one pointers pointing to it if its local depth is less than the global depth.
2. When overflow condition occurs in a bucket, all the entries in the bucket are rehashed with a new local depth.
3. If Local Depth of the overflowing bucket is equal to the global depth, only then the directories are doubled and the global depth is incremented by 1.
4. The size of a bucket cannot be changed after the data insertion process begins.

Advantages

1. Data retrieval is less expensive (in terms of computing).
2. No problem of Data-loss since the storage capacity increases dynamically.
3. With dynamic changes in hashing function, associated old values are rehashed w.r.t the new hash function.

Limitations Of Extendible Hashing

1. The directory size may increase significantly if several records are hashed on the same directory while keeping the record distribution non-uniform.
2. Size of every bucket is fixed.
3. Memory is wasted in pointers when the global depth and local depth difference becomes drastic.
4. This method is complicated to code.

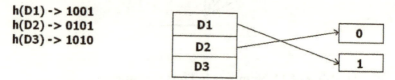

```
h(D1) -> 1001
h(D2) -> 0101
h(D3) -> 1010
```

But the problem is that No bucket address is remaining for D3. The bucket has to grow dynamically to accommodate D3. So it changes the address have 2 bits rather than 1 bit, and then it updates the existing data to have 2 bit address. Then it tries to accommodate D3.

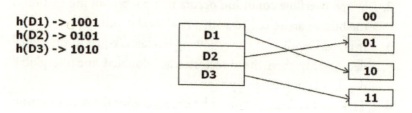

```
h(D1) -> 1001
h(D2) -> 0101
h(D3) -> 1010
```

10.9   LINEAR HASHING

Linear hashing is a dynamic hashing technique. It allows a file to extend or shrink its number of buckets without a directory as used in Extendible Hashing. Suppose you start with a number of buckets N to put records in the buckets 0 to N-1. Let this be round i which will be 0 initially. You start with an initial mod hash function $h_i(K)$ = K mod 2^iN. When there is a collision, the first bucket, i.e., bucket 0, is split into two buckets: bucket 0 and a new bucket N at the end of the file.

The records in bucket 0 are redistributed between the two buckets using another hash function h_{i+1} = K mod $2^{(i+1)}$N. Important property of the hash function is that records hashed into bucket 0 based on h_i will be hashed to bucket 0 or bucket N based on the new hash function h_{i+1}. Still there could be overflow buckets that are attached to main buckets as usual. As more records are inserted, rest of the buckets 1 to N-1 are split in the linear order and the file will have now 2N buckets and at this point hash function h_{i+1} can be used to search for any record. This is starting of round i+1 or just 1.

In order to keep track of which hash function is needed to be used we use a split pointer s that points to next bucket that will be split. This is initially set to 0 and incremented every time a split occurs. When s becomes N after incrementing, this signals that all buckets have been split and hash function h_{i+1} applies to all buckets. At this point the split pointer s is reset to 0. After this, next collision hash function to be used would be h_{i+2} = K mod $2^{(i+2)}$N.

Searching for a bucket with hash key K can be done as following. Apply current hash function h_i. If bucket b = $h_i(K)$ < s, then apply hash function h_{i+1} because bucket b is already split.

Here is a simple example of using linear hashing to store 14 records with number of initial buckets N = 4.

Bucket#		Buckets			
0	s = 0	32	44	36	
1		9	25	5	
2		14	18	10	30
3		31	35	7	11

10.9.1 An Example

This example shows various aspects of linear hashing with more data. Initially the file (at least logically) will be empty. As records are inserted into the file, buckets are added to the file. Key of each record could consist of one or more fields of the record. We assume that a hash function is used to come up with a number before hashing function specified in the linear hashing is used.

Let each bucket has capacity for storing 4 records.

Let initial number of buckets N be 4.

Record key values could be numbers, names or a combination of these depending on fields you select as key for the file. If a key contains more than one field or a key field is not a number, we have to use a hash function to get a number because we are going to use other hash functions to map record keys to bucket numbers..

10.9.2 Inserting Records

1. Insert record with keys 32, 44, 36, 9, 25, 5, 14, 18, 10, 30, 31, 35, 7 and 11

   ✧ Current round i = 0.
   ✧ Split pointer s = 0.
   ✧ Hash function to be used $h_0(K) = K \bmod 4$.

✧ $h_0(32) = 32 \bmod 4 = 0$. Insert record in bucket 0.

✧ $h_0(44) = 44 \bmod 4 = 0$. Insert record in bucket 0.

Similarly you can find out hash values for other keys and insert in appropriate buckets as shown in the following diagram:

Bucket#	Buckets				
0	s = 0	32	44	36	
1		9	25	5	
2		14	18	10	30
3		31	35	7	11

2. Insert record with key 43.

   ✧ Current round i = 0.

   ✧ Hash function to be used $h_0(K) = K \bmod 4$

   ✧ $h_0(43) = 43 \bmod 4 = 3$. Insert record in bucket 3. But the bucket is full.

   ✧ Add an overflow page and chain it to 3.

Bucket#	Buckets					
0	s = 0	32	44	36		
1		9	25	5		
2		14	18	10	30	
3		31	35	7	11	→ 43

⅄ Because there is an overflow, split bucket 0 pointed to by s and add a new bucket 4.

⅄ Redistribute bucket 0 contents between buckets 0 and 4 using next hash function $h_1(K) = K \bmod 2 * 4$.

⅄ Increment split pointer.

Bucket#	Buckets

```
0              | 32 |    |    |    |

1     s = 1    | 9  | 25 | 5  |    |

2              | 14 | 18 | 10 | 30 |

3              | 31 | 35 | 7  | 11 | → | 43 |    |    |    |

4              | 44 | 36 |    |    |
```

3. Insert record with key 37.

▲ Current round $i = 0$.

▲ Hash function to be used $h_0(K) = K \bmod 4$

▲ $h_0(37) = 37 \bmod 4 = 1$. Insert record in bucket 1.

Bucket#	Buckets

```
0              | 32 |    |    |    |

1     s = 1    | 9  | 25 | 5  | 37 |

2              | 14 | 18 | 10 | 30 |

3              | 31 | 35 | 7  | 11 | → | 43 |    |    |    |

4              | 44 | 36 |    |    |
```

4. Insert record with key 29.

✧ Current round $i = 0$.

✧ Hash function to be used $h_0(K) = K \bmod 4$

✧ $h_0(29) = 29 \bmod 4 = 1$. Insert record in bucket 1. But the bucket is full.

✧ Split bucket 1 pointed to by s.

✧ Add new bucket 5.

✧ Redistribute bucket 1 contents and 29 between buckets 1 and 5 with new hash function $h_1(K) = K \bmod 2 * 4$.

✧ Increment split pointer

✧ No overflow page is needed because we are splitting the same bucket to which the key was mapped with the original hash function.

Bucket#   Buckets

0 | 32 | | | |

1 | 9 | 25 | | |

2   s = 2 | 14 | 18 | 10 | 30 |

3 | 31 | 35 | 7 | 11 | → | 43 | | | |

4 | 44 | 36 | | |

5 | 5 | 37 | 29 | |

5. Insert record with key 22.

  ✧ Current round i = 0.
  ✧ Hash function to be used $h_0(K) = K \bmod 4$.
  ✧ $h_0(22) = 22 \bmod 4 = 2$. Insert record in bucket 2. But the bucket is full.
  ✧ Split bucket 2 pointed to by s.
  ✧ Add new bucket 6.
  ✧ Redistribute bucket 2 contents and 22 between buckets 2 and 6 with new hash function $h_1(K) = K \bmod 2 * 4$.
  ✧ Increment split pointer
  ✧ No overflow page is needed because we are splitting the same bucket to which the key was mapped with the original hash function.

Bucket#   Buckets

0 | 32 | | | |

1 | 9 | 25 | | |

2 | | 18 | 10 | |

3   s = 3 | 31 | 35 | 7 | 11 | → | 43 | | | |

4 | 44 | 36 | | |

5 | 5 | 37 | 29 | |

6 | 14 | 30 | 22 | |

6. Insert record with key 66.

  ✧ Current round i = 0.

- ❖ Hash function to be used $h_0(K) = K \bmod 4$
- ❖ $h_0(66) = 66 \bmod 4 = 2$. Insert record in bucket 2.
- ❖ Since $2 < s$, we have to use h_1 hash function.
- ❖ $h_1(66) = 66 \bmod 8 = 2$. The same bucket number and hence insert record in bucket 2.

Bucket#	Buckets			
0	32			
1	9	25		
2	66	18	10	
3 s = 3	31	35	7	11 → 43
4	44	36		
5	5	37	29	
6	14	30	22	

7. Insert record with key 34.

- ❖ Current round $i = 0$.
- ❖ Hash function to be used $h_0(K) = K \bmod 4$
- ❖ $h_0(34) = 34 \bmod 4 = 2$. Insert record in bucket 2.
- ❖ $2 < s$, hence need to use h_1 hash function.
- ❖ $h_1(34) = 34 \bmod 8 = 2$. Again the same bucket. Insert record in bucket 2.

Bucket#	Buckets			
0	32			
1	9	25		
2	66	18	10	34
3 s = 3	31	35	7	11 → 43
4	44	36		
5	5	37	29	
6	14	30	22	

8. Insert record with key 50.

    ✧ Current round i = 0.
    ✧ Hash function to be used $h_0(K)$ = K mod 4
    ✧ $h_0(50)$ = 50 mod 4 = 2. Insert record in bucket 2.
    ✧ As 2 < s, use h_1 for hashing.
    ✧ $h_1(50)$ = 50 mod 8 = 2. The same bucket. Insert record in bucket 2.
    ✧ But the bucket is full.
    ✧ Split bucket 3.
    ✧ Add new bucket 7.
    ✧ Redistribute bucket 3 contents and 50 between buckets 2 and 7 with new hash function $h_1(K)$ = K mod 2 * 4.
    ✧ Add an overflow bucket, insert 50 in it and chain it to bucket 2
    ✧ Increment split pointer. It will be 4.

    + Since it is equivalent to initial number of buckets N = 4, reset it to 0.
    + Use has function to be used as $h_1(K)$ = K mod 2 * 4 for further insertion of records.
    + Set next round i to i + 1. Now the round i will be 1.

Bucket#		Buckets								
0	s = 0	32								
1		9	25							
2		66	18	10	34	→	50			
3		43	35		11					
4		44	36							
5		5	37	29						
6		14	30	22						
7		31	7							

9.   Insert record with key 45.

   ✧ Current round i = 1.
   ✧ Hash function to be used $h_1(K) = K \bmod 2 * 4$.
   ✧ $h_1(45) = 45 \bmod 8 = 5$. Insert record in bucket 5.

Bucket#	Buckets
0 s = 0	32
1	9 25
2	66 18 10 34 → 50
3	43 35 11
4	44 36
5	5 37 29 45
6	14 30 22
7	31 7

10.   Insert record with key 53.

   ✧ Current round i = 1.
   ✧ Hash function to be used $h1(K) = K \bmod 21 * 4$
   ✧ $h1(53) = 53 \bmod 8 = 5$. Insert record in bucket 5. But the bucket is full.
   ✧ Therefore, split bucket 0 as pointed to by split pointer.
   ✧ Add new bucket 8.
   ✧ Redistribute its contents between buckets 0 and 8 with new hash function $h2(K) = K \bmod 22 * 4 = K \bmod 16$.

      ✦ $h_1(32) = 32 \bmod 16 = 0$. Hence 32 remains in the same bucket

   ✧ Add an overflow bucket, insert 53 in it and chain it to bucket 5
   ✧ Increment split pointer. It will be 1.

OVERVIEW OF STORAGE AND INDEXING   **367**

```
0              ┌──┬──┬──┬──┐
               │32│  │  │  │
               └──┴──┴──┴──┘

1      s = 1   ┌──┬──┬──┬──┐
               │ 9│25│  │  │
               └──┴──┴──┴──┘

2              ┌──┬──┬──┬──┐   ┌──┬──┬──┬──┐
               │66│18│10│34│──▶│50│  │  │  │
               └──┴──┴──┴──┘   └──┴──┴──┴──┘

3              ┌──┬──┬──┬──┐
               │43│35│  │11│
               └──┴──┴──┴──┘

4              ┌──┬──┬──┬──┐
               │44│36│  │  │
               └──┴──┴──┴──┘

5              ┌──┬──┬──┬──┐   ┌──┬──┬──┬──┐
               │ 5│37│29│45│──▶│53│  │  │  │
               └──┴──┴──┴──┘   └──┴──┴──┴──┘

6              ┌──┬──┬──┬──┐
               │14│30│22│  │
               └──┴──┴──┴──┘

7              ┌──┬──┬──┬──┐
               │31│ 7│  │  │
               └──┴──┴──┴──┘

8              ┌──┬──┬──┬──┐
               │  │  │  │  │
               └──┴──┴──┴──┘
```

11. Insert record with key 48, 64, 80

    ✧ Current round i = 1.
    ✧ Hash function to be used $h_1(K) = K \bmod 2^1 * 4 = K \bmod 8$.
    ✧ $h_1(48) = 48 \bmod 8 = 0$. Insert record in bucket 0.
    ✧ Since 0 < s, $h_2(48) = 48 \bmod 2^{2*4} = 48 \bmod 16 = 0$. Insert record in bucket 0.
    ✧ $h_1(64) = 64 \bmod 8 = 0$. Insert record in bucket 0.
    ✧ Since 0 < s, $h_2(64) = 64 \bmod 2^{2*4} = 64 \bmod 16 = 0$. Insert record in bucket 0.
    ✧ $h_1(80) = 80 \bmod 8 = 0$. Insert record in bucket 0.
    ✧ Since 0 < s, $h_2(80) = 80 \bmod 2^{2*4} = 80 \bmod 16 = 0$. Insert record in bucket 0.

0	32	48	64	80

| 1 | s = 1 | 9 | 25 | | |

| 2 | 66 | 18 | 10 | 34 | → | 50 | | | |

| 3 | 43 | 35 | | 11 |

| 4 | 44 | 36 | | |

| 5 | 5 | 37 | 29 | 45 | → | 53 | | | |

| 6 | 14 | 30 | 22 | |

| 7 | 31 | 7 | | |

| 8 | 40 | | |

12. Insert record with key 40

  ❖ Current round i = 1.
  ❖ Hash function to be used $h_1(K) = K \bmod 2^1 * 4 = K \bmod 8$.
  ❖ $h_1(40) = 40 \bmod 8 = 0$.
  ❖ Since $0 < s$, $h_2(40) = 40 \bmod 2^2 * 4 = 40 \bmod 16 = 8$. Insert record in bucket 8.

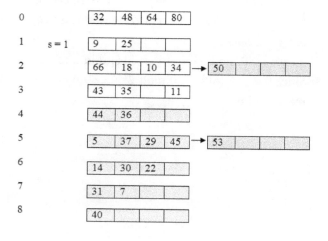

10.9.3 Searching

Searching can be done as following. If current hash function is $h_i(K)$, let bucket b = $h_i(K)$. If b < s, then let b = $h_{i+1}(K)$. Search for the record with K in bucket b.

In the above example, current hash function is $h_1(K)$ = K mod 2^1*4 = K mod 8.

Examples

Search For Record With Key 35

Bucket b = 35 mod 8 = 3 and 35 is in bucket 3.

Search for Record with Key 64

Bucket b = 64 mod 8 = 0. Since 0 < s, b = 64 mod 16 = 0. Again bucket 0 and 64 is in bucket 0.

Search for Record with Key 40

Bucket b = 40 mod 8 = 0. Since 0 < s, b = 40 mod 16 = 8. 40 is in bucket 8.

Search for Record with Key 52 (does Not Exist)

Bucket b = 52 mod 8 = 4. 42 is not in bucket 4 as expected.

10.9.4 Notes

1. In a round, if a bucket to which a key is hashed is full, buckets are split in the order of bucket numbers 0, 1, 2, 3, etc., irrespective of whether or not the buckets are full.

2. When a key is hashed to bucket b that is full, bucket pointed to by the split pointer is split and not the bucket b. An overflow page is chained to b or its existing overflow page to accommodate the new key.

3. In a round, when split pointer is equal to number of buckets present at the beginning of the round, it is reset to 0, a new round is started, buckets are split again starting from bucket 0 and new hash function $h_{i+1}(K)$ is used.

4. If hashed bucket for key K is less than split pointer bucket, key has to be rehashed using $h_{i+1}(K)$ to know bucket number of the key.

5. When all initial buckets are split, number of buckets will be double the number of initial buckets.

6. Number of initial buckets need not be multiple of 2.

Distributed Database

11.1 INTRODUCTION

A **distributed database** is a collection of multiple interconnected databases, which are spread physically across various locations that communicate via a computer network.

Features

- ▲ Databases in the collection are logically interrelated with each other. Often they represent a single logical database.
- ▲ Data is physically stored across multiple sites. Data in each site can be managed by a DBMS independent of the other sites.
- ▲ The processors in the sites are connected via a network. They do not have any multiprocessor configuration.
- ▲ A distributed database is not a loosely connected file system.
- ▲ A distributed database incorporates transaction processing, but it is not synonymous with a transaction processing system.

11.2 DISTRIBUTED DATABASE MANAGEMENT SYSTEM

A distributed database management system (DDBMS) is a centralized software system that manages a distributed database in a manner as if it were all stored in a single location.

Features

▲ It is used to create, retrieve, update and delete distributed databases.

▲ It synchronizes the database periodically and provides access mechanisms by the virtue of which the distribution becomes transparent to the users.

▲ It ensures that the data modified at any site is universally updated.

▲ It is used in application areas where large volumes of data are processed and accessed by numerous users simultaneously.

▲ It is designed for heterogeneous database platforms.

▲ It maintains confidentiality and data integrity of the databases.

Factors Encouraging DDBMS

The following factors encourage moving over to DDBMS –

▲ **Distributed Nature of Organizational Units** – Most organizations in the current times are subdivided into multiple units that are physically distributed over the globe. Each unit requires its own set of local data. Thus, the overall database of the organization becomes distributed.

▲ **Need for Sharing of Data** – The multiple organizational units often need to communicate with each other and share their data and resources. This demands common databases or replicated databases that should be used in a synchronized manner.

▲ **Support for Both OLTP and OLAP** – Online Transaction Processing (OLTP) and Online Analytical Processing (OLAP) work upon diversified systems which may have common data. Distributed database systems aid both these processing by providing synchronized data.

▲ **Database Recovery** – One of the common techniques used in DDBMS is replication of data across different sites. Replication of data automatically helps in data recovery if database in any site is damaged. Users can access data from other sites while the damaged site is being reconstructed. Thus, database failure may become almost inconspicuous to users.

⅄ **Support for Multiple Application Software** – Most organizations use a variety of application software each with its specific database support. DDBMS provides a uniform functionality for using the same data among different platforms.

11.3 ADVANTAGES OF DISTRIBUTED DATABASES

Following are the advantages of distributed databases over centralized databases.

Modular Development – If the system needs to be expanded to new locations or new units, in centralized database systems, the action requires substantial efforts and disruption in the existing functioning. However, in distributed databases, the work simply requires adding new computers and local data to the new site and finally connecting them to the distributed system, with no interruption in current functions.

More Reliable – In case of database failures, the total system of centralized databases comes to a halt. However, in distributed systems, when a component fails, the functioning of the system continues may be at a reduced performance. Hence DDBMS is more reliable.

Better Response – If data is distributed in an efficient manner, then user requests can be met from local data itself, thus providing faster response. On the other hand, in centralized systems, all queries have to pass through the central computer for processing, which increases the response time.

Lower Communication Cost – In distributed database systems, if data is located locally where it is mostly used, then the communication costs for data manipulation can be minimized. This is not feasible in centralized systems.

11.4 ADVERSITIES OF DISTRIBUTED DATABASES

Following are some of the adversities associated with distributed databases.

- **Need for complex and expensive software** – DDBMS demands complex and often expensive software to provide data transparency and co-ordination across the several sites.
- **Processing overhead** – Even simple operations may require a large number of communications and additional calculations to provide uniformity in data across the sites.
- **Data integrity** – The need for updating data in multiple sites pose problems of data integrity.
- **Overheads for improper data distribution** – Responsiveness of queries is largely dependent upon proper data distribution. Improper data distribution often leads to very slow response to user requests.

11.5 TYPES OF DISTRIBUTED DATABASES

Distributed databases can be broadly classified into homogeneous and heterogeneous distributed database environments, each with further sub-divisions, as shown in the following illustration.

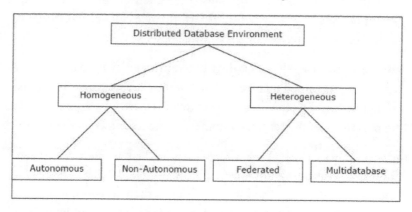

1. Homogeneous Distributed Databases

In a homogeneous distributed database, all the sites use identical DBMS and operating systems. Its properties are –

- ▲ The sites use very similar software.
- ▲ The sites use identical DBMS or DBMS from the same vendor.
- ▲ Each site is aware of all other sites and cooperates with other sites to process user requests.
- ▲ The database is accessed through a single interface as if it is a single database.

Types of Homogeneous Distributed Database

There are two types of homogeneous distributed database –

- ✧ **Autonomous** – Each database is independent that functions on its own. They are integrated by a controlling application and use message passing to share data updates.
- ✧ **Non-autonomous** – Data is distributed across the homogeneous nodes and a central or master DBMS co-ordinates data updates across the sites.

2. Heterogeneous Distributed Databases

In a heterogeneous distributed database, different sites have different operating systems, DBMS products and data models. Its properties are –

- ✧ Different sites use dissimilar schemas and software.
- ✧ The system may be composed of a variety of DBMSs like relational, network, hierarchical or object oriented.
- ✧ Query processing is complex due to dissimilar schemas.
- ✧ Transaction processing is complex due to dissimilar software.
- ✧ A site may not be aware of other sites and so there is limited co-operation in processing user requests.

Types of Heterogeneous Distributed Databases

- ▲ **Federated** – The heterogeneous database systems are independent in nature and integrated together so that they function as a single database system.
- ▲ **Un-federated** – The database systems employ a central coordinating module through which the databases are accessed.

11.6 DISTRIBUTED DBMS ARCHITECTURES

DDBMS architectures are generally developed depending on three parameters –

- ▲ **Distribution** – It states the physical distribution of data across the different sites.
- ▲ **Autonomy** – It indicates the distribution of control of the database system and the degree to which each constituent DBMS can operate independently.
- ▲ **Heterogeneity** – It refers to the uniformity or dissimilarity of the data models, system components and databases.

Architectural Models

Some of the common architectural models are –

- ▲ Client – Server Architecture for DDBMS
- ▲ Peer – to – Peer Architecture for DDBMS
- ▲ Multi – DBMS Architecture

Client – Server Architecture for DDBMS

This is a two-level architecture where the functionality is divided into servers and clients. The server functions primarily encompass data management, query processing, optimization and transaction management. Client functions include mainly user interface. However, they have some functions like consistency checking and transaction management.

The two different client – server architecture are –

✧ Single Server Multiple Client
✧ Multiple Server Multiple Client (shown in the following diagram)

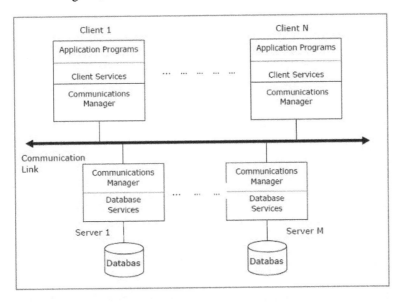

Fig.11.1: Client Server Architecture of Ddbms

Peer – to-Peer Architecture for DDBMS

In these systems, each peer acts both as a client and a server for imparting database services. The peers share their resource with other peers and co-ordinate their activities.

This architecture generally has four levels of schemas –

✧ **Global Conceptual Schema** – Depicts the global logical view of data.
✧ **Local Conceptual Schema** – Depicts logical data organization at each site.
✧ **Local Internal Schema** – Depicts physical data organization at each site.
✧ **External Schema** – Depicts user view of data.

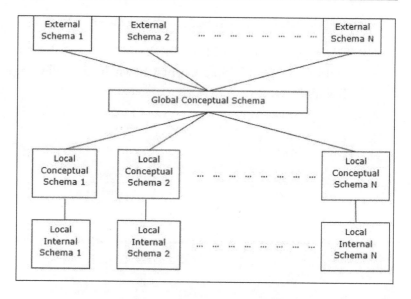

Fig.11.2: Peer –To-Peer Architecture Of Ddbms

11.7 MULTI – DBMS ARCHITECTURES

This is an integrated database system formed by a collection of two or more autonomous database systems.

Multi-DBMS can be expressed through six levels of schemas –

- ✧ **Multi-database View Level** – Depicts multiple user views comprising of subsets of the integrated distributed database.
- ✧ **Multi-database Conceptual Level** – Depicts integrated multi-database that comprises of global logical multi-database structure definitions.
- ✧ **Multi-database Internal Level** – Depicts the data distribution across different sites and multi-database to local data mapping.
- ✧ **Local database View Level** – Depicts public view of local data.
- ✧ **Local database Conceptual Level** – Depicts local data organization at each site.

❖ **Local database Internal Level** – Depicts physical data organization at each site.

There are two design alternatives for multi-DBMS –

❖ Model with multi-database conceptual level.
❖ Model without multi-database conceptual level.

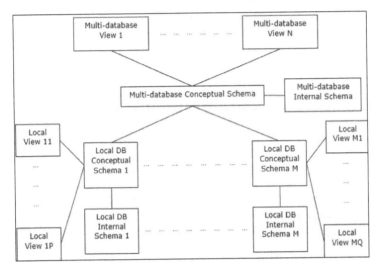

Fig.11.3: Model With Multi-Database Conceptual Level

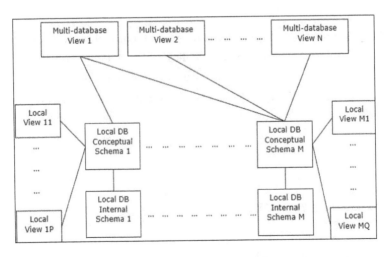

Fig.11.3: Model Without Multi-Database Conceptual Level

11.8 DESIGN ALTERNATIVES

The distribution design alternatives for the tables in a DDBMS are as follows –

- Non-replicated and non-fragmented
- Fully replicated
- Partially replicated
- Fragmented
- Mixed

Non-replicated & Non-fragmented

In this design alternative, different tables are placed at different sites. Data is placed so that it is at a close proximity to the site where it is used most. It is most suitable for database systems where the percentage of queries needed to join information in tables placed at different sites is low. If an appropriate distribution strategy is adopted, then this design alternative helps to reduce the communication cost during data processing.

Fully Replicated

In this design alternative, at each site, one copy of all the database tables is stored. Since, each site has its own copy of the entire database, queries are very fast requiring negligible communication cost. On the contrary, the massive redundancy in data requires huge cost during update operations. Hence, this is suitable for systems where a large number of queries is required to be handled whereas the number of database updates is low.

Partially Replicated

Copies of tables or portions of tables are stored at different sites. The distribution of the tables is done in accordance to the frequency of access. This takes into consideration the fact that the frequency of accessing the tables vary considerably from site to site. The number of copies of the tables (or portions) depends on how frequently the access queries execute and the site which generate the access queries.

Fragmented

In this design, a table is divided into two or more pieces referred to as fragments or partitions, and each fragment can be stored at different sites. This considers the fact that it seldom happens that all data stored in a table is required at a given site. Moreover, fragmentation increases parallelism and provides better disaster recovery. Here, there is only one copy of each fragment in the system, i.e. no redundant data.

The three fragmentation techniques are –

✦ Vertical fragmentation
✦ Horizontal fragmentation
✦ Hybrid fragmentation

Mixed Distribution

This is a combination of fragmentation and partial replications. Here, the tables are initially fragmented in any form (horizontal or vertical), and then these fragments are partially replicated across the different sites according to the frequency of accessing the fragments.

11.9 DATA REPLICATION

Data replication is the process of storing separate copies of the database at two or more sites. It is a popular fault tolerance technique of distributed databases.

Advantages of Data Replication

▲ **Reliability** – In case of failure of any site, the database system continues to work since a copy is available at another site(s).

▲ **Reduction in Network Load** – Since local copies of data are available, query processing can be done with reduced network usage, particularly during prime hours. Data updating can be done at non-prime hours.

▲ **Quicker Response** – Availability of local copies of data ensures quick query processing and consequently quick response time.

▲ **Simpler Transactions** – Transactions require less number of joins of tables located at different sites and minimal coordination across the network. Thus, they become simpler in nature.

Disadvantages of Data Replication

▲ **Increased Storage Requirements** – Maintaining multiple copies of data is associated with increased storage costs. The storage space required is in multiples of the storage required for a centralized system.

▲ **Increased Cost and Complexity of Data Updating** – Each time a data item is updated, the update needs to be reflected in all the copies of the data at the different sites. This requires complex synchronization techniques and protocols.

▲ **Undesirable Application – Database coupling** – If complex update mechanisms are not used, removing data inconsistency requires complex co-ordination at application level. This results in undesirable application – database coupling.

Some commonly used replication techniques are –

   ✧ Snapshot replication
   ✧ Near-real-time replication
   ✧ Pull replication

11.10 FRAGMENTATION

Fragmentation is the task of dividing a table into a set of smaller tables. The subsets of the table are called **fragments**. Fragmentation can be of three types: horizontal, vertical, and hybrid (combination of horizontal and vertical). Horizontal fragmentation can further be classified into two techniques: primary horizontal fragmentation and derived horizontal fragmentation. Fragmentation should be done in a way so that the original table can be reconstructed from the fragments. This is needed so that the original table can be reconstructed from the fragments whenever required. This requirement is called "reconstructiveness."

Advantages of Fragmentation

▲   Since data is stored close to the site of usage, efficiency of the database system is increased.
▲   Local query optimization techniques are sufficient for most queries since data is locally available.
▲   Since irrelevant data is not available at the sites, security and privacy of the database system can be maintained.

Disadvantages of Fragmentation

▲   When data from different fragments are required, the access speeds may be very high.
▲   In case of recursive fragmentations, the job of reconstruction will need expensive techniques.
▲   Lack of back-up copies of data in different sites may render the database ineffective in case of failure of a site.

1. Vertical Fragmentation

In vertical fragmentation, the fields or columns of a table are grouped into fragments. In order to maintain reconstructiveness, each fragment should contain the primary key field(s) of the table. Vertical fragmentation can be used to enforce privacy of data. For example, let us consider that a University database keeps records of all registered students in a Student table having the following schema.

Student

Regd_No	Name	Course	Address	Semester	Fees	Marks

Now, the fees details are maintained in the accounts section. In this case, the designer will fragment the database as follows –

CREATE TABLE STD_FEES AS SELECT Regd_No, Fees FROM STUDENT;

2. Horizontal Fragmentation

Horizontal fragmentation groups the tuples of a table in accordance to values of one or more fields. Horizontal fragmentation should also confirm to the rule of reconstructiveness. Each horizontal fragment must have all columns of the original base table. For example, in the student schema, if the details of all students of Computer Science Course needs to be maintained at the School of Computer Science, then the designer will horizontally fragment the database as follows –

CREATE COMP_STD AS SELECT * FROM STUDENT WHERE COURSE = "Computer Science";

3. Hybrid Fragmentation

In hybrid fragmentation, a combination of horizontal and vertical fragmentation techniques are used. This is the most flexible fragmentation technique since it generates fragments with minimal extraneous information. However, reconstruction of the original table is often an expensive task.

Hybrid fragmentation can be done in two alternative ways –

✧ At first, generate a set of horizontal fragments; then generate vertical fragments from one or more of the horizontal fragments.

✧ At first, generate a set of vertical fragments; then generate horizontal fragments from one or more of the vertical fragments.

11.11 DISTRIBUTION TRANSPARENCY

Distribution transparency is the property of distributed databases by the virtue of which the internal details of the distribution are hidden from the users. The DDBMS designer may choose to fragment tables, replicate the fragments and store them at different sites. However, since users are oblivious of these details, they find the distributed database easy to use like any centralized database.

The three dimensions of distribution transparency are –

✧ Location transparency
✧ Fragmentation transparency
✧ Replication transparency

1. Location Transparency

Location transparency ensures that the user can query on any table(s) or fragment(s) of a table as if they were stored locally in the user's site. The fact that the table or its fragments are stored at remote site in the distributed database system, should be completely oblivious to the end user. The address of the remote site(s) and the access mechanisms are completely hidden.

In order to incorporate location transparency, DDBMS should have access to updated and accurate data dictionary and DDBMS directory which contains the details of locations of data.

2. Fragmentation Transparency

Fragmentation transparency enables users to query upon any table as if it were unfragmented. Thus, it hides the fact that the table the user is querying on is actually a fragment or union of some fragments. It also conceals the fact that the fragments are located at diverse sites. This is somewhat similar to users of SQL views, where the user may not know that they are using a view of a table instead of the table itself.

3. Replication Transparency

Replication transparency ensures that replication of databases are hidden from the users. It enables users to query upon a table as if only a single copy of the table exists. Replication transparency is associated with concurrency transparency and failure transparency. Whenever a user updates a data item, the update is reflected in all the copies of the table. However, this operation should not be known to the user. This is concurrency transparency. Also, in case of failure of a site, the user can still proceed with his queries using replicated copies without any knowledge of failure. This is failure transparency.

Combination of Transparencies

In any distributed database system, the designer should ensure that all the stated transparencies are maintained to a considerable extent. The designer may choose to fragment tables, replicate them and store them at different sites; all oblivious to the end user. However, complete distribution transparency is a tough task and requires considerable design efforts

www.ingramcontent.com/pod-product-compliance
Lightning Source LLC
Chambersburg PA
CBHW031235050326
40690CB00007B/815